To Morton —
Thanks, + good
to meet again — a
fine dinner [signature]

D1256781

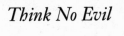

Think No Evil

ALSO BY C. FRED ALFORD:

What Evil Means to Us, 1997

The Man Who Couldn't Lie: An Ancient Quarrel between Philosophy and Poetry, 1995

Group Psychology and Political Theory, 1994

The Psychoanalytic Theory of Greek Tragedy, 1992

The Self in Social Theory, 1991

Melanie Klein and Critical Social Theory, 1989

Narcissism, 1988

Science and the Revenge of Nature: Marcuse and Habermas, 1985

Think No **evil**

KOREAN VALUES IN THE
AGE OF GLOBALIZATION

C. FRED ALFORD

Cornell University Press

ITHACA AND LONDON

Copyright © 1999 by Cornell University

All rights reserved. Except for brief quotations in a review, this book, or parts thereof, must not be reproduced in any form without permission in writing from the publisher. For information, address Cornell University Press, Sage House, 512 East State Street, Ithaca, New York 14850.

First published 1999 by Cornell University Press

Printed in the United States of America

Library of Congress Cataloging-in-Publication Data
Alford, C. Fred.
    Think no evil : Korean values in the age of globalization / C. Fred Alford.
      p. cm.
    Includes bibliographical references and index.
    ISBN 0-8014-3666-4 (cloth)
      1. Postmodernism—Social aspects—Korea (South) 2. Korea (South)—Civilization—Foreign influences. 3. Korea (South)—Social conditions. 4. Internationalism. 5. International economic relations. I. Title. II. Title: Evil.
    HM449.A44 1999
    306'.095195—dc21   99-30527

Cornell University Press strives to use environmentally responsible suppliers and materials to the fullest extent possible in the publishing of its books. Such materials include vegetable-based, low-VOC inks and acid-free papers that are recycled, totally chlorine-free, or partly composed of nonwood fibers. Books that bear the logo of the FSC (Forest Stewardship Council) use paper taken from forests that have been inspected and certified as meeting the highest standards for environmental and social responsibility. For further information, visit our website at www.cornellpress.cornell.edu.

Printed in the United States of America

Cloth printing   10 9 8 7 6 5 4 3 2 1

FSC FSC Trademark © 1996 Forest Stewardship Council A.C.
SW-COC-098

TO THOSE KOREANS

WHO SHARED THEIR

HOPES AND FEARS

WITH ME

Contents

Preface

The Shilla Hotel sits on the side of Mount Namsan, right in the middle of Seoul. Mount Namsan was the location of the Korean Central Intelligence Agency, where the most important interrogations and tortures were conducted during the years of the dictators. Almost as big as the Shilla Hotel is the duty-free store next door. Like the hotel, possibly the finest in Korea, it too is owned by the Samsung *chaebŏl* (conglomerate). Many Koreans take pride in knowing which chaebŏl owns what. It can get complicated, the top four chaebŏl owning so many diverse businesses that together they produce almost 50 percent of the GDP.

Inside the duty-free store are Chanel perfumes, Gucci purses, and Coach leather bags—not one item a person could truly need. All this in the midst of an austerity campaign in which Koreans are encouraged to use their pencils down to the nub.

Adjacent to the hotel is an outdoor sculpture garden, the collection of the founder of Samsung. At the top of the jogging trail that passes through the sculpture garden stands a life-size statue of the founder. Wearing glasses and a Western suit, he stretches his arms out as if calling the poor of Korea to him. As I was looking at the statue, evidently in puzzlement, a jogger stopped for a moment, glanced up at it, and said, "We have been poor for five thousand years. It's our turn to be rich for a little while."

In front of the hotel, a bald man in a gray *hanbok* (loose-fitting traditional clothing) is talking on a cellular phone. Inside at the bar a Korean woman dressed in an electric blue silk miniskirt is singing Western lounge-lizard songs. From the picture windows overlooking the city below one can see Dongguk, a Buddhist university. All Korea is here, or so it seemed for a moment. In reality there is so much more.

Why study something so obscure as the Korean concept, or rather, non-concept, of evil? Three of the most important reasons follow.

1. Half the world believes in evil. *What Evil Means to Us* (1997c) is my study of some of those who believe. That leaves the other half. One cannot hope to study half the world, but only one place. For me, Korea is that place. It is a country still more dedicated to the teachings of Confucius than any other, and it is going through enormous conflict as it tries to simultaneously resist and embrace globalization. Korea is a crossroads for conflict: military, economic, psychological, social. If we want to understand the modern non-Western world, there is no better place to start.

2. How Koreans do not believe in evil is as important as why. How one might study something that is nothing raises fascinating questions of philosophy and method. For Koreans do not merely disbelieve in evil. They have constructed a world in which it cannot exist. I am very interested in how one can study silence. If Eskimos have a dozen words for snow, then presumably snow is important. What if the words a culture does not have are even more important? But how could one know?

3. Globalization is the future. For Koreans it promises freedom, and yet it threatens a world of icy polar darkness of unrelatedness and alienation. For many Koreans globalization is tantamount to what the West calls evil, though they dare not call it that. Globalization also holds out the possibility that men and women might experiment with new identities, new selves. If there is any meaning left to the idea of enlightenment, this is it. How men and women might work through experiences of evil, whatever they are called, in order to create new, more fulfilling identities seems important. How the culture can help, and why it generally does not, also seems important.

"Korea" always refers to the Republic of Korea (ROK), that is, South Korea, unless it is being explicitly contrasted with North Korea, the Democratic People's Republic of Korea (DPRK) as it is called.

The term "informants" is the one generally used for those I spoke with. The term is common among anthropologists, and that is why I use it. If I had to characterize my approach in a few words, I would call it an anthropological approach to philosophy.

All unattributed quotations in my text come from author interviews. Korea is a small country, and the names of many informants are widely known. Although I did not promise anonymity to those informants who would qualify as experts, it seems best to grant anonymity to every informant. Thus, all names are pseudonyms. Those readers familiar with public life in Korea may be able to identify some informants by the descriptions of their lives and positions. Sometimes the reader will be wrong. The one exception to the granting of anonymity concerns those informants who are also authors of cited works when the interview serves to expand on the work.

A Senior Fulbright Research Fellowship to Korea made possible the original research on which my work is based. The Comparative Cultural Studies Center at Yonsei University and *chontong kwa hyondai* provided the opportunity for a return visit in the summer of 1998. The Division of Behavioral and Social Sciences at the University of Maryland, College Park, provided additional resources, without which I could not have completed my work.

Moon Chung-in, director of the Graduate School of International Studies at Yonsei sponsored my project and taught me much. So did Hahm Chaibong, senior editor of *chontong kwa hyondai*. Research such as mine requires the cooperation of many, and I was fortunate.

Horace G. Underwood of Yonsei University invited me to present my results to the Korean Branch of the Royal Asiatic Society. Frank Tedesco invited me to submit some preliminary findings to *Korea Journal*. I took advantage of both opportunities, which provided an occasion for additional conversations with Koreans about my findings.

My working hypothesis, discussed at length in Chapter 4, was suggested by Frederick Carriere, executive director of the Korea Society. Although I did not corroborate it, the hypothesis was sufficiently subtle and complex that it never got in the way of my experience. What else could one ask for from a hypothesis?

One unfortunate result of granting anonymity to my informants is that I cannot thank them publicly. Those whom I can thank are those who facilitated my research.

David Kosofsky, of Hankuk University of Foreign Studies, made several of his classes available for my research project. In addition, we discussed things Korean and American for hours. He taught me a great deal.

Amir Jahansir, a former student, was teaching English in Korea, and he made his classes and his friends available to me.

I am fortunate in having the former U.S. ambassador to Korea, James R. Lilley, as a colleague. He introduced me to Horace G. Underwood and to Mujin sŭnim, of the Lotus Lantern International Buddhist Center in Seoul. In addition to introducing me to many Koreans, Mujin made me feel at home. Nowhere else in Korea was I more comfortable than at the Lotus Lantern.

Ray Weisenborn, former executive director of the Korean-American Educational Commission, and Horace H. Underwood, the current executive director, both made my visit more pleasant and productive.

Kim Mann-kyu, professor of political science at Inha University, and Kim Euikon, associate professor and chair, invited me to speak to their students, from whom I learned much.

Kim Yong-shin, a former graduate student, sponsored my first trip to Korea several years ago. Had he not done so, I would not have known of this passage to the East.

Above all, I owe a debt to Lee Yoonkyung of Yonsei University's Graduate School of International Studies, currently a graduate student in political science at Duke University. She is my ideal native informant, helping me every step of the way. Without her assistance, this would have been a lesser work.

Fred Dallmayr's *Beyond Orientalism* influenced my thinking.

Jim Glass first pointed out to me the connection between globalization and evil.

S. Robert Ramsey, professor and chair of Asian and East European Languages and Culture at the University of Maryland, College Park, helped me with the McCune-Reischauer System of Romanization, which I have employed. Any errors are those of this slow learner.

My wife, Elly, excelled me in learning Korean, accompanied me on the first part of my journey to Korea, and discussed many of the issues with me. I would not have felt as at home in Korea without her. Nor would I have learned as much.

C. FRED ALFORD

College Park, Maryland

Think No Evil

CHAPTER ONE

"Tell Me the Relationship . . ."

Solomon is a popular image of wisdom for many Koreans. For the woman I was talking to, Solomon represents Western wisdom at its best—and worst. "The Western Solomon figured out which prostitute was lying by almost chopping the baby in half. Then he killed the pretend mother, giving the baby to its real mother. A Korean Solomon would have found a compromise. He would have made the two women sisters, so they could have cared for the child together."

Often we learn most from what is misremembered or misunderstood. The biblical Solomon (1 Kings 3.16–28) does not kill the false mother, nor does he almost chop the baby in half. He only pretends in order to discover the true mother. But the Korean woman who misremembers the story is making an important point about how she sees East and West. The West divides, chopping things—and people—up. The East creates relationships modeled on the family. From her perspective, the Korean Solomon has not achieved a compromise. A compromise would be chopping the baby in half. The Korean Solomon has made the conflict disappear by placing it within a relationship in which it can be resolved by the expectations inherent in traditional relationships, such as older and younger sisters.

Most of the themes regarding good and evil that I encountered in Korea are inherent in this simple story. Evil depends on the creation of dualisms, oppositions between people and ideas. Instead of evil, Koreans find and create relationships among people, relationships that are woven so tightly that the duality on which concepts like evil depend cannot appear. Conversely, evil depends on a type of separation and division that is so terrifying it cannot be allowed to exist. The result is that Koreans do not believe in evil. Or if they do, they believe in it contingently. Evil is created by the Western tendency toward dualism and will disappear when this alien intellectual inclination is abandoned. Evil is not a moral category; it is an intellectual one, the result of erroneous dualistic thinking.

Some "anthropologists of evil" (yes, there is such a subfield) argue that every society has a concept of evil. Evil is a virtually universal category. But what they generally mean by "evil" is something very bad (Parkin 1985, 1–23; Southwold 1985, 128–133). Certainly Koreans possess terms for "very bad." *Ak* and *saak* are among the strongest. What Koreans lack is a sense that all, or even many, very bad things possess something in common, what we would call "evil." If one were to translate "ak" as evil, then "evil" would become just a word, with nothing in common to link its objects, much as bad day, bad hair, bad dog, bad boy, and bad air lack a common denominator, other than being bad.

What else is new, you might ask? Of course Korea lacks a Western concept of evil. Korea is East. Evil is part of a whole set of Western distinctions, such as that between Being and becoming, form and void, that has never been convincing to the East. Ruth Benedict made this point in 1946 in *The Chrysanthemum and the Sword*, her study of Japanese culture, and she was not the first.[1] Not the absence of evil, but the meaning of its absence, is my concern.

Most research is aimed at simplifying an enormously complex reality so that we might make sense of it. My research was aimed at taking a reality that seemed fairly obvious, Koreans' widespread disbelief in evil, and making it complex, trying to get at the how and why. "Keep watch over absent meaning," says Maurice Blanchot (1986, 42). One way to do this is to consider that the words a culture does not have may be more important than the ones it does. Eskimos are said to have a dozen words for snow, as the Japanese have a dozen words for seaweed. But what about the words they don't have? What reality do they reveal, and could we even know it? Absent words are not necessarily absent meaning. Not only because we can have experiences without words but also because meaning can be conveyed by indirectness, by a series of words that encircle reality, none naming it directly, but all working together to convey its form.

Do people who do not believe in evil see the world through rose-colored glasses? Do they not have the same experiences as those who believe in evil? Do they view human nature more benignly? Or do they just refuse to do the addition, so to speak, refusing to assimilate bad Japanese, bad North Koreans, and bad morals into a single quality of extreme badness? In other words, do people who do not believe in evil order their world differently, or just the terms they use to describe it? Does the woman who says a Korean Solomon would have made the two women sisters live in a less dualistic world (whatever that means exactly), or just a world in which dualistic terminology is absent? Whatever the answer is, it will touch on not only the concept of evil but also the role of language in world making.[2]

Korea is possibly the most religiously diverse but ethnically homogeneous country on earth. In most countries, religious diversity stems from ethnically mixed populations who bring their religions with them. Often and eventually the religions mix. In Korea religions have proliferated within a remarkably homogeneous population. It is a perfect place to study what anthropologists have called 100 percent + 100 percent cultures, in which the adoption of new beliefs does not mean displacement of the old. The world does not fit together as tightly as we sometimes think it must, and Korea is a case in point. Korea is not religiously syncretic; it is religiously eclectic, a much more interesting state.

Korea is at a point where it will never be again, where few nations ever are. Modernization has accomplished in thirty years in Korea what it took two hundred years to accomplish in the industrialized West. Until recently, Korea was the most rapidly modernizing country on earth. It is a perfect place to see globalization at work, the old and new side by side for a few years more.

I use the concept of evil to examine the process of globalization in a country in which many not only remember the old Korea, as it is called, but live it. The older generation even looks different from the younger. Not just worn and elderly, but inches shorter, the result of widespread malnourishment during the years of the Japanese occupation and after. Old

Koreans even move differently, not just taking shorter steps but taking up less space in the world, what it once meant to be respectful.

In half a generation these old Koreans will be gone, and with them the living embodiment of old Korea. It is a good time to talk with them. When one takes the time, a surprising thing emerges. Though neither old nor young Koreans say that globalization is evil (Koreans don't say that anything is evil), it is actually younger Koreans whose comments about globalization are more readily translated into terms Westerners would recognize as being about evil.

This difference is not, I believe, due to younger Koreans being more conversant with Western views of evil. They are (many older Koreans were unfamiliar with the concept), but more to the point, younger Koreans live in a world in which the meaning of what it is to be Korean is daily becoming less clear, the border between Korea and the rest of the world ever more permeable.

For older Koreans, the meaning of what it is to be Korean is clear: to be Korean is to suffer. Younger Koreans lack even this connection to the old Korea. Their suffering, which is real, does not attach them to their history but rather to a future that promises to relieve them of their suffering at the cost of their Korean identity. That is an evil bargain in any language.

Empiricism and Essentialism

For a Western academic, it was easier to gain access to the new Korea than the old. "I don't know everyone who is important," said one colleague. "But if I don't, I know somebody who does. Just ask, and I'll introduce you." It was true. In many ways Korea is a small country. I spoke with more generals and politicians than I knew what to do with, and I could have spoken with more. It was a blessing and a curse. Here was the weightiest research problem I faced: how to speak with as wide a variety of Koreans as possible, especially with those who might not ordinarily be interviewed by foreigners, denizens of not just the old Korea but the margins of the new? Following are some of the measures I took to speak with more than 250 Koreans from all walks of life. (Demographic and methodological details are discussed in the Research Appendix.)

The most enjoyable approach was to invite a group of Koreans to dinner. I paid for dinner and drinks, and they talked among themselves about evil, the Korean self, globalization, and much else besides. I listened and asked questions. Often my guests were students. On one occasion they were generals and politicians. These dinners provided an opportunity to listen while Koreans talked. After a couple of hours and some drinks, they said things to each other they did not say to me.

If "evil dinners" were the most enjoyable approach, probably the most useful was visiting restaurants in the middle of the afternoon, when the staff was not so busy, in order to talk with older, generally less educated women. In the evenings I visited coffeehouses and talked with the patrons.

Pagoda (T'apkol) Park in Seoul is a favorite place for older men to spend their days. Many were eager to talk at length. I returned almost a year later to conduct follow-up interviews. Although I did not talk with any of my original informants, I spoke with many whose views were similar. Seoul Station has become a place for the homeless to congregate since the economic crisis, and I spoke with a number of newly unemployed and homeless individuals there.[3] I also talked with taxi drivers, some of whom were the only informants I paid, as the driver ran his (or occasionally her) meter while we talked.

Handbills were posted at several universities and other public places inviting people to talk about evil. Former students doubted if any would respond. "Koreans do not do things that way," said one. In fact, a number did respond. Several teachers at English language institutes (hagwŏn) allowed their adult upper-level classes to become seminars on evil, the Korean self, and globalization. Most of the students were employed professionals. They had a chance to practice their English, and the researcher learned much. One hundred fifty students from Hankuk University of Foreign Studies wrote essays on evil, the Korean self, and globalization. Koreans are often more self-revealing in writing than in conversation. Those whose essays were particularly striking were interviewed individually or in small groups. I visited a dozen different classes at three universities, one outside Seoul, and talked with the students. Several called me later, and we met and talked further.

Several shamans, a half-dozen blind fortune-tellers, and other "scientists of divination" were interviewed, most at length. I made special efforts to interview Buddhist monks, Confucian scholars, Christian ministers, and Catholic priests. Almost two dozen were interviewed. One priest talked about confessions he had heard (in general terms, of course), which afforded access to guilty feelings about evil thoughts and deeds that would otherwise have been unavailable.

I interviewed several dozen professionals and experts in relevant fields, such as psychiatrists, philosophers, and sociologists, and a number of these same professionals were interviewed a second (and sometimes third and fourth) time after the economic crisis broke.

Roughly a quarter of the Korean population lives in Seoul. In order not to exclude others, I traveled to a small town in the Chŏlla provinces to talk with rural Koreans. In addition, I conducted many interviews in Pusan. A former student was running for the Korean parliament, so I joined him on the campaign trail and spoke with several politicos about evil, the Korean self, and globalization. As a member of a panel whose task it was to select younger international education administrators to receive grants to work in the United States, I interviewed a number of Koreans on "the front line of globalization," as one put it.

Sometimes I fantasized that if I were a good enough listener, I could hear all of Korea in one interview. The notion is untrue, of course, and denies real differences among Koreans. At the same time, it does contain a partial truth. Many informants were subtle and complex, with many Koreans and Koreas running through their conversations.

At other times I fantasized that if I listened to myself long and hard enough, I could hear all of Korea there too. Such fantasies are the stuff of Orientalism, as Edward Said (1994) calls it, as though Korea were little more than my lost exotic self. Nevertheless, even this fantasy contains a grain of truth. If there were not something in me prepared to hear it, I could not have heard it at all.

How Koreans talked about evil varied significantly, not so much by religion, but by age. Even Korean Christians sounded more like Koreans than Christians when it came to the subject of evil, which means, in practice, that they sounded like Buddhists. Although age made a difference in how Koreans talked about evil, what they said was remarkably similar across all the usual demographic categories, including age. There is, I believe, something it makes sense to call a Korean view of evil.

When a writer says things like this, the reader often sees red flags, as well he or she should. In writing that Koreans believe this and that about evil or globalization, I suppress the fact that at least some Koreans do not believe this and that but something else. Most readers will be aware of this and will make allowances.

Should they also make allowances for the fact that in drawing conclusions about Korean culture at a particular point (right now), I am assuming that Korean culture and society is more unitary than it is? As though Koreans do not believe many different and contradictory things at the same time, the result of layers of historical compromise, though perhaps peaceful (and sometimes not so peaceful) coexistence might be a better term. In this regard the common designation of Korean religious culture as syncretic is especially misleading, as though the result were a blend. The term "eclectic" comes closer to the mark, though even it plays down the terrible conflicts.

A recent review of a couple of new books on Korea concluded that "there is no Korean model. There is only Korean history" (Kagan 1998, 46). Even this is not quite right. There are only Korean histories. History is the history of compromise and struggle. What looks like a single narrative, the history of Korea, is in actuality a series of contestations and compromises among contending factions, contending stories. Society and culture do not exist except as compromise, or should I say the prevailing balance of forces?

I know of no way around this problem; the only recourse is awareness. First, keep in mind that my project is not an interpretation of Korean history. It is an interpretation of my experience of aspects of Korean history at a certain point: immediately before and after the economic collapse. It is the experience of one who is an outsider, not just to Korea but to Korean studies. It is the experience of an outsider who has come upon Korea at a singular moment, when the triumph of the Korean economy was giving way to an economic crisis that involves far more than economics. This approach does not mean that I ignore history but only that I do not imagine that I have explained the Korean view of evil. Rather, I have mapped its absence. This map is fundamentally a Western overlay, showing where East does not match West. It is all I could do, all any Westerner can do, I believe. The trick is to know it.

The other point I have tried to be aware of is that not only culture is built on conflict, but so is the self who lives, breathes, and makes this culture. Chapters 2 and 3 are about this self, the psyche of every Korean at war with itself because every psyche everywhere is at war with itself. The only difference is where the fault lines run. In a similar fashion, I find great conflict and ambivalence about globalization.

About evil I find less conflict and contestation. It is here, I believe, that I am most open to the charge of essentialism. Among Koreans of all ages, religions, and walks of life I discovered remarkable agreement about the nonexistence of evil, less but still substantial agreement about why they do not believe in evil. Not because Koreans are religiously syncretic (a generalization that is both untrue and unnecessary to explain this unanimity), but simply because Koreans agree on evil. Although I posit several explanations, one of which refers to philosophical shamanism (popular Taoism), my argument does not rest on the explanation, but on more than 250 interviews.

"Essentialism," and its cousin "ontologizing," are terms tossed around loosely these days, in part because it is assumed that one's text is the world, or rather, that it is impossible to know and tell the difference, text being the only world the critic could know—as though to say "X" is to make it so forever in the only place that counts, the pages of a book. It is possible that I am mistaken about the unanimity with which Koreans view the nonexistence of evil. If that were so, it would be an empirical failure on my part: a failure to interview enough different Koreans, a failure to listen attentively, or whatever. This is why I discussed my research methods so early in the chapter. It is, in any case, not a question of essentializing or ontologizing anything. It is simply a question of whether I have looked and listened with sufficient subtlety to be faithful to a complex and fascinating reality. About this only the knowledgeable reader can decide.

The Imagination of Innocence

Koreans believe that they have a choice about concepts such as evil, essentially dualistic concepts that divide the world in two.[4] Many Koreans, such as the Solomon woman, talk as if they and their culture have chosen to reject such concepts because they are superficial, false, and destructive. This hatred of dualism is, of course, not without irony, Korea being home to the most heavily fortified border in the world.

One young Buddhist put it this way. "The West is infected with dualism. You Americans destroyed the Indians because of dualism. The West had two world wars because of dualism. You are always finding and fighting an enemy."

What about the Japanese occupation of Korea, I asked? Wasn't that dualism?

He thought a moment. "No, the Japanese didn't want to fight us. They wanted to absorb us. It's just the opposite."

Not so different, perhaps, for the "absorbees," but that is hardly the point. The point is that it is possible to organize what seem to be very similar experiences, such as Western and Japanese colonialism, under vastly different categories, even apparently opposite ones.

Although this knowledge no longer astounds in our postmodern world, it is necessary to make a distinction between the situation I am describing and older and more familiar accounts of liberal tolerance. Herodotus writes of an encounter between Greeks, horrified at the thought that Indians eat their dead, and Indians, horrified to learn that the Greeks burned their dead. This difference in cultures is not analogous to the situation I am describing. Greeks and Indians both recognize the sacred significance of death. They just commemorate it differently.

A more relevant example would be romantic love. It is not, evidently, a universal experience. It emerged in the West in the late medieval period with the troubadours and was expressed in romances such as Tristan and Iseult and Troilus and Cressida. For most societies most of the time, including the West, romantic love has been an alien experience, an unknown category. Or so it seems. Many so-called primitive societies have no category akin to romantic love. Yet members of these same societies seem to have experiences that we would place under the category of romantic love, such as intense jealousy, infatuation with the beloved, and so forth. Nor is it simply a question of translation, of finding the right word. Members of these societies express incredulity and disbelief when confronted with the concept of romantic love. How could anyone believe or practice such a thing? Yet, when we look from the outside, we see (or think we see) experiences and practices that fit our category. Have we divided the world differently? If so, what is the principle of division? Or is someone in denial? But who?

When is denial more than denial? When it constructs a world that serves to make impossible not merely the existence but even the concept of something such as evil, or romantic love. When is denial less than denial? The answer is the same. Denial presumes the existence of something to be denied. If it is denial to construct a whole world in such a way that something cannot appear, then it is denial on a whole new scale: metaphysical incredulity, it might be called.

It is, by the way, quite likely that every culture is metaphysically incredulous. Culture is the rules by which some things are brought into existence by disallowing the existence of other things. Culture makes a world by processes of inclusion and exclusion at the level of being—that is, of existence.

Thought is dualistic: this exists, that doesn't. Complex thought is not necessarily less dualistic; it just plays with dualism, often by multiplying it. Consider, for example, words like "suture," which means both a drawing together of separate things and the separation itself. Cross-cultural study is concerned with how we draw boundaries and create spaces: spaces in which things can appear and spaces in which they cannot. I call this study of boundary and space making "cultural mapping."

How internally coherent must maps be? Benedict (1946, 11–12) argues that cultures demand coherence. People will do anything to make their values fit together. "They integrate them no matter what the difficulties." This propensity for coherence, of course, makes easy work for the mapmaker, as though culture were characterized by a Rosetta stone: find the key and one can decipher everything about the culture.

I hope I have not suggested that the nonconcept of evil is a Rosetta stone to Korean culture. For me it has been useful, but Korean culture does not fit so tightly together as all that.[5] I study evil not because it is the key, but because it is an important concept that is related to other important concepts, such as how Koreans view the self, how they are joining a larger world, and how exciting and scary this union is. Perhaps it matters little where one begins, as long as one follows the threads, one concept to another. This statement assumes that concepts such as evil, self, and globalization are related, but that is all it assumes. Related is not the same thing as internally consistent.

Evil Is Unrelatedness

I argue that Korean disbelief in evil is not an essentially linguistic phenomenon. It is a social one, the result of the way in which interpersonal relationships are organized. Linguistic practice is significant as it reveals and reflects these relationships. It is not the thing in itself.

When I argue that the absence of evil is the result of the way in which interpersonal relationships are organized, I am not making a causal statement, but a phenomenological one. Because Korean relationships are organized in such a way that evil cannot be known does not mean that these relationships are organized like this because Koreans wish to deny evil. Quite likely this is only one of several reasons. My concern, in any case, is not so much with the why as the how.[6]

"Tell me the relationship and I'll tell you what's evil" is what one Korean said to me. Many said something similar. In many ways it is the signature response, the motto of the Korean worldview, but only as this view meets the Western world. Koreans do not say "tell me the relationship . . ." among themselves. (I have some idea of what Koreans say among themselves, thanks to the "evil dinners.") They say it to a researcher whom they are trying to relate to. What Koreans meant is that evil cannot be defined independently of who is relating to whom because the relationship defines everything. The result, I argue, is that evil no longer means what it means in the West. I could get Koreans to use the term, but not like Westerners do. If there were a proof of my argument, this difference would be it.

If "tell me the relationship and I'll tell you what's evil" defines evil, then the real evil must be the evil that cannot be spoken: unrelatedness, the dread of absolute alienation and unconnectedness, pure loneliness, absolute difference. This, I argue, is how Koreans would define evil if they could. It is how they in effect define evil by organizing so much of their cultural life in the service of its denial.

Few Koreans said as much. They do not put their dread into words in the same way Westerners do, or at least not into the same words. My argument is a conclusion I have drawn from their silence. The denial of evil creates an evil-shaped hole in the world, the presence of something that is nothing. While most of my research was aimed at divining the shape of this hole, I also turn my attention to its content: the fear of absolute otherness and difference. It is not a fear *of* the other. That is the Western academic version. The Korean version is the fear of becoming other to oneself. It is from this perspective that I conclude this book with a consideration of why globalization is so frightening to Koreans—because it threatens to create a world in which Koreans no longer recognize themselves, in which Koreans are other to themselves.

Becoming other to oneself is, I think, a universal fear. Koreans can speak it in a way that Westerners cannot because Koreans experience themselves as living in a fleshy human web, closer to the disaster and more protected from it at the same time. Koreans just cannot call it evil. Little would be gained if they could. Much would be gained if Koreans could connect this experience to their fears about globalization, the better to be able to talk about choices regarding how to do and be in the new Korea.

Studying Evil Is Studying Globalization

By now it should be apparent that I am not just studying the Korean concept of evil. I am interested in the way that evil serves as a prism through which to view Koreans' experience of what is called globalization. Globalization is experienced by Koreans as posing the gravest danger to the self, the danger of becoming other to one's self, self's stranger. Most of the ways in which Koreans appear to embrace globalization are in fact strategies to keep globalization at bay. Conversely, many of the terrible things Koreans say about Confucianism have the quality not so much of nostalgia but secret attachment, as though Koreans were saying to themselves, "If I disparage Confucianism long and loud enough, maybe I can get to keep it. Who else would want such a terrible thing? Who else would care?"

If Koreans were merely afraid of globalization, it would not have the quality of evil. The evil of globalization stems from its attractiveness as much as its terror. Globalization promises freedom and enlightenment. To become other to oneself is terrifying, but it may also be the path to a richer, more complex and manifold self. One has to lose oneself to become new.

Many Koreans know this too. Those of us who have become cynical about globalization, seeing the choices it offers as tantamount to the choice between Coke and Pepsi, have lost the sense of wonder that begins with the shattering of the old order.

At several points throughout this book I suggest the appositeness of ancient Greek terms to translate contemporary Korean experiences. Here is a good place to start. *Deinon* is the term used by Sophocles in *Antigone* (332ff) to praise man. "Wonderful" is a common translation, but "terrible" and "fearful" are just as plausible. "Awesome" might be a good translation of "deinon," as long as we recall the terror of the transcendent the term originally evoked. It is with this awe that Koreans regard globalization. As I argue in Chapter 6, it is an awe that comes terribly close to what we in the West know as evil.

Only the last two chapters are explicitly concerned with globalization. Most who write about globalization write about the phenomenon at a remarkable level of abstraction. In so doing they imitate the phenomenon they would criticize. Homogenized analysis of global processes of homogenization is the problem, not the solution. In using the Korean disbelief in evil as a prism through which to view the experience of globalization, I avoid this problem by focusing on something unique and particular. Not that evil is somehow less abstract and more concrete a concept than globalization, for it is obviously not, but in studying evil I am talking to real people about real experiences, not theorizing about them at a distance. It is these real experiences that I bring to bear on the problem of globalization as a problem of life.

For the same reason that I do not write about globalization as abstract process, I do not write about "the East," even as I make a number of comparisons between Korea and Japan. I believe that the experience of globalization as evil held by many Koreans is an experience that is widely shared throughout the world. Globalization promises freedom and enlightenment, and it threatens alienation and estrangement from self and world. It is not just Koreans who are facing this terrible temptation, but it is about Koreans that I write. The only other possible approach would be to compare Korea with another country. Any other approach would be to lose the particular.

For many academics, globalization is about more than the convergence thesis: the argument that modern, industrial societies are becoming more and more alike, wherever they happen to be located. Globalization is the end of history that Francis Fukuyama writes of, the synthesis of centuries of conflict. To be sure, many who hold this thesis are less enthusiastic about it than Fukuyama, though Fukuyama's ambivalence should be noted. Universal freedom may be boring (1992, 199–208).

Not every grand perspective emphasizes synthesis. Some emphasize conflict, such as Benjamin Barber's recent *Jihad versus McWorld: How Globalism and Tribalism Are Reshaping the World* (1995). Another conflict-oriented perspective is Huntington's *Clash of Civilizations*. It makes less difference than one might suppose whether one chooses conflict or synthesis. Not conflict versus synthesis but distance at which the analysis takes place is most important. When we start with grand categories, be they globalization as the telos of history or globalization as the clash of civilizations, we guarantee that we shall not see anything new. We guarantee that we shall not see anything not already implicit in our categories.

It is not enough to know that diverse cultures exist. One must know and love the details, or at least be fascinated by them. This focus on detail is particularly important in a world that appears to be growing smaller, the lives of its inhabitants more similar. Cornelius Castoriadis puts it this way:

> If we look at the life of the thirteenth century . . . [comparing] this extraordinary diversity with the present state of the world, where countries are not really different from each other in terms of their present—which, as such, is everywhere the *same*—but only in terms of their past. *That* is what the developed world *is*. (1991, 196)

From Castoriadis's perspective, globalization is tantamount to modernization, and modernization is everywhere the same: industrialization, capitalism (including the state capitalism of China), labor as a commodity, the organizational capacity to put an entire population under surveillance, control of the means of violence, the industrialization of war, and the dominance of the nation state. To this list one should add the experience of modernization as juggernaut, beyond the control of state or citizens (Featherstone 1995, 145). Individuals and nations can either adapt or be pushed to the margins of existence. Let us call this the homogenization perspective.

From another perspective, one that idealizes the abstract idea of difference, globalization is about the experience of diversity, an encounter with a world of otherness in which the categorical imperative is reduced to tolerance of difference: resist the desire to assimilate otherness and difference into familiar categories of experience.

Multiculturalism is an instance of such a perspective: as the world grows smaller, we will encounter more and different cultures in our everyday lives. This is so whether we never leave the city of our birth, say Los Angeles, or whether we are globe-trotting travelers. Appreciate other cultures at a distance, seeking neither assimilation nor the denial of difference. Above all, do not demonize the other. At the same time, do not downplay otherness and difference. They are real, but not as scary as you think. Know the world as a carnival of difference.

Once this perspective was called cultural relativism—until, that is, people figured out that from relativism one could derive anything and everything, including intolerance, as some, such as skinheads and neo-Nazis have. Now it is called cultural pluralism, tolerance of difference and otherness being the only virtue.

The remarkable thing about the diversity perspective is its lack of specificity. In this it shares much with the homogenization perspective. Both make sense only at a vast distance. Each is treated as a universal principle in which the actual content of particular views and ways of life do not enter into the picture. For good or ill (as if these categories still applied), the particular is not important, except as illustration of the value of the idea of particularity.

Particularity and diversity are the way otherness and difference are valued from the perspective of homogenization. When do we value particularity and diversity for their own sake? When do we value not particular diverse ways of life but the abstract ideal of particularity and diversity itself? Only from the standpoint of homogenization, only from a perspective that sees homogenization as the danger, particularity and diversity the solution. In fact, to see the Ideas of particularity and diversity as the solution is to have already fallen victim to the belief in homogenization, the world as a single place.

Those who are truly interested in different ways of life don't talk about difference and diversity; they talk about the details. Nor do they "interrogate the discourses of globalization" to show how professionals in "the academic discipline of international relations" are doing ideology without knowing it (Youngs 1996, 58–61). This is the West turned back on itself, interrogating itself endlessly as the alternative to talking with and listening to others. No wonder the world starts to seem like a single place.

The trick, it is apparent, is to get the distance right. Too close and there is only one way of life, one's own, one's people identified with humanity. Everyone else is mere barbarians, the term the ancient Greeks used to refer to all who spoke another language, a language that sounded like everyone was saying bar-bar, bar-bar. Too distant and the world is a vast sea of difference (a perspective that combines homogenization and difference in one telling oxymoron), every particularity just like every other, because that is all one is interested in—the Idea of particularity, not its reality.

> Oh, East is East, and West is West, and never the twain shall meet,
> Till Earth and Sky stand presently at God's great Judgment Seat;
> But there is neither East nor West, border, nor breed, nor birth,
> When two strong men stand face to face, though they come from the ends
>   of the earth!

Rudyard Kipling's lines from *The Ballad of East and West* capture this strange but far from new tendency to get it wrong twice: overemphasizing the difference *and* overemphasizing the similarity, abstract diversity and homogenization being two sides of the same coin.

In their critique that came to be known as the Dialectic of Enlightenment, Max Horkheimer and Theodor Adorno (1972) argued that although Western reason may appear to originate in wonder, it actually originates in fear. In the end, reason measures everything by the standard of utility, whatever works to get the job done of mastering reality in all its guises. Not only is the process of globalization an extension of the standard of utility, what Max Weber called rationalization, to every corner of the globe, but the analysis of globalization threatens to ease, rather than criticize, the process.

Globalization is the production of order, not just an empirical order of instrumental relationships, market forces, and the dominance of multinationals, but a theoretical order that subjects the globe to a single analytic framework. The analysis of globalization risks becoming the intellectual justification of the process not because it necessarily sees globalization as desirable, or even inevitable, but because it takes the same perspective, ignoring the particular even as it idealizes particularity.

While theorists of globalization frequently state that globalization is an experience of rupture and discontinuity, they often write about it in such a way that it is neither. Instead, they write about it as if it were the rationalization of the world. In so doing, they emulate the worst aspects of enlightenment thought, idealizing the particular in such a way as to render it universal. Particularity becomes the fungible unit of universal experience. It is this strange legacy of the Enlightenment, the tendency to universalize about particulars, that I shall endeavor to avoid throughout this book. This tendency is, I believe, an attempt to recapture aspects of enlightenment self-certainty while pretending to have transcended it.

Globalization as Enlightenment?

Under what conditions would it be meaningful to claim that cross-cultural understanding (including, I hope, the understanding represented in this book) contributes to enlightenment? "Enlightenment" is not only an ambitious term but today a suspect one, as it should be. Nevertheless, it will not do to hand the term over to the cynics, just as we should not abandon it to those who would measure enlightenment by the standard of utility, whatever works to master the environment. Cross-cultural understanding does not contribute to enlightenment when we learn new things about another culture, even if they are striking and important. Cross-cultural understanding contributes to enlightenment only when we learn of new ways of organizing the basic experiences of our lives.

Wisdom, says Peter Winch, a student of Wittgenstein, is learning new possibilities for good and evil, not just in the sense of moral rightness and wrongness, but in the larger sense of what it is to live a good and meaningful life. "From other cultures, we may learn different possibilities of making sense of human life, different ideas about the possible importance that the carrying out of certain activities may take on for a man, trying to complete the sense of his life as a whole" (Winch 1964, 321).

Postmodernism stresses the insight and understanding that stems from taking structures, be they texts or societies, apart, showing how the pieces are fit together by force, even the force that masquerades as knowledge. True enough, but wisdom is also about putting the pieces together again, albeit in new ways, for which no one has the pattern. In the ruins one finds not merely fragments to play with but possibilities for constructing lives that are fuller and more meaningful than before because they combine elements previously thought to be incompatible.

The principle is clear but abstract. An example might help to make it concrete, drawn from an interview with a sage. The interview began in the faculty lounge of the Confucian University, eight big fat leather chairs with red cushions arranged around a classic Chinese table. Off in the corner a man in a dark blue suit did calligraphy with a big brush. One man wore black robes; all the rest were dressed in dark suits, white shirts, and serious ties. After introductions and tea, we were directed to what looked like a reconstruction of a classical Confucian village. Two plaques were attached to pillars on either side of the wood gate. One read "Alumni Association of the University of Confucian Studies," the other "Main Office of the Association of the Confucian Way." We were headed there.

The courtyard was defined by a series of perhaps thirty small rooms set around a quadrangle, a Confucian version of Jefferson's University of Virginia, or should I say vice-versa? Doors were of the sliding, wooden-framed variety, with paper panes instead of glass. Construction was mortar and beam, classic Confucian. It was not, however, quite what it seemed. Pairs of expensive athletic shoes stood before several of the doors. Empty plastic soda and water bottles littered the dirt courtyard. A motorcycle was parked in front of one door, and rock music playing softly came from another. The university allows students to use these rooms as study carrels.

My interview was with a Confucian scholar, designated as an "intangible cultural asset" by the government, granted an office and a stipend to instruct those who will teach *chesa*, ritual feeding of the ancestors, to schoolchildren in various after-school cultural enrichment programs. Proud that the government sponsors him, and Confucianism, he takes pains to explain that he is no professor, but a living cultural resource.

Confucianism flows from one generation to another through the blood, he says. Apparently the blood is thinning, or there would be no need for after-school programs like his. He does not see the contradiction. Confucianism is very clear to him, the practice of life more than a philosophy.

About sixty, with handsome gray hair and blue suit, only his white Armani socks clash with his grave demeanor. On the coatrack hangs a dark overcoat and a Christian Dior scarf. He wears a tasteful gold signet ring. The sage had *mŏt*, that difficult-to-translate Korean word that means both style and harmony. Throughout our interview he was bombarded with telephone calls, most from instructors on technical aspects of the ritual. He never failed to pause and excuse himself gently before getting up and walking fluidly across the room to answer the insistent phone, hurrying neither his callers nor his guests.

One call was from an instructor who wanted to know what happens when a son's father remarries and then dies. Can mother and stepmother both attend when the son holds chesa? Yes, the sage of chesa answers. Because it is the male who defines who is related to whom, the son's stepmother becomes a virtual blood relative of his mother, so both may attend. The sage sounds like a rabbi, giving instructions to his flock on how to conduct the Passover seder. He is not, however, just giving advice. He is preserving an agnatic society in a changing world (agnation defines descent in terms of a common male ancestor through male relatives only); in other words, he is finding new ways to define woman in terms of man. One is reminded of Aeschylus' *Eumenides*, in which Apollo argues that it is father, not mother, who is the true blood relative of the son.

Confucianism came late to Korea; it was not until the eighteenth century that one could say that Korea was a truly Confucian society. It was then that the Chosŏn state succeeded in restructuring family along patrilineal and patriarchal lines. But if Confucianism came late, it came to stay. "Korea has long been popularly viewed as the nation that adhered to Confucian principles more faithfully than any other" (Janelli 1993, 109). One wonders, however, if its stay is not almost over. Not yet over is the patriarchy it quickened.

Won't the influence of Confucianism wane in the coming years with the next generation, I asked?

"No, it will never change. Confucianism is not just ritual. It is built into the nature of the cosmos, including man. Man is a little cosmos, and his happiness depends on following the principles of the big cosmos. Loyalty to the state isn't just good ethics. It is the path of self-realization and self-development.

"Confucianism is the only complete worldview," he continues after taking another call, "and the West is suffering, with crime, drugs, and the rest, because it has deviated from universal principles. Only Confucianism can set the world to rights, because it is universal, not for a particular place or class."

His teachings recall the less attractive aspects of Plato, metaphysics untempered by eros. The sage of chesa was untroubled by conflict or contradiction. All mysteries had long ago been resolved. The best teachings, the ones that remain alive, contain their own contradictions, as Plato's eros denies his rationalism. Try as hard as he might to make eros a vehicle for reason, Plato could never fit them together, which is why his work lives on. Several Koreans to whom I made this argument replied that Korea is itself this complex tradition, weaving the ultimately incompatible doctrines of Confucianism, shamanism, Buddhism, and more recently Christianity into a richly contradictory whole.

As we got up to leave after a long interview, the Confucian sage gave my assistant a copy of a Confucian manual of manners for young women. I wondered if it was a veiled insult, but she seemed pleased.

Leaving the sage, we traversed again the dirt quadrangle of the reconstructed Confucian village, the sterility of the sage's Confucianism relieved only by the student slum that most of the buildings had become, the living detritus of modernity rendering a worn tradition more intriguing. Photographers love shots like this, nuns on motor scooters, Confucian villages turned into student slums. Presumably it is the contrast that intrigues. The question, of course, is whether it is anything more than contrast. Under what conditions can Koreans make something new of Confucianism?[7] Or is the very idea of making something new out of a tradition an oxymoron, the problem not the solution? Under what conditions, in other words, can these ruins—the ruins on which postmodernism loves to tread—contribute to enlightenment?

The answer depends, in part, on what one means by enlightenment. In his surprisingly traditional answer to the question "What is Enlightenment?" Michel Foucault (1984) says that it is the project of defining who we are by experimenting with the limits of identity. We know who we are only by trying to overcome what we think we know about ourselves. Enlightenment is not a body of knowledge, or even the practice of criticism, though that comes closer: the criticism of this or that limit as a given, a part of nature. Enlightenment is the practice of creating new identities out of old ones. It is, he continues, a practice that takes place at the margins and interstices of a society.

There are currently more margins and interstices in Korean life than ever before, more than there will be again for years. Globalization has created a ragged, running edge dividing tradition and modernity, one that provides new opportunities to experiment with identity, as well as new scope for identity's destruction. Soon the suture will close, globalization triumphant, tradition safely enshrined in museums and intangible cultural assets. Is this not the time for Foucauldian experimentation in Korea? Is this not what enlightenment must mean there too?

If one were to judge by the shelf space occupied by his books in the major bookstores of Seoul, the answer could only be yes. There are more works by and about Foucault than any other Western author. Almost all are in English, or translations into English; virtually none are in Korean or French. The trouble is, Foucault does not translate readily into Korean. Here I am not talking about the words, but the concepts, the ideas.

Take Foucault's leading idea, that in the modern world self-creation is an aesthetic act, "existence, a work of art." Baudelaire, not Kant, is the model. An aesthetic of self-creation must, in the end, be irrelevant to social life, the world divided between the bourgeois and the dandy, each more alienated than the other. "This transfiguring play of freedom with reality, this ascetic elaboration of the self—Baudelaire does not imagine that these have any place in society itself, or in the body politic. They can only be produced in another, a different place, which Baudelaire calls art" (Foucault 1984, 42).

Such a conception would be thoroughly intelligible to a Korean, with one vital distinction. Aesthetic creation is a social act, not an individual one. The object of creation is not the beautiful and free individual but the beautiful—that is, harmonious—relationship. The Korean aesthetic, devoted to relationships rather than individuals, is always already social. In this regard, the Korean aesthetic is more concerned with responsibility than freedom, even as it combines moral and aesthetic categories in ways more postmodern than Kantian. For Kant, one is ultimately responsible to universal principles, such as the categorical imperative. From the perspective of a social aesthetic, one is responsible for beautiful relationships.

Viewing relationships as aesthetics is actually enormously helpful in understanding the Korean nonconcept of evil. Evil is not the infamous other. Evil is a lack of harmony, ethics come closer to aesthetics than most in the West, including Foucault, have ever imagined. But it is not an insight that can be gained by "applying" Foucault. On the contrary, applying Foucault only guarantees that we miss the decisive difference.

It is one of the virtues of the East that it has never been as interested in the project of philosophical fundamental grounding as the West. It is the West, not the East, that has tended to confuse ethics with metaphysics. Similarly, if one does not believe in the abstract, autonomous individual in the first place, Foucault's demonstration that he or she does not exist is not so much shocking as equivocal.

Foucault may sound radical, but how's this for a truly radical thesis? From a Korean perspective, it is not just the rationalization associated with modernity but the universalism associated with enlightenment that is evil. The Kantian categorical imperative, as well as its more circumspect cousins, the theories of Kohlberg, (1983), Donagan (1977), Gewirth (1978), and Rawls (1971), are evil to the degree that they dissolve and devalue particular relationships, unique connections. Kant (1959, 16) is the worst, of course, referring to the "pathological love" that might lead one to favor family over strangers. But the tendency to esteem universals over particulars seems inherent in the Enlightenment itself.

One might argue that I have here confused modernity with enlightenment, universal empirical tendencies such as rationalization and globalization with universal principles. It is modernity that brings us the flattening universalism that Max Weber refers to, the iron cage that results from the transformation of human relationships into functional ones. In recognizing the moral personhood of every individual, enlightenment universalism actually resists the homogenizing power of rationalization.

The trouble with this answer is that it assumes that the fundamental unit to be protected is the individual him- or herself. If the unit of value is actually the intimate *relationship*, then enlightenment universalism must function much like Weberian rationalization, shattering particular connections, which is why the student interviewed in Chapter 4 had to get Kohlberg just backward in order to grasp his meaning. When Zygmunt Bauman (1991) writes about modernity in terms of the production of order, he is not just referring to natural laws and clocks, but to those social laws that shade into, and take their inspiration from, the universal laws of the Enlightenment.

This universalism, though, is not the only aspect of the Enlightenment. There is a counter-Enlightenment within enlightenment itself, the enlightenment represented by Foucault, but also aspects of Kant. This enlightenment involves experimentation rather than knowledge. It concerns the mixing and matching of elements previously thought incompatible. It understands that this mixing and matching takes place in the relationship of self and society. These are the leading categories of enlightenment, both Kantian and Foucauldian, that I use to make sense of Korean experience. In other words, these are the categories that I use to make sense of my experience of Korea.

From one perspective, every chapter of this book could be seen as an application of Foucauldian categories of enlightenment to Korea. No topic was more precious to Foucault than the transvaluation of good and evil, and this is the topic of Chapters 4 and 5. No topic appeared in Foucault's later works more often than the question of individual identity and whether it may meaningfully be said to exist. This is the topic of Chapters 2 and 3. No image of modernity was more central to Foucault than that of discontinuity, a rupture in time and tradition. Globalization is this experience, and it is the topic of Chapters 6 and 7.

From another perspective, my view of enlightenment differs from Foucault's. Globalization may offer a new and fuller image of human freedom and fulfillment without allowing us to realize that image in more than bits and pieces. From this perspective, globalization as enlightenment involves regret. To be truly *muendig*, the term Kant uses to denote mature autonomy, is to be in possession of a richer sense of regrets. This tone of regret is mostly missing in Foucault's account. In Chapter 7 I define what I mean by enlightenment. I am not just hitchhiking on a term.

Globalization is not just the topic of the last two chapters. It is in some ways the climax, intended to show that my analysis of the Korean nonconcept of evil illuminates social reality, revealing the dread behind the apparent eager embrace of social change there. My other purpose is to consider how Koreans, and others in similar circumstances, might use globalization as an opportunity to experiment with new social identities.

If evil is about the threat of becoming other to oneself, then experiences of evil provide not only new occasions for dread and terror, but new occasions to rebuild and reform the self. Experienced rather than denied or projected, evil may contribute to enlightenment. This experience does not require that Koreans posit evil. It may require that Koreans confront the dread of otherness that in the West is called evil and in Korea is called globalization.

Evil West

So far I have been working with an undefined term: "evil." To detect its absence in the East presumes its presence in the West, or at least its presence in Western history. I believe it is still present in the West, though it would take a book to prove it. *What Evil Means to Us* (Alford 1997c), a study of what a diverse group of Westerners think about evil, is that book. Following is a brief summary of what I take to be some of the more subtle and salient aspects of the Western concept of evil. It is to these aspects that I will be comparing and contrasting Korean views.

1. Evil is pleasure in hurting and a lack of remorse. In one way or another, most people "operationalize" evil in this way. Sadism is evil.
2. For many, evil is not just about malicious acts, but a spirit of malicious pleasure, a delight in destruction and pain for its own sake. For some this spirit is transcendent, a presence in the world. Some call it Satan. For others the spirit is immanent, a tendency in human nature. One does not have to be religious to believe in evil.
3. Not only is good the opposite of evil, but good and evil are Siamese twins. Without one we could not have the other; without one we could not know the other. Good and evil are in constant conflict in every human heart. For many, this conflict is the engine of history.
4. Evil is not just repellent, but attractive. Many of the great culture heroes of the West, from Milton's Satan to Goethe's Faust, are evil, or flirt

with it. When Blake says of *Paradise Lost* that Satan got all the best lines, he means that evil is more closely associated with creativity than is good. If evil were not attractive, it would not cause such problems.

5. Evil is not just what we do but what we suffer. This is not a view that is dominant in the West today, but it goes back to the Hebrew Bible. *Ra*[c] refers to anything bad, displeasing, or harmful to man (Isa. 45.7; Jer. 4.6; Amos 3.6; Mic. 2.3, Eccles. 1.13; Job 2.10). For more than a century, the Lisbon earthquake of 1755 was the paradigm of evil. Now it is the Holocaust (not in Korea, however, as one might expect). Think about how differently one must see evil to see it in a geological event. This is an experience still present in the West, but one not much attended to.

6. Evil both creates and solves the problem of theodicy, which has haunted the West for centuries. Many informants, not just conventionally religious ones, were troubled by it. How could an all-good and all-powerful God allow the suffering of innocents? Evil creates the problem because an all-good and all-powerful God should be able to eliminate it. Evil solves the problem by separating badness from God. Or rather, evil is a first step toward a solution.

7. When asked to talk about evil, most people refer not to an ethically horrendous act, such as mass murder, but to an experience of dread and terror. The most common example of evil among those I interviewed in the United States (and this included a number of Korean Americans) was the experience of going down into a dark basement as a child, the fear that something dark and dangerous was lurking about.

In *The Symbolism of Evil*, Paul Ricoeur (1969, 30, 347) writes about this dimension of evil in terms of what he calls ethical dread, terror at the inability to connect with the human world. The result is the loss of root and bond, a feeling that one is no longer anchored in the world. Evil is quite literally no-thing: the fear of nothing, absolute alienation from everything human. To experience evil is to fall into absolute otherness, an otherness that does not recognize the self as human.

It is this experience of evil, I believe, that is being reflected in the countless robots and vampires that emerged in the narratives people told when asked to make up a story about evil. It is the same type of experience to which Kafka refers in "The Metamorphosis." Gregor Samsa becomes a giant insect because he is regarded that way by his family, treated strictly as an instrument of its status and comfort. If we can understand why this experience of utter alienation is called evil by so many, not just bad or horrible, then we shall know much. Not just about Evil West, but about the present absence of Evil East.

Steps in the Argument

It is apparent that the concept of evil is intimately related to the experience of self in the world. Ricoeur writes of the prehistory of evil, located in a sense of rootlessness, a loss of connection with the human world. Koreans talk about what seem to be similar experiences without referring to evil, except when they are talking with a Westerner. Then they say, "Tell me the relationship and I'll tell you what's evil." Evidently the relationship comes first.

The next two chapters are devoted to the concept of the Korean self, which means Korean relationships. Only after that discussion do I turn to the concept of evil, the topic of Chapters 4 and 5. In Chapter 6 I consider why Koreans regard globalization as evil, and how evil is related to enlightenment. In Chapter 7 I consider further how globalization might contribute to enlightenment.

Although I believe my argument is more subtle and complex than the steps that represent it, this book is first of all an argument. Its steps, outlined below, roughly correspond to the order of the chapters.

1. Koreans do not believe in evil because they are so enmeshed in relationships that to call anything evil is to call everything near and dear evil.

2. One sees the origins of this way of thinking in the Korean view of the self, the topic of the first two chapters.

3. While Koreans do not believe in evil, they have experiences that we would call evil in the West.

4. If Koreans had the concept of evil available to them, most would call globalization evil because it threatens to transform even burdensome traditional relationships into strictly instrumental ones, an even worse fate for most Koreans. It is this fate that I call becoming other to oneself.

5. It would help Koreans to know why they find globalization so threatening. This understanding does not require the concept of evil, however. The concept is not crucial to making sense of experience or to avoiding evil.

6. I say that the concept of evil is unnecessary not because I am a nominalist but because I follow the Tao, which says that names are guests of realities.

7. Reality is ambiguous enough to admit of several interpretations—not *any* interpretation, but several.

8. Here is the opening to a concept of enlightenment that finds it not in universals or their ruins but in ways of life that combine elements previously thought to be culturally incompatible, such as the fortune-telling therapist discussed in Chapter 7.

9. In this sense, globalization creates new possibilities for enlightenment as well its destruction.

10. We see these new possibilities best when we assume neither that enlightenment is an incredible metanarrative nor that it must make us free. If Minerva's owl flies at dusk, then regret is key to enlightenment.

CHAPTER TWO

The Self Is a Conflict, Not a Continuum

"Tell me the relationship and I'll tell you what's evil" is not just a statement about evil. It is a statement about the self who experiences evil, and how it does so, from a location deeply embedded in particular relationships. Only this does not put it quite right, for it assumes clear distinctions among self, the concept of evil, and the people with whom the self is in relationship. When the self is the relationship, and the relationship defines the evil, none of these distinctions can be assumed, which is not to say that Koreans do not draw distinctions among self, other, and relationship, for of course they do. They just draw them differently, the topic of this and the next chapter.

"Koreans have a group self. They don't think of themselves in terms of 'I,' as centers of action and initiative. They think of themselves as we, and worry about how well they will fit in with the group."

One might think that a statement like this would be an instance of psychological Orientalism, and perhaps it is. Read from the perspective of Foucault (1980), who reminds us how often the power to control masquerades as knowledge, the statement could be seen as an attempt not merely to devalue Orientals but to deindividuate them. Singly at least, Koreans do not exist as Westerners do, for they do not know themselves as individuals. Hence their lives lack individual value. It would not matter in this regard that this statement was made by an Oriental, a Korean, as it was. Orientalism has long worked through its subjects.

What if it were the case—as it is—that every Korean psychologist, psychiatrist, and professor held such a view: that Koreans think of themselves as possessing a group self? Furthermore, only a tiny minority consider this a subject for regret.[1] Although not every expert traced the group self to the Confucian heritage, as its critics do, the vast majority regarded the group self not as a hindrance but a value worth protecting. So did the vast majority of informants.

Psychology of the Korean People: Collectivism and Individualism, published by the Korean Psychological Association, contains about two dozen papers on the topic, all by Koreans. For all their differences, every paper agrees that Koreans have a group self, or we-self, though what they mean by it differs. In addition, almost all find this self to be a value worth preserving (Yoon and Choi 1994). Such unanimity is actually disturbing, suggesting either that the group self is a meaningless construct or that it is an empty value, or perhaps both. What the unanimity does suggest is that the group self is not merely an empirical assessment of Koreans' psyches. It is a value.

One psychologist uses an analogy in arguing for the existence of a group self, stating that Korea's traditional philosophers were wise to accept Mencius's doctrine of innate goodness. They knew that the theory by which we explain human nature helps make that theory come true. Similarly, Korean psychologists should write about the group self as if it exists. In so doing they may help create and preserve it (Lee Soo-Won 1994, 88).

Westerners may scoff, though it is worth considering what it says about Western values that the academic reward system in the West works on almost opposite principles. Here the prize goes to the one who can come up with the darkest, most selfish, and greediest view of human motivation, be it Hobbes, formal theory (game theory), or even John Rawls's *Theory of Justice* (1971), which assumes that individuals decide what's fair based on their fear of ending up on the bottom of the social heap. Also relevant here is Foucault's idea of power/knowledge, that all knowledge is drawn into the project of domination.

Why the West esteems cynicism in its intellectual life is unclear. Like most cynicism, it is likely a dualistic (splitting) defense against disappointment. If humans cannot be good, then they must be bad. What cannot be allowed is that humans confront the terrible disappointment of not living up to their human potential, what Confucius meant when he said that men are close by nature, but by practice far apart *(Analects*, 17.2). Our practices have betrayed our natures, so the West does not talk about human nature anymore either.

Ruth Benedict (1946, 1–2) writes about Japanese human nature in *The Chrysanthemum and the Sword*, or at least she tries, running into a wall of contradictions. The Japanese are aggressive and unaggressive, insolent and polite, rigid and adaptable, submissive and rebellious, loyal and treacherous, brave and timid, conservative and open to new ways. They are the sword and the chrysanthemum at the same time, a nation of fantastic "but also's," as in militaristic but also aesthetic.

In a similar fashion, I argue that the Korean self is profoundly collectivist while deeply committed to individual self-assertion. The difference between my approach and Benedict's is that I do not assume that contradictions like this are unique to Korean, or Oriental culture. They are just easier to see there, at a distance. My other difference is that unlike Benedict I do not assume that there is a code, a key value that resolves the conflict. All selves are built up from incompatible elements, and they stay that way. The only question is whether the conflict becomes impossible to bear. *Hwabyŏng* disease, the topic of the next chapter, is what happens to some Koreans when it does.

There is no "Korean self," of course, only Korean selves. What I shall talk about is not so much a modal self as an ideal one, reflecting the ideals of Korean culture. Although Koreans are quite clear about the role of the "group self" in this ideal, it seems that it is Westerners who are better able to see (or perhaps just more willing to write about) the "but also" of the individual self that stands in constant tension with its groupish twin.

No one has emphasized Korean individualism more than Paul Crane. "The most important thing to an individual Korean" is recognition of his selfhood (1978, 25). Emotional stability, prestige, and awareness of being recognized as a person by others all determine a Korean's self-esteem, which is frequently expressed with the term *"kibun."* Crane runs several different senses of "selfhood" together, of course. Kibun is not so much state of the self as state of the self in society. But my point is not that Koreans lack a collective self but only that Westerners are inclined to see the individualism in the collectivism ("the most important thing to an individual Korean") in a way that Koreans are not. It is not really a question of psychology. It is a question of values.

Although not denying the communitarian values generally associated with Confucianism, the anthropologist Vincent Brandt (1971) points out a deep, countervailing tendency in Korean culture toward individual self-assertion. The culture, he argues, is best understood in terms of the conflict of opposing values, the tension between individualism and collectivism, rather than in terms of communitarianism alone. It is this conflict that best explains Korea's unique economic development, combining aggressive entrepreneurship with close government-business relationships (Eckert 1990, 409).

I argue in Chapter 6 that it is this same conflict that makes it so difficult for Koreans to take the next step toward globalization: the introduction of what the West calls market discipline in the economy. Market discipline is not just economic reform. It threatens the balance between individualism and collectivism that is at the heart of what it means to be a Korean.

Roger Janelli (1993) does not quite see the conflict between individualism and collectivism, arguing that the Confucian values of the Lucky Goldstar chaebŏl, where he worked for a year, are hollow. Respect for hierarchy, seniority, and group harmony are the language individuals use in order to pursue their own individual interests. Older employees believe in these values more than the younger, but only because the belief suits their interests. It would be easier for Koreans if Janelli's were the whole story, collectivism a false value. Adherence to false values does not cause the intense psychological conflict that adherence to contradictory values does.

Koreans appear to be remarkably individualistic and competitive, more so than many students at my state university in the United States, where many seem to have settled for mediocre academic and professional achievement years before they arrive there. Or rather, they see no connection between individual effort and reward, as though success all depends on who you know. "It's not what you know but who you know" is how many of them put it, a statement that sounds like a motto for the group self. It is not. You would rarely hear a Korean say it. To do so would devalue the group and its goals, as though it did not need each member's efforts.

Consider, by contrast, the system of competitive exams for university admission on which so much of a Korean's future depends. Families will frequently spend 30 to 40 percent of their income over a number of years to provide their son or daughter the private tutoring he or she needs to be admitted to one of the big three universities, Seoul National, Yonsei, or Korea. What is more individualistic and competitive than that?

Why do Westerners see the individualism, whereas Koreans do not, at least not in the same way? Several Korean psychologists have argued that Westerners fail to understand Korean collectivism because the West starts from an assumption of separate individuals who are subsequently glued together in the group. In reality, Koreans are so thoroughly we-selves that the Western model of the collective as a group of glued-together individuals does not go far enough. "The individualist perspective [on] collectivism hardly does justice to the indigenous psychology of collectivism, as far as that of the Korean society is concerned. The notion of a person as an autonomous, individuated human entity is not compatible with the sociocultural and psychosocial context of Korean society" (Choi and Choi 1994, 58).

Koreans are not separate individuals to begin with, so the individualistic competition you see is not really competition among individuals at all, but among families, the individual always representing more than him or herself. Every student sitting for a national examination is accompanied, as it were, by his family. (And not just in the subjunctive; many parents wait for hours in the halls outside the examination room.) The fact that this idealization has an economic basis makes it more persuasive. Until recently, one family member's entry into the salaried middle classes could carry his or her extended family there.

Bruce Cumings calls it "amoral familism" (1997, 334–335), not because he believes it is amoral, but to emphasize the difference from liberal individualism. Beginning as an economic project (laissez-faire, laissez-passer), liberalism quickly became a moral and philosophical project as well: the individual as the locus of moral worth, and the locus of truth as well. Empiricism is a liberal doctrine. "Amoral familism" makes the family the locus. Does this not make evil impossible too? This would seem to be my argument, and yet we must not jump to conclusions. Something like amoral familism was the way of the West for more than 2,000 years, during which the concept of evil emerged. The Korean story must be more complex.

Linguistic Analysis or Linguistic Metaphor?

The collectivism of the Korean self is often argued for by referring to the Korean language, in which the pronouns "I" *(na-nun)* and "me" *(na-ege, na-rul)* are used infrequently, and then usually to take responsibility, as in "my fault" *(nae chalmot)* or "my responsibility" *(nae ch'aegim)*. Instead, Koreans use the terms "we" *(uri)* and "our" *(uri-ŭi)*. Thus, Koreans will frequently say "our wife" *(uri puin)*. The linguistic practice originated, said many Koreans, in the ethic of village life, in which to say "my wife" would be considered selfish and individualistic, separating both husband and wife from the community.

The question, of course, is what it means today. When people use the language of traditional community long after the community is gone, it may mean that traditional values persist. It may also mean that words can lose their meaning, becoming empty forms. Say any word real fast a couple of dozen times and it will start to sound strange and alien. Is there really such a word, you will ask yourself? Something like this may happen over an extended period of time, several hundred years. The word remains, but it loses its meaning, except that it happens so slowly we never notice the strangeness.

Postmoderns write about the "I" as a slippery signifier, slipping around the group, depending on who is speaking. One might argue that in Korea the "I" is downright elusive. That would not be correct, just as it would not be correct to argue that Koreans define evil in terms of relationships. The "I" is not so much elusive as nonexistent, being replaced by the decidedly unslippery "we" and "our," which do not change their meaning when they are used by different members of the group. Or if they do (and I believe this is the case), then this change in meaning cannot be tracked linguistically. It must be tracked psychologically and socially, by what people say and do, not the words they use.

Koreans frequently point out that a Korean term for humans (the term is gender-neutral), *in'gan*, is composed of two Chinese characters. One put it this way. "*In* was made to show two people leaning against each other, and implies dependency or mutuality of human relationships. The character *gan* means between. From this, we can say that Koreans, and maybe Chinese, thought people are people only when they exist between people."[2] My informant's interpretation is not a uniquely Eastern thought. Aristotle made much the same point when he said man was by nature a "*zoon politikon*," a political animal (*Politics*, i.2.1253a). This example is important, because it means that one can draw quite different conclusions from the same premises, that it is human nature to live among humans. The Greeks, after all, were the first Western individualists, or so we say.

Consider some of the different Korean terms for "uncle": *ajŏssi* (familiar, a nice way to address an older man of same or lower class); *paekpu* (father's older brother); *kŭnabŏji* (familiar for father's older brother); *chungbu* (father's second brother); *sukpu* (father's younger brother); *komobu* (father's sister's husband); *oesamch'on* (mother's brother); *sŏnsukpu* (own deceased uncle); *paekpujang* (others' father's eldest brother); *sonpaekbujang* (others' deceased father's eldest brother). The list is not exhaustive, and most terms for relatives have similar permutations, some many more. Certainly this shows that Koreans are sensitive to the complexities and permutations of relationships in ways that Americans, for example, are not. What else it shows, however, is quite unclear.

We should be very cautious about using what appears to be a linguistic analysis as a mere linguistic metaphor, as though the presence of so many words for a particular relationship, and the relative infrequency of the terms "I" and "me," tells us more than it does. Furthermore, if we are to use language as a metaphor, it is a game that can be played both ways. Consider, for example, that when I say "I am an American" in Korean, it is rendered simply "American person" (*miguk saram*). The "I" does not really disappear; it is suppressed in the language, evidently because it is deemed unnecessary. Everyone knows who I am referring to.

I make much the same argument about the Korean self: it is not so much absent as suppressed. One sees its presence everywhere, even if it is rarely mentioned. In this regard my argument here is different from the one I make in Chapter 4. Unlike "evil," the term "I" does not disappear, it just recedes into the background. This comparison, though, would be just another linguistic metaphor, not a genuine explanation. Particular terms are not terribly helpful in explaining what people are thinking, mostly because linguistic forms can become empty over time, eventually being repopulated with new meanings. But although terms are not important, the pattern of terms we call conversation is crucial. That pattern has been my concern.

I asked informants why Koreans say "we Koreans" (*uri han'guk saram*) so much. Most said they did it to be polite. Others said they never thought about it. One put it this way: "Sometimes people say 'we Koreans' because they mean it, they feel a part of our nation, or want to. But usually they say it to hide their personal ambition behind the group. That way they can pretend to want what's best for the group, but seek what's best for themselves." The heavy presence of we-words in Korean society demonstrates that "we-ness" is a value. It does not demonstrate *why* it is a value: because it is observed, because it is not, or because it serves to deny the presence of its opposite. Younger Koreans are making an effort to say "in my opinion" (*che saenggak-enŭn*) in place of "we Koreans think." Does this mean they have become more individualistic, or simply more aware of the hypocrisy of "saying we but doing I"? Or is this perhaps what individualism means? The answer will not come from the words, but from talking with the people who use them.

The Self Is Not a Continuum, but a Conflict

Just as the absence of a single word for "I" does not tell us anything by itself, so we should not assume that the separate individual is the real material entity, the group self a metaphor. The separate individual is as much (and as little) a fiction as the collective self: they are both metaphors. Are humans first of all between others (in'gan), or do we stand alone? It depends on our metaphor.

What seems clearly mistaken is the claim of still another Korean psychologist that although there may be different perspectives, there is only one human nature. Each theory has its own way of approaching human nature. One theory may be egoistic, another altruistic. But human nature itself cannot be both. There can be competing theories, but only one reality, one true human nature (Lee 1994, 86–87). The psychologist is mistaken not only, or even primarily, because human nature is itself a construct, but because the construct we call human nature is, above all, marked by conflict, and the collision of opposites. It is what Benedict means when she refers to the "but also's" that characterize the Japanese. Unlike the yin and the yang, these opposites do not nest neatly together. Sometimes they tear the individual, and the society, apart.

The most obvious and compelling thing to say about "human nature" is that it is both egoistic and altruistic, and frequently at the same time. Who has not experienced both in oneself, or another, frequently almost at the same time, for example driving aggressively one moment, stopping to help a stranded motorist the next? What is necessary is an account that puts this *conflict* at the center, rather than seeking to resolve it by saying human nature is really one or the other, or Koreans are really one or the other. The conflict is important because it creates psychological and social structures, like that referred to earlier: a highly regulated economy depending heavily on individual entrepreneurship. These structures produce and reproduce generations of individuals with like conflicts, individuals who in turn reproduce the social structures that produced them.

The second most obvious and compelling thing to say about "human nature" is that it is complex; the individualism-collectivism continuum is unlikely to capture this complexity. As soon as a scholar, in this case a Western one, says "the individualism-collectivism continuum has been isolated by many intercultural theorists as a powerful and robust source of cultural variation," we should become suspicious (Knutson 1996, 7). Not only because terms like "powerful and robust" are used in an almost magical way, granting a puny theory the aura of Atlas. (Isn't every theory puny, generalizing from a relatively few instances to a whole world?) But also because the author wants to explain the variation before understanding the variable, which is nothing less than a self. The author wants to use his measuring instrument, the continuum, before he knows what to measure.

What does it mean to be a self? How does the self organize itself in terms of such values as individualism and collectivism? Putting it this way suggests that a self could score highly on *both* individualism and collectivism, which is in fact what happens in Korea, as will be discussed later. Koreans are both individualistic and collectivistic, and it is the conflict between their individualistic and collectivistic selves that is central to the culture, as well as the psyche of every Korean.

This statement, though, can be made about every culture, and every human. The conflict between individualism and collectivism is the human conflict par excellence, what it means to live as a human in a world with others. Different cultures resolve the conflict in different ways, none, however, simply by placing themselves in a different position on a continuum that looks like this:

individualism ———————————————————— collectivism

as though we could put the United States toward the left, Korea to its right, and the Japanese still further to the right. Such a spatial formulation omits (or rather, suppresses) the most important thing of all, the conflict between them, the individualist and the collectivist at war in every human soul. It is not, after all, Ruth Benedict's point that we should place the Japanese somewhere on a continuum between chrysanthemum and sword. They are both at once, which is what makes them interesting.

"We are the Latinos of Asia," said one Korean. "We are more emotional, more individualistic, more self-assertive. We laugh and we cry out loud." Dozens of Koreans made similar remarks. "The Irish of Asia" is a frequent variant. Several referred to themselves as the Jews of Asia. (Is there something about being a member of a historically oppressed group that leads its members to think of themselves as more emotional and closer to nature than their hard-willed oppressors? Does it matter that the oppressors frequently share the stereotype?)

Certainly this self-characterization of Koreans is born out by the soap operas, as we call them, that run on all the television stations every night, dozens in the course of a week, each a catharsis of laughter and tears, mostly tears. For hours each night the camera lingers lovingly on the faces of the protagonists, as though not to miss a single millisecond of emotion.

A Korean television crew went to Japan in 1997 and filmed a pedestrian crosswalk in the middle of the night in Tokyo. Every car stopped and waited at the red light, even if no one was waiting to cross the street. At a crosswalk in Seoul not a single car stopped! (They don't stop in the day-time either.) The Koreans whom I spoke with, and others who wrote about it in the newspapers, loved it.

Something complex and puzzling is going on. Koreans characterize themselves as possessed by a group self, a mark of the most Confucianized country on earth. At the same time, Koreans assert a strong individuality, taking pride in it, particularly as it distinguishes them from the Japanese. There is no logical contradiction here. The contradiction is psycho-logical, insofar as it leads to certain patterns of individual and group conflict, and certain modal psychological disorders, that look different than in the United States. The trick is to focus on the conflict, stay with it, and not try to resolve it into this or that end of this or that continuum.

So far the terms "individualism," "collectivism," and "group self" have been employed casually, as reflects their status and values and stereotypes. Before going on to characterize these terms more precisely, in order to talk about them as attributes rather than slogans, it will be useful to look at some Korean short fiction. Nowhere else do we see the psychological conflict as a conflict between these values more clearly.

The Korean Short Story: Isolated in a "Uri" World

Until the last several decades, Koreans did not read many novels.[3] Fiction's genre was the short story, itself the product of Western inspiration, beginning about the turn of the century. Not only are there a lot of Korean short stories, but the most well known are widely known. A half dozen of my favorites, classics evidently, were known to most educated Koreans with whom I spoke and to a number with no university education at all. I cannot imagine a comparable group of Americans being familiar with similar short stories or novels, unless perhaps they are lowest common denominator works, what Americans call page-turners.

Until very recently, the aesthetic of the Korean short story has been social realism. Korean literary critics are frequently embarrassed, writing of the overemphasis on social realism in contemporary literature while hoping for the development of a more literary aesthetic (Lee Tae-dong 1996, 90). Be this as it may, social realism makes the Korean short story a marvelous mirror of the culture, its authors no alienated postmodern existentialists (if that is not a contradiction in terms) like Frederick Barthelme, but men and women immersed in the mainstream of the culture. To be sure, the Korean short story does not reflect the culture entire. Until recently it reflected a culture under the social and psychological domination of first the Japanese and then the Korean War and the military dictatorships that followed.

The realistic short story was itself a political and social act of liberation, the first and most important act of all: truth telling. "One result of this pressure on writers to portray familiar situations of human pain has been to devalue the role of the literary imagination. Literature has at times been treated as merely a means of social documentation" (Lee Tae-dong and Bro. Anthony 1996, 3). It is to this document that I turn.

Attributes of the short story itself influence the story it tells. In his study of the short story "The Lonely Voice," Frank O'Connor argues that the very form of the short story, characterized by its entry into the narrative in medias res, encourages a story line that is detached from community: romantic, individualistic, and insubordinate. It is, however, not just a question of narrative form but of national culture and character. In the United States one might describe the writer's attitude toward society as "It may work." In England the attitude would be "It must work," and in Ireland it would be "It can't work." Since Koreans are frequently compared to the Irish, in this case by Kevin O'Rourke (1981, 1–4), one might expect to see a similar attitude among Korean writers. In fact, this is just what one sees in the Korean short story: alienated individuals who can't get anything to work in their lives in a country that does not seem to work either. The result is *han*, that combination of frustration and resentment so difficult to render in English.

The other leading characteristic of the Korean short story (again it is hard to tell how much this is an attribute of the short-story form, how much of national character) is the absence of what the West calls tragic heroes, who destroy themselves while struggling against society and nature. Instead, one encounters protagonists who give up before they begin, or so some Korean literary critics say about their own literature. In the Korean short story, there is reconciliation before conflict, peace before the tragic end. The hero is resigned to failure before he or she has begun to fight

(Chung 1995, xli). Since the late 1960s the emphasis has changed, the protagonists of the Korean short story being less resigned to failure. They struggle not for survival but identity. They are "trying to define the protean identity of the true Korean" (p. xli). Above all, Koreans talk about who they are, and they talk about it a lot.

One other attribute of the Korean short story, and those who write about it, must be mentioned. Many stories reflect an attitude of self-denigration and self-contempt, as though both the genre and the nation have failed to measure up. Self-doubt is not bad, but good. But only when one believes that self-understanding could lead to self-transformation. Under the rule of dictators foreign and domestic, many Koreans seem to have experienced their doubts as impuissant, as though they lack the power to change anything, even themselves. "Society defeats is the ever recurring theme" (O'Rourke 1981, 11). Or as the protagonist of "Wings," by Yi Sang, puts it, "I looked down into the bustling streets. The tired pedestrians jostled wearily, like the fins of the goldfish. Entangled in a slimy rope, they could not free themselves. . . . All of a sudden my armpits began to itch. Ah, these are the traces of where my man-made wings once grew, the wings I no longer possessed. Torn shreds of hope and ambition shuffled like dictionary pages in my mind" (1990, 64–65). That's it, the end, no more, finis.

Not every Korean short story is like this. The most famous of all, perhaps, "The Buckwheat Season," by Yi Hyosŏk (1990), expresses the hope of a traveling peddler who has nothing, not even wife or child, only his memory of one radiant liaison lasting only a night that still illuminates his life. "Echoes," by O Yong-Su (1995), tells the story of a refugee couple who leave the city to build a utopian community in the countryside, complete with an ex-communist who joins them. The young couple's sexuality mirrors that of the nature that surrounds them, and the mountain god blesses their union. These, though, are hardly the average Korean short story, nor are these two stories terribly realistic in the mode of social realism, the documentation of reality, though they are hardly experimental fiction, at least as the term is used in the West.

Following are brief plot summaries of a dozen Korean short stories, most published between the end of the Korean War and the late 1970s, but several more recently. They are among the most well known, and widely reprinted, Korean short stories, and that is why I have chosen them. If they are social documentation, we should consider what they are documenting.

"Wings," by Yi Sang (1990). The protagonist's wife is a casual whore who may be trying to poison him, or at least put him to sleep while she brings men home. The protagonist rebels, coming home at awkward times, refusing to eat, but he is unable to leave or kick his wife out. The story ends as noted earlier.

"The Rock," by Kim Tongni (1990). A leper's son has gone off, perhaps taken by the occupying Japanese army. Her husband is long gone. Communing daily in the center of town with a rock reputed to have magical qualities, she acts as if rubbing it will cause her son to reappear. He does, only to leave again, but perhaps it was just a dream. The villagers are disgusted at the dirty leper fouling their wonderful rock. She dies while rubbing the rock, her tears transformed into crystals that cover the rock.

"Cranes," by Hwang Sunwŏn (1990). Two young men, childhood friends, are now on different sides in the Korean War. Which side is which hardly matters. Once they hunted cranes together. Now one is taking the other to be shot. As they pass a marsh, they decide to go on one last crane hunt together. It is a chance for the soldier to let his prisoner escape. He does.

"The Gray Club," by Ch'oe Inhun (1990). A group of young men allows a young woman to join their literary club, a private *tabang* (tea house) where they enjoy art, music, and literature, a sanctuary in Seoul. Soon the club begins to fall apart, apparently a result of the jealousy the woman engenders. Hyon, who invited the woman to join, is hauled off by the police, who think his effete group is a communist cell. Eventually he is released, and the club falls apart, but Hyon is liberated, free to see beyond ideology to individuals.

"Seoul: Winter, 1964," by Kim Sŭngok (1990). In a cold city two failed students drink and eat charred sparrows in a tiny bar. There they meet up with a man who, having just lost his wife to cancer, has sold her body to the medical school to pay for the burial and a few drinks. They get so drunk they end up taking a hotel room together. When they awaken their new friend has killed himself.

"A Cup of Coffee," by Kim Sŭngok (1980). A failed cartoonist plagued by diarrhea journeys around Seoul, trying to find a new job, only to be told that he is not a great talent and that the newspaper has decided to use franchised American cartoons. He loves his wife, from whom he is so alienated they barely talk. He fears that sometime in the future he may come home drunk and beat his wife, like the man next door, whose farts, beatings, and sexual struggles with his wife echo through their apartment so loudly the cartoonist is not quite sure they do not live with him.

"The Target," by Yi Ch'ŏngjun (1990). A young lawyer comes to small town, where he wants to impress his seniors. The best way, he decides, is to study with the famous monk and archer who lives and teaches on the mountain. One day he brings his colleagues with him. Preoccupied with making a good impression, he shoots and kills the son of the archery master.

"A Dwarf Launches a Little Ball," by Cho Sehŭi (1990). Driven mad by the bureaucracy that is condemning his house, as well as the factory he works in, all to build something new, a dwarf dreams he will retire to the moon. There he will polish the lenses of telescopes, keeping them free of dust in a place where there is none. Climbing the factory smokestack in the middle of the night, he falls in, his body only discovered by the demolition crew days later. His daughter saves the house by prostituting herself to the landlord in order to steal back the deed. There is, she suggests, not much difference between Korea in feudal times and the Korea of 1976.

"The Beating," by Yun Hŭnggil (1990). Run-down regulars at a run-down tabang become fascinated with the new cook. Telling all sorts of stories about him, they imagine he is a thief in hiding. A waitress finally dials a radio call-in show, telling the disc jockey she is going to kill herself, and giving the address of the tabang. The disc jockey calls the police, who rush over to the tabang. Seeing the police come running in, the cook jumps out the window, killing himself. Everything goes back to dull normal, and the regulars seem relieved.

"Another Eve," by Kang Sinjae (1990). Responsible for a retarded thirty-year-old woman-child, the nanny Agatha encourages her charge to drink all of her "quiet medicine" so her nanny can have some peace. The woman-child dies, and Agatha feels sorry for herself, regretting that she has lost a cushy position. Told entirely in Agatha's voice, she is revealed to be utterly narcissistic, caring for no one and no thing but her own comfort and well-being.

"In Search of a Bird," Kim Joo-young (1997a). The protagonist recalls a game he used to play as a child, looking for a bird in the thatch of his house.

The memory overlaps with his search for his tour group from work, which has gone to visit a Buddhist temple. Chasing after the group in a taxi, wandering all over the town, he, and we, begin to wonder if the group exists. As he finally finds his group, he also finds his bird, transformed into a pinecone.

"Searching for Ch'ŏrwŏn," by Kim Joo-young (1997b). The narrator and his friend set out in search of Ch'ŏrwŏn, a town of sixty thousand a few hours from Seoul. Why they want to go there is never quite clear. As they get near, everyone they ask says they have just passed it, it is just ahead, or down some side street. They never find it and end up taking some comfort with a pair of women they meet in a restaurant. Humans and bodies are, it seems, the only thing that is truly real, the only thing worth searching for.

Originally published in the late 1980s, the last two stories by Kim Joo-young have a more existential feel, the absurdity and illusion more explicitly drawn. They could be read as a critique of what it means to pursue the Buddhist ideal of nothingness in contemporary Korea—all you get is nothing. In substance, however, the two stories are of a piece with the preceding ten, about the inability of the narrators to connect with the world that is all around them. The result is an encounter with meaninglessness that threatens to destroy the narrators.

The most obvious and striking thing about these stories is that the collectivism that is supposed to be such a comfort to Koreans is nowhere to be found. Almost every Korean short story, with a few exceptions like "Echos," concerns lonely and alienated protagonists searching for something they never find. Although this theme is not quite so characteristic of the novel, whose devotion to social realism is less, it may be found there too, as *The Poet*, a recent and wildly popular novel by Yi Mun-yol (1995), reveals.

One might argue that the theme of the Korean short story is thoroughly compatible with collectivism. The protagonists are displaced and alienated because they, like so many Koreans in the contemporary world, have been cast out of the collective, while lacking the internal resources of individualism to cope with their new world. If so, one should then ask why the protagonists of so many Western novels and short stories, such as those by Barthelme, Philip Roth, John Updike, to mention just a few, seem equally lost. Nor are the characters of these Western authors recognizably more heroic.

In *Values of Korean People Mirrored in Fiction*, Kim Tae-kil (1990, 91) interprets postwar Korean fiction as a lament for the loss of genuine collective values. Korean fiction shows that although traditional family values remain influential in the countryside and among the old, selfish individualism reigns among the city dwellers and the young. I would put it somewhat differently, though certainly some of the difference stems from having looked at different representative works—thousands of Korean short stories were published in the postwar era. For both generations, collectivism and individualism were esteemed values in conflict. What has changed is the nature of the conflict between them.

For the older generation, the conflict took the form of individual versus the crushing weight of tradition, and family members who used traditional values to pursue selfish goals. "Yun Hung-gil's 'Emi' exposes the selfishness of some rural people who stress kinship only in words" (Kim Tae-kil 1990, 89). Today the conflict is between family and individual on the one side, the fragmenting forces of modernization and urbanization, which threaten both individual and family, on the other. This threat, though, does not draw family and individual closer. On the contrary, it divides them still further. In this regard Koreans may be quite cynical. "Although a Korean society is family-centered, the Koreans do not really enjoy getting together with their family members. . . . Our society is not one built family by family, but rather Korean society is constructed by each family member escaping from the family in his own way according to his age and sex" (Park 1994, 111).

Take Mr. Chi. When asked if he is married, he responds simply "of course." Rather than talking about his wife, he talks about his three daughters. He seems proud, but his mother says three daughters are heaven's punishment for having married a Christian. Mr. Chi left a succession of jobs before this one, which is going well. "This time I might voluntarily quit." Before this job he had not been able to hold a position for more than a year. He considered suicide. What saved him is Buddhism and golf. During the six-day week he works from dawn to dusk. When he comes home he fixes dinner for his daughters and goes to bed. His wife works late at the store she owns, not returning until ten-thirty. They meet each other climbing in and out of bed.

"Sundays belong to me," he says with a wry smile. Arising a little later, he has the house to himself for a couple of hours while his wife and girls are at church. He gets in his car and drives an hour and a half to a "mosquito course," a golf driving range covered with nets, so the golf balls don't go flying out into houses and cars. He plays on a real course only three times a year. It costs about $150 dollars a round, and he knows the dates of the last dozen times he actually played. He is working on breaking 140.

On the way back from the driving range, he stops by the Buddhist temple. There he has found inner peace. "It's the only time during the week I have a chance to relax." He loves the meditation, but sometimes he dozes. A number of foreigners attend this temple, and he likes to talk with them. "It gives me a different perspective on the world, before I go home and begin another week."

Mr. Chi might be a character in a Korean short story, but he is not. He is a Korean friend. The most striking thing about him is how alone he is in a "uri" world, the world of "we Koreans." Looking at the externals of his life, one would have to characterize him as woven into his world, enmeshed in religion, family, and society. At work he has become successful salesman. He is even participating in the globalization of Korean society, learning English, meeting foreigners. The impression he gives, however, is of a man alone, not so much alienated as simply disconnected, floating in a space bounded by his relationships but not connected with them. In this regard, he is like the protagonists of so many Korean short stories.

What are we to make of the Korean we-self in this light, the collective self that seems to so many psychologists and others to characterize the Korean character and culture? We should consider it a value rather than a description, an ideal that has become stronger even as (or rather, because) it is threatened with extinction. Globalization has little room for we-selves. The stories, or rather the world of experience these stories represent, are not evidence that Koreans are more lost than Westerners because they depend on the collective more and are so more devastated at its loss (although Koreans do report being more lonely than Americans in one of the few cross-cultural studies on the topic [Park 1994, 228]). The contemporary fiction of the West concerns protagonists at least as lost, and even more alienated.

What the Korean short stories do suggest is a different solution. Romance and adventure are the preferred solution for most Westerners: intense romantic union with another coupled with the anodyne thrill of adventure. The contemporary American novelist Paul Theroux captures this Western solution as lucidly as any, both in his novels and his life, judging from his autobiographical works and comments.

Koreans long for a solution with softer edges, to be enmeshed once again in the collective arms of society, in which the world once again becomes a meaningful whole. Until then they remain on the edges, looking in, waiting, hoping. One might attribute this difference to differences in child rearing, though such explanations have their limits. "Most Korean children have almost unlimited access to mother the first two or three years," says one Korean psychiatrist. "As a result they develop a confidence in the world most Westerners don't know. Life's hard, and the confidence doesn't last. But it stays with us as hope for the future."

Better seen as a trope than as an explanation, Korean child-rearing practices represent not so much an empirical reality (though they are that too) as a cultural ideal and hope: that there remains a world in which the lost wanderer might find a home. This world cannot, however, be sought, except perhaps in a dilatory fashion, like the narrator and his friend who set out in search of Ch'ŏrwŏn. It can only be waited for, as it can only be given. Hope for that which can only be waited for, coupled with a disgust at the self for being so passive, leading to energetic efforts to do something that can only seem ultimately pointless because it cannot restore lost unity: this is the theme of the Korean short story.

Confucius Says: The Location of the Self

In their recent translation and rearrangement of the *Analects*, Brooks and Brooks (1998) put book 4 first, arguing that it and only it contains the sayings of the original Confucius. The rest of the book is commentary by his successors over several centuries. This is not as radical a thesis as it may sound; many have wondered if the *Analects* contains any of the sayings of the original Confucius. But it leads to a fascinating reinterpretation that solves the problem of *jen* and *li*. Jen *(ren)* is often translated as benevolence, the goodness of the human heart. Li is generally translated as ritual, the proper observance of manners and customs. Which is more important in our understanding of Confucius is an old debate. The answer of Brooks and

Brooks is simple. Jen is Confucius, li, about which not a word is written in book 4, is Confucianism, the development of his followers.

I am not going to try to evaluate the historical accuracy of Brooks and Brooks's rearrangement and reinterpretation. Instead, I am going to use it as metaphor, another way of rethinking the relationship between individual and group self that is more complex and subtle than the continuum approach.

Plato and the original Confucius wrote within a hundred years of each other. They wrote under similar circumstances, when feudalism was being transformed into something else. It is what this something else was that differed. For Plato, this something else was urban democracy, which had emerged at Athens no more than sixty years before his birth in 427 B.C. For Confucius, this something else was court bureaucracy, the institutions of patrimonial government.

Plato's contribution to his transformation was to reinterpret the meaning of *arete*, which since Homer's day had meant noble words and great deeds, the excellence of the Homeric warrior. Such values were ill-suited to the city, leading to no end of strife. Although Plato writes of philosopher-kings as an ideal and apparently means it, his lasting contribution was to transform arete into *sophrosune*, excellence in self-mastery. Here is the history of Western philosophy in a nutshell, arete transformed from the values of a contest with others to a contest that takes place almost entirely within oneself.

Jen, argue Brooks and Brooks, had for the original Confucius much the same meaning as Homeric arete, at least in so far as it retained strong links to the values of a military elite. Rather than making this comparison, however, Brooks and Brooks note jen's similarity to the chivalric virtues of the Western Middle-Ages: bravery, duty, courage, fidelity, honor, and comradeship. In a sense, jen is already more civilized than Homeric arete. Although Achilles was concerned with bravery, courage, and honor, his sense of duty was deficient. Achilles' honor was his personal glory, not his duty to his comrades, at least not when these values came into conflict.

The transformation of jen parallels, in only some respects, the transformation of arete, so that by the later books of the *Analects*, one sees under the influence of Mencius that jen becomes benevolence (12.22). It is not, however, the transformation of the content of jen with which I am most concerned, but its form. Whereas Plato would internalize arete, making it the self-mastery of the exceptional individual, jen is internalized without losing its external quality.

This unique location of jen, at once inside and outside, is Confucius's contribution, suggest Brooks and Brooks. The transformation of jen was not his work but that of his successors. What Confucius did was to change jen's locus, rendering jen a virtue of the human heart in such a way that it never loses its original quality of being defined entirely in terms of one's relationships. Arete becomes a strictly internal virtue, that of self-control, the mastery of the desiring self by the rational self. Jen, on the other hand, remains defined by the quality of one's interactions with others, while at the same time becoming a virtue that can be individually cultivated. It has the quality of "honorific individualism," to which I shall refer in the next chapter.

The psychoanalyst D. W. Winnicott (1986) writes of transitional objects and spaces. The first transitional objects are usually blankets and teddy bears, toys that represent mother while at the same time pointing beyond her to a larger world of relationships. The point of the transitional object is that it is both mother and not-mother at the same time, so that the child may have the comfort of mother while separating from her. Transitional spaces have a similar quality, the quality of being in between: neither one thing nor another, neither inside nor outside, neither fish nor fowl. Transitional space is the locus of all creativity, and all newness. The Tao, pregnant with nothingness that gives birth to everything, is the original transitional space, at least in the East. More than one, less than two, is its motto.

Confucian jen has the quality of transitional space. Arete does not. Arete is defined by an inner conflict, above all that between reason and desire. Jen is defined in terms of acts but valued in terms of its indwelling in man (*Analects*, 4.6). Almost three thousand years later, the difference remains, not in the concepts of arete and jen, which are no longer popular virtues, but in the concepts of the self they reflect. Neither arete nor jen was a partial virtues, such as wisdom or bravery. Both summarized all of virtue, all of what it once meant to be an excellent human being. Today an excellent Western human being is inner-directed, master of self. Today an excellent Korean is not merely good at interpersonal relations. He or she *is* the interperson, the self located in the transitional space between self and other. This is the meaning of in'gan. It is, I suggest, not the same thing as the group self. It is instead a richer way to think about the relationship between individualism and collectivism than the standard continuum approach that still dominates cross-cultural social psychology.

Individualism and Collectivism

The standard formulation of the distinction between individualism and collectivism runs as follows:[4]

Collectivism	*Individualism*
1. Ingroup is extension of self	1. Self is distinct from ingroup
2. Ingroup is center of psychological field	2. Person is center of psychological field
3. Subordination of personal goals to group	3. Ingroup and personal goals are unrelated
4. Ingroup regulation of behavior	4. Individual regulation of behavior
5. Interdependence	5. Self-sufficiency
6. Ingroup harmony is important	6. Confrontation with ingroup may be good
7. Sense of common fate with ingroup	7. Personal fate
8. Shame control	8. Guilt control

Imagine, for a moment, how Confucius might fall on the continuum represented by these extremes. Exactly in between, one might answer, except that would miss the point entirely. To locate Confucius in between would take the complex, multidimensional interperson and flatten him so as to fit on a continuum that only applies, and only can apply, when the concept of transitional space does not exist. Confucius has to be made flat and one-dimensional in order to fit, which is just another way of saying that we have to think about the self in flat and one-dimensional ways in order to use the continuum.

We might contrast Confucius with Steven Lukes's *Individualism* (1973), his study of the history of the concept in Western thought. Among other things, individualism is an account of the dignity of humanity, with roots reaching back to the Hebrew Bible, an epistemological doctrine of the origin of knowledge in individual perception, a metaphysical assumption that it is the separate individual who is most real, and an ethical doctrine that morality rests on individual decision. Individualism is also an economic and political ideal. As such, it has been historically combined with collectivist trends, such as the cry of the French Revolution, "liberty, equality, and fraternity," a doctrine that mixes individualism and collectivism in ways not dreamed of by the continuum or dichotomy approaches. Rousseau's "general will" is an ideal of liberal individualism—that it need not forever conflict with the group.

The reader might wish to stop me at this point, arguing that I am subjecting what is merely a social-psychological operationalization, the individualism-collectivism continuum, to an impossibly high ideal: the rich complexity of the philosophical traditions of East and West. I would respond that social psychology, like every human study, should be subject to the great traditions, not because the rich complexity of the traditions is important, but because the traditions are as complex as the humans they write about, and that complexity is important. Nevertheless, it is possible to make this same point in a more down-to-earth fashion.

The individualism-collectivism continuum is misleading because it almost succeeds in rendering incomprehensible a fascinating empirical finding: Koreans who score highest on many measures of individualism also score highest on many measures of collectivism. Not just philosophers, but average Koreans, mix individualism and collectivism in ways that the continuum can only obscure. Not only that, but the continuum eliminates the possibility of psychic and social conflict between individualism and collectivism, as scoring high on one automatically means scoring low on the other. The result is that a fascinating anomaly almost disappears from view.

In a series of psychological tests given to Korean workers, those who score highest on measures of competitiveness and internal locus of control, measures closely associated with individualism (numbers 4–7), also score highest on collectivism (Cho Nam-Guk 1994, 229). This outcome is just the opposite of what happens in the West.

Consider some answers that contribute to a high competitiveness score:

a. Winning is best.
b. Doing your best is not enough; it is important to win.

c. To be superior a man must stand alone.

d. In the long run the only person you can trust is yourself.

Consider the answers that contribute to a high internal locus of control score:

a. Promotions are earned through hard work and persistence.

b. In our society, a person's earning power depends on his or her ability.

c. I am the master of my fate.

What are these scores doing highly correlated with "collectivism"? Is this not counterintuitive, even illogical? Only in the West.

The Korean psychologist who discovered this anomaly does not know what to make of it, concluding that Koreans are really collectivist, their individual power and ability placed strictly at the service of the group (Cho Nam-Guk 1994, 229). This conclusion does not seem wrong, but it does not seem quite right either. The problem is that the psychologist writes as though he is forced to choose, as though it must be one or the other, and not both, as though an individual could never be both individualistic and collectivistic at the same time. The conflict would be too great. What is needed is a more subtle and sophisticated view of the self, one who could be both individualistic and collectivistic and more. What follows is one suggestion in this direction.

In the West, Margaret Mahler's (1968) account of psychological development remains the single most influential model, far more widely held than Freud's. Mahler writes of the phase of separation-individuation, which lasts from about six months to two years of age. (Two Western years, three Korean years: Koreans are one year old when born, which already tells us something about separation and individuation.) Mahler joins the separation-individuation stage with a hyphen, as though they were one inseparable process. Perhaps they are not. The separation stage "refers to those intrapsychic processes through which the child emerges from the symbiotic dual unity with mother." Individuation "refers to those processes by which the child distinguishes his or her own individual characteristics, so that the self becomes differentiated from the object and is represented intrapsychically as a series of self-representations" (Moore and Fine 1990, 180–181).

Must the two stages always be joined? Alan Roland argues they need not be (1988, 100–101). In India and Japan, individuation takes place without separation. The child, and later adult, develops a fairly consistent set of self-representations without the separation we expect in the West. It is Roland's most exciting finding, suggesting that we need not reject our commonsense experience of this category because we lack the theoretical subtlety to explain it. Certainly it seems to fit Korea as well, even in regard to something so simple and apparently straightforward as age. If a child is already one year old when born, then his status as an individual does not depend on separation from mother. He was already an individual even in the womb, the original collective, the most "uri" of worlds.

Let us make the theory just a little more complex. Most psychoanalysts, including Heinz Kohut (1984), upon whom Roland draws, hold that the self is constructed out of paired images of self and other, self and self-object as it is called in the literature. Some of the most severe psychological disorders, the borderline disorders they are called, stem from the inability to distinguish self and object representations. This inability, however, does not mean that self and object are ever truly separate. Everything we know, feel, and imagine about ourselves stems from a series of internalized self-object representations, in which the self knows itself in and through the mirror of the other.

The self is not an image in the psyche opposed to its knowledge of others. The self is an internalized series of images reflecting our encounters with lots of others—lots of other people, and lots of different aspects of the same people, each twinned with a different dimension of self. Norman O. Brown puts it this way. "The existence of the 'let's pretend' boundary [between selves] does not prevent the continuance of the real traffic across it. . . . 'There is a continual unconscious wandering of other personalities into ourselves.' Every person, then, is many persons; a multitude made into one person" (1966, 146–147).[5] Brown is not talking about Eastern selves or Western selves, just selves.

Gilbert Rozman thinks he is talking about the "Asian self." He is actually talking about every self. "In the formative years, the child . . . learns to conceive of the self not as an abstraction, but in reciprocal terms appropriate to specific relationships. There is no independent ideal of an individual prepared to conquer a succession of worlds. Instead, one's identity is changeable, depending on the others who are present. Linguistically, in Japanese, this flexibility is reflected in the many terms employed to designate 'I' and 'you' " (Rozman 1991, 27).

Quite aside from the question of how useful it is to use language to decode self-structure, the remarkable thing about Rozman's comment is the way he assumes that the Asian self is somehow fundamentally different, dependent on relationships for its identity in a way the Western self is not. Where he may be correct is his assumption that degree of abstraction is important. Rozman, however, assumes that the abstraction at issue is the ability of the self to abstract itself *from* relationships. The real question is how the self uses abstractions *of* relationships.

We are all psychological collectivists, our psyches a maze of pairs, and pairs of pairs. The difference is that some cultures encourage individuals to have more abstract, imaginary relationships with their self-objects than others. We should not, however, assume that more abstract relationships are more compatible with individual autonomy. Quite the opposite may be the case. It is a point made by Alexis de Tocqueville more than 150 years ago, and it is the topic of the next chapter.

CHAPTER THREE

"Why Do Koreans Always Say 'We' and Do 'I'?"

What follows is a reinterpretation of three widely held views about individualism and collectivism. The point in all three cases is to confound the conventional wisdom and further confound the conventional distinction.

First is Tocqueville's study of the tendency of isolated Americans to think like everybody else, showing that group-think and separation are as likely to go together as separation and individuation. Second is a study of the distinction between shame and guilt, in which it is argued that the shame felt by members of a collectivistic culture may be more psychologically profound than guilt. Third is a report on an interview with a Korean psychologist, who recommends an upbringing that in the West is closely associated with individual autonomy but in Korea with being a good member of the group.

Following those reinterpretations is a more general discussion of the dilemma of the Korean self. Koreans are in the position of being forced to use valued relationships in an instrumental fashion, leading them to "say 'we' but do 'I.' "

The chapter concludes with a discussion of a form of mental illness unique to Korea, *hwabyŏng* disease. Hwabyŏng disease is one way people go crazy in a group culture, and it is contrasted with the modal psychological disorder in the United States, the borderline or narcissistic personality disorders. Although these dissimilar modal disorders reveal substantial differences between Korean and American selves, these differences are more subtle and complex than can be captured by a simple individualism-versus-collectivism continuum. There is much to be learned about the different ways people go crazy.

The Isolated Self Thinks Others' Thoughts While Calling Them His Own

It would be hard to find a self less ostensibly collective than the selves about whom Alexis de Tocqueville wrote in *Democracy in America*. No theorist has better appreciated the terrible loneliness to which men and women were subject upon the breakup of traditional society. Tocqueville was awestruck by the way a new race of people had become isolated from time, place, family, community, and society. "The woof of time is every instant broken and the track of generations effaced. Those who went before are soon forgotten" (Tocqueville 1956, 193–194). He was, in other words, struck by a society in which the communitarian self no longer existed, the form of society in which most selves have lived since the beginning of time. He was filled with fear and hope.

His hope was not purchased cheaply. Tocqueville knew that a society of men and women cut off from each other—what he termed "individualism"—was not more, but less likely to produce men and women both autonomous and free. He understood better than we how collectivism might actually support individualism, rather than being its opposite. Not only does democracy (by which he means not so much the institutions of majority rule, but the relative equality of citizens) make a man forget his ancestors and ignore his fellows, but it "throws him back forever upon himself alone, and threatens in the end to confine him entirely within the solitude of his own heart" (1956, 194).

The result is not merely that man "exists for himself alone" (the opposite of the group self), but that he is actually more dependent on the opinions of others, more inclined to follow the crowd. "The same equality which renders him independent of each of his fellow citizens, taken sever-ally, exposes him alone and unprotected to the influence of the greater number" (1956, 148). When Tocqueville says "unprotected," he means un-protected from the threat of isolation and alienation that is always just around the corner in a nontraditional world. And if one does persist in thinking differently? "You are free to think differently but you are hence-forth a stranger among your people. . . . I have given you your life, but it is an existence worse than death" (1956, 117–118).

Neither democracy, nor equality, nor liberty is Tocqueville's primary concern, but rather isolation, the isolation of the individual in the modern world. Isolated from the march of generations, from place, from an or-ganic community: this is the individual he writes about, not just in *Democracy in America* but in *The Old Regime and the French Revolution* and else-where (Tocqueville 1980).

> Aristocracy links everybody, from peasant to king, in one long chain. Democracy breaks the chain and frees each link. . . . Not only does democ-racy make men forget their ancestors, but it also clouds their view of their descendents and isolates them from their contemporaries. Each man is for-ever thrown back on himself alone, and there is danger he may be shut up in the solitude of his own heart. (1956, 193–194)

Tocqueville calls it democracy, and he is not wrong, but it is not just democracy, it is the modern world he is writing about, the modern West-ern world that is. Is it becoming the modern Eastern world as well? It is a world that fills Tocqueville with religious terror. In Chapter 1, I called this terror *deinon*, referring to the awe with which Koreans face globalization. How can a human survive in such a world and keep his or her soul? A soul that for thousands of years has defined itself in terms of place: in the world, in the march of generations, in the community, in the Great Chain of Being, in the web of relationships that marks every traditional society.

When asked "What is the worst thing that could happen to you?" Kore-ans answer like this: "Neglect is the worst thing, because to neglect some-one is to make someone's existence valueless. . . . The worst thing is if I am forced to live alone and have to live by myself for good like Robinson Cru-soe. . . . I hate to be left alone. The worst thing I can think of is losing the people I love. First I thought of me getting murdered, but the pain will only last for that moment, while the pain caused by losing the people one loves could last forever. I hate to imagine when all the people I love have died. I don't think I could ever recover from it."

This was said by a half dozen Koreans, their remarks here strung together to form a pattern. It is the single strongest pattern of my research. For about 60 percent of Koreans, and about 70 percent of Korean college students, "the worst thing that could happen to you" is to be "outside of all relationships, isolated and alone," alive in a world in which everyone one knows and loves is dead.[1] Another study reaches a similar conclusion (Park 1994, 228).

Only a few Koreans talked about their dread of isolation and aloneness as a source of conflict, as though their intense need of others threatened a hard-won sense of independence and freedom. For the rest it was simply self-evident that isolation and loneliness were the worst thing. The difference from the Americans whom Tocqueville wrote about is that the Koreans were aware of their interdependence, and its costs, including how often they suppressed their own opinions and beliefs in order to fit in with the group. A number felt angry at themselves for what they were willing to do to fit in, but it was not really a conflict. It was a regret that they cannot have all of every good thing. As one put it, "I do what I have to do to fit in. I don't always like myself for doing it, but I'd like myself even less if I didn't."

Americans, suggests Tocqueville, were especially vulnerable to the tyranny of the majority because Americans were unaware of their need to fit in. Unlike the Korean students who knew what they were willing to sacrifice to join the group, Americans thought they were thinking their own thoughts. This is background to Tocqueville's statement that "I know of no country in which there is so little independence of mind and real freedom of discussion as in America" (Tocqueville 1956, 116), not because Americans consciously tailor their beliefs to others in order to fit in, but because they don't, because it is almost automatic, each so alone with others. Without the intellectual, social, and cultural resources of the aristocracy, all Americans can do is think others' thoughts after them . . . and call them their own. Actually, they do not know the difference.

Who is actually more dependent on the group, the Koreans who know something of what they will do to fit in, or the Americans (at least the

Americans studied by Tocqueville) who have no idea that they are thinking others' thoughts after them and calling them their own?

Eunyoung attended her first two years of college at a prestigious university in Massachusetts, the same institution that one of the Japanese students mentioned in Benedict's *Chrysanthemum and the Sword* attended. Like Benedict's student, Eunyoung felt not merely out of place, but that the values she most esteemed left her without a compass in the new world.

Eunyoung's father is involved in international trade; she spent most of her high school years in the United States. While at college her English class read Edith Wharton's *Age of Innocence*, at just about the same time the movie came out. The other students just couldn't understand, she said, why Daniel Day Lewis (the actor who plays Newland Archer) married a woman he didn't really love because his family approved of her and disapproved of another, whom he did love. " 'Who cares what other people think?' " they said. " 'Just do what you want to do.' " At this point Eunyoung decided to return to Korea and finish college there. "I understood why he didn't; I understood perfectly well. When the other students didn't get it, right then I knew I had to leave. How could I be around people who had no understanding of the world I lived in?"

Why didn't Archer marry the girl he really loved, I asked?

"If he elopes and goes to France, how does he live when the passionate love is gone? You have to measure, passionate love on the one side, his whole life, country, parents, and everything on the other. You can't live on love. But you can live on *chŏng*. I know what I would do. I don't always like it very much. Sometimes I wish I weren't this way, but I am. I couldn't give it all up, not for love, not for anyone." She sounds like she knows what she is talking about, like she is speaking from experience.

Lee Soo-Won (1994, 95) uses "chŏng" to characterize the collective self, "exchange theory" to characterize the individual self. "It is chŏng that enables us to overcome our own point of view in relationships" and so fit into the group. Lee is less discriminating than Eunyoung, failing to distinguish between good (*koun*) and bad (*miun*) chŏng, and thus between affection and attachment, including those attachments that may be destructive. The question Eunyoung is willing to confront, even if she does not always like the answer, is whether it is worth it. It depends, she seems to conclude, on whether it is good chŏng or bad chŏng. She values both, but she wouldn't give up a romantic attachment for bad chŏng. But for good chŏng, "now that's another matter."

Does it make any sense to say that Eunyoung has a weak or porous ego, that she is less autonomous and free than one who gives up everything for love? Does it not make more sense to say that she knows her values, what she cares about, and that one cannot have all of everything one wants, and she is aware of how she would choose? Are these not the attributes of a strong self who knows that reality means choices among values? That hers is a strong group self makes no difference in this regard. Hers is still a strong self: highly individuated without being fully separated.

One observer says that Koreans are actually more self-aware than Americans because they are more aware of their relationships. Think of what this means. Self-awareness is not awareness of the pristine self. There is no such thing. Self-awareness is awareness of the self in interaction with others, including those others who exist only in our memories. Koreans do not have "Emersonian moments," says another observer. But there are other forms of self-awareness, forms that actually come much closer to what it means to be a self in the world.

Shame versus Guilt Cultures

Shame is the mark of a collectivistic culture, guilt the mark of an individualistic one. Or so the stereotype goes, point number eight in the collectivism-versus-individualism outline (Chapter 2). A shame culture, it is argued, depends very little on the ability to abstract and generalize from concrete relationships. If one is not actually seen doing something bad by another, then it hardly matters. It is as though one had not done anything bad at all. Conversely, a guilt culture presumes the ability to internalize actual relationships as general principles, so that it makes no difference whether someone actually sees or not. One can see this difference reflected in the quote from Rozman on "Asian selves." Depending as it does on imaginary relationships with a universal other, one might argue that the guilt culture is more advanced. Again, it is not so simple.

The locus classicus of the distinction is Benedict's *Chrysanthemum and the Sword.*

In a culture where shame is a major sanction, people are chagrined about acts which we expect people to feel guilty about. . . . So long as his bad behavior does not "get out into the world" he need not be troubled. . . . Shame is a reaction to other people's criticism. (1946, 222–223)

To be sure, the distinction between shame and guilt cultures is not simply a distinction between East and West. Alvin Gouldner (1965) is one of several who have argued that ancient Greek culture was a shame culture. It took Plato to transform the primitive shame culture idealized in the *Iliad* and *Odyssey*, and much Greek tragedy, such as Sophocles' *Ajax* (in which intentions count for nothing, results everything), into a guilt culture. Plato did so by constructing a complex, three-part psyche at war with itself, transforming arete into self-mastery, as discussed earlier. Only such a complex psyche possesses the categorical richness to feel anger at itself for disobeying abstract principles of justice. More than two millennia later, Freud would use a similar model of a three-part mind, a model so similar he acknowledges his debt to Plato (Freud 1962, xviii).

One may summarize the teachings of Confucius in a single sentence: to teach men to have proper shame at the proper things. One who does is called a gentleman (*junzi*), "a man who has a sense of shame in the way he conducts himself" (*Analects*, 13.20). We in the West tend to see the gentleman as admirable but hardly profound in his virtue, which rather tends toward the conventional. The tendency is thus to equate Confucianism, shame culture, and an excessive, or at least somewhat superficial, concern with appearances. In fact, shame may be at least as profound as guilt. Not only because shame may run "deep," but because guilt may be quite "shallow."

At its stereotypical worst, the shame-guilt distinction argues that the inhabitants of a shame culture feel embarrassment, the "loss of face" that is said to overcome Easterners when are confronted with wrongdoing, such as taking more than their share. If no one sees them, if no one knows, then they feel nothing at all. From this perspective, a shame culture is immature, its members unable to internalize the culture's values as guilt, responding only to the public humiliation that disclosure brings, a humiliation that stems from fear of ostracism, being excluded from this group.

A guilt culture is a sign of progress in individual autonomy, the guilty person internalizing the values of society so successfully that remorse, the pangs of conscience, arise even when no one knows, when no one could know. To be sure, the denizen of a shame culture may feel shame even when he knows no one is watching because he fantasizes an observer. But this kind of shame is not the same as guilt. Confucius, so the story goes, did not sleep naked even when alone, because he could imagine the censure of ideal others even when they were absent. This imagined other, though, is not the same thing as a conscience. Not just because the observer is more abstract, a principle not a human, in the case of conscience, but because conscience is about states of mind, not just acts of body.

Confucius naked is a misleading story. His idea was that people should be educated so as to feel shame at not living up to the highest ideals of benevolent humanity (jen). Here shame runs as deep as the narcissistic soul of humanity, which is about as deep as it goes, only it is no mere narcissism of the omnipotent infant but the narcissism of the ego ideal, which aspires to live up to the highest standards and feels ashamed when it falls short. (Narcissism is negative only when it lowers its standards to suit the self, rather than raising the self to meet them [Alford 1988].) Is feeling shame when one does not live up to the highest human standards really an inferior ideal?

Contrast what Freud says about guilt. Guilt, the voice of the superego, is not society's highest values internalized in oneself. That sounds nice, but it is not what Freud said. He said that the superego represents the aggression one would have liked to turn against others, turned back against the self, so as not to lose the love of powerful authorities, above all father. The discontent of civilization is the discontent of the guilty conscience, angry that it could not destroy all those who stand in its way, turning this anger against itself, experiencing this introjected anger as malaise.

> His aggressiveness is introjected, internalized; it is, in point of fact, sent back to where it came from—that is, it is directed towards his own ego. There it is taken over by a portion of the ego, which sets itself over against the rest of the ego as super-ego, which ... in the form of "conscience," is ready to put into action against the ego the same harsh aggressiveness that the ego would have liked to satisfy upon others. ... Civilization, therefore, obtains mastery over the individual's dangerous desire ... by setting up an agency within him to watch over it, like a garrison in a conquered city. (Freud 1961, 84)

Which is really more profound and mature? The shame one feels at not living up to the highest ideals of benevolent humanity, or the guilt one feels that is the result of aggression turned inward, ruling over the self like a garrison in a conquered city?

Why would someone do this, treating him- or herself like an occupying power, an analogy Freud draws from Plato? The answer, says Freud, is fear of loss of love. Helpless and dependent, the child depends on others for survival. To keep the other's love he turns his hatred against himself (Freud 1961, 85). Guilt here begins to sound remarkably like the stereotypical account of the shame culture, concerned with being found out, excluded, deprived from protection, and isolated from the group. Conversely, it is Confucius's concept of shame that begins to sound like the ideal of guilt, the distress one feels when not living up to the highest ideal standards.

"If I do something bad, really bad, and my friends and family find out, they will no longer respect me. They will have no place for me." One Korean said this. Another said "My acts are not just my acts, they reflect upon my entire family. If I act bad, they look bad." Is this shame talking? Presumably, as the referents are particular others, and how they will respond to the would-be perpetrator. But the psychology is no mere saving face, but rather a sense of personal failure at having failed to live up to common standards. Is this really less "mature" than the guilt that stems from a fear of loss of love?

In listening to Koreans talk about these things, I came to a point where I could no longer make the distinction, shame and guilt running together in ways that seemed impossible to sort out. I did not experience this difficulty because the concepts became confused in the minds of Koreans, but because the concepts, or rather the distinction, is unclear to begin with, and has been for 2,500 years. Plato did not replace a superficial concern with saving face with a profound concern for universal principles. Nor did Freud. They turned the aggression one would vent on others back against the self, occupying the self as though it were a foreign power. The result, frequently, is a heightened ability to act unselfishly (that is, against the interests of the desiring self) in the absence of external guardians, but we should not make more of this strategy than it is. Certainly we should not somehow make it out to be more profound that a proper sense of shame.

Bourgeois Ego or Group Self?

It could hardly be said that Max Horkheimer and Theodor Adorno, intellectual founders of the Frankfurt School of Critical Theory, valued the guilty man about whom Freud wrote. But they valued him more than the one who followed, mass man, whom Nietzsche called the last man. When Herbert Marcuse (1970), another member of the Frankfurt School, wrote of "The Obsolescence of the Freudian Concept of Man," he was not rejoicing. Freudian man may be obsolescent, but what comes after is worse, the man who feels not guilt but anxiety when he does not fit in with the crowd.

The source of the Frankfurt School's reluctant admiration for the guilty bourgeois stems strictly from Freud. In the typical bourgeois family, the son (they talk only about sons) comes to fear that his father will castrate him for his Oedipal pretensions, as well as for his murderous fantasies against his father. As a defense, the son internalizes the father's authority, taking over the father's values and attitudes as his own. It is this process, according to their interpretation of Freud, that is the foundation of the superego: society's values, embodied in the father, are internalized in the son.

The result is a strong but guilty conscience, producing the so-called guilt culture. As Horkheimer (1972, 125) put it, "the self control of the individual, the disposition for work and discipline, the ability to hold firmly to certain ideas, constancy in practical life, application of reason," are all developed through the child's relationship with the father's authority. Similarly, Adorno (1968, 85) sees the Oedipal conflict as a source of adult spontaneity and nonconformity, apparently because the resolution of this conflict can take such idiosyncratic forms, among which Adorno seems to include neurotic protest against society, which is better than no protest at all.

Applying this argument to Western Europe and the United States in the 1950s and 1960s, Herbert Marcuse (1970) argued that obsolescent Freudian man has been replaced by mass man, whose values have been preformed by the mass media, and early socialization by the institutions of the larger society. Father is weak, absent, a source of affectionate humor. In such a world, authority is nameless, faceless, "just the way things are." Freudian man, however guilty and driven, at least had the potential to rebel against society, as he understood himself to be in opposition to society, as once he stood in opposition to his father, representative of the larger world. Mass man, on the other hand, has nothing to rebel against. In "society without the father," to use Alexander Mitscherlich's phrase, everything just is, naturelike in its givenness, so that it does not even occur to one to rebel, just as one does not rebel against the mist.

"All they have to do is study, or pretend to, and mommy does everything for them. No one ever says no. They never learn boundaries, they never learn that the world does not exist to please them. In my clinic we even have cases of children who beat their mothers when they fail in school. And some of the mothers say they deserve it. Can you imagine?" The man talking is a psychiatrist, director of the most prestigious mental health institute in Korea. He is concerned about the "prince and princess syndrome" he sees emerging among the younger generation, who have never been disciplined by their parents.

Alan Roland (1988, 108) could imagine, writing of a similar syndrome of parent abuse in Japan, involving teenage boys who beat up their mothers. Deeply dependent on their mothers, whose ideals and expectations they have adopted as their own, these boys are in a rage over their failure, as well as their entrapment in a relationship that prevents their success. A common feature in both the Korean and Japanese cases is the absent father, so involved at work that he leaves mother and son to turn in on themselves.

An older middle-aged man with grown children, the Korean psychiatrist goes on to reflect about his own very different upbringing. "I never saw my father laugh. He was a stone face, like a god." A harsh god, perhaps, but not a brutal one, always waiting until mother was home to punish him or his brothers, so the child could go running to mother for comfort. Wrapping himself in his mother's skirts, his desire to kill his father slowly lessened.

"The way we were brought up has a name, ŏmbu chamo. It means literally strict father, tender mother. Without it there is no discipline in society. With it society is strong. Without it people behave like horojasik, a fatherless child, the worst insult you can call someone, at least in his generation. With ŏmbu chamo one gets respect for authority combined with tenderness. You get respect for authority without authoritarianism. It takes two parents with different roles: mother alone can't scold and love very well. Neither can father."

The same family constellation that produced a strong, independent bourgeois ego for the Frankfurt school produces a responsible and responsive "group self" in Korea. How can this be? In fact, it is not precisely the same family constellation. The Korean psychiatrist places almost equal emphasis on the mother, whose absence in the Frankfurt School's account has been noted by Jessica Benjamin, who argues that Horkheimer and Adorno have confused the process that produces a strong (primarily in the sense of harsh, demanding, and punitive) superego with the process that produces a strong ego. Horkheimer and Adorno confuse the Oedipal conflict, in which the son's sexual identity is consolidated, with an earlier process, relation to and separation from mother, in which the basis of individuality and autonomy is laid down (J. Benjamin 1977; 1978).

There is no need to proceed further with Benjamin's argument, which can quickly become very technical. The point is clear. Father's authority is not enough. It must be supplemented with love. When it is, the result is children (not just sons, as is the case when the Oedipal conflict is the crux) able to discipline themselves and respect others. The result, in other words, is a strong ego as well as a strong superego. Only we have seen that this teaching is most tellingly expressed by a Korean psychiatrist talking about his own child rearing during the Japanese occupation, when Korea was by most standards a traditional culture. The group self and a strong ego are not, it appears, contradictory, but complementary.

I am not arguing that there is no important difference between Korean and Western patterns of child rearing. Earlier I have pointed out significant differences, especially in the young child's early access to mother. What is apparent is that these differences are not well explained in terms of compliant group selves on the one hand, autonomous individual selves on the other. What one gets in Korea is an autonomous group self, to put it a little too simply. One gets the anomaly discussed previously, high individualism coupled with high collectivism. It is a recipe not just for psychological conflict, but social conflict as well.

Korean Family Values

Consider the following circumstances:

1. Koreans are the most individualistic of Asians, or at least they understand and value themselves that way.

2. Koreans are frequently personally ambitious. Whether this ambition is strictly for themselves, or whether they see themselves as striving for the greater good and glory of their families, makes no difference here. The vehicle for both is personal achievement.

3. Personal ambition can only be pursued through the cultivation of relationships with those in a position to bestow benefits, usually older and senior people. It is rare for a poet or artist to succeed by going directly to the public, even by way of the critics. "In the Korean literary world, you are not recognized as a real poet unless your poems are commended by some renowned writer" (Kim Young-Moo 1993, x). If the sponsorship of senior successful poets and artists is needed in the world of poetry, one of the more anarchic and less hierarchically organized areas of life, then how much more it is needed elsewhere. The pattern is not unique to Korea, of course, but it is significantly harder in Korea than in the United States to move from margin to mainstream. Those who define the mainstream control access to it to a greater degree than here, even in areas that might themselves appear marginal and eccentric, such as poetry.

4. Ambition is exercised through the creation and maintenance of relationships of obligation incurred by duties performed or favors bestowed. Consider a strictly market relationship on the one hand, goods or services for cash. Consider a strictly family relationship on the other, defined not so much by love as loyalty. This includes the fear of the consequences of disloyalty: marginalization and exclusion, lack of access to the benefits family brings, a combination of resources and emotional support. Even in traditional societies, many relationships involve a mix of both. In Korea, the family relationship dominates, almost always as an ideal, but frequently in practice as well.

Put these four factors together, and the unavoidable implication is that individual achievement invites, even requires, the exploitation of personal relationships. Nor should the practice be confused with what is called "networking" in the United States, cultivating those who might be in a position to exchange cash, including a paycheck, for services. In Korea one cultivates people without whose support one is not in a position to be a member of the larger "family" within which one may display loyalty and perform duties for superiors in the first place. One cultivates relationships to enter, remain within, and advance in the "family" that is the professional association, university, firm, or market. Outside it, there is no one to display deference toward, no one to whom it would matter. In Korea, one does not "network" to advance, one networks so as not to fall outside the web of the world. It is a life's work.

Not only is it a life's work, but managing personal relationships comes to redefine all work: or rather, it becomes this work. One Korean professional says that "Koreans cannot tell the difference between managing personal relationships and their jobs. There isn't any." The job of a professional is to manage his personal relationships. Period. This is why, I argue in Chapter 7, the most creative work in Korea is being done closer to the margins, where there are fewer relationships to manage.

The psychiatrist interviewed earlier tells a story. A distant relative got sick and was admitted to a hospital where the psychiatrist attends. The doctor's telephone didn't stop ringing for days, not until the relative finally went home from the hospital. "Koreans don't trust doctors, they don't trust hospitals, they don't trust bureaucracies. They only trust personal relationships. The only way [my relative] could get proper care was if people outside the hospital called on everyone they knew inside the hospital to take care of him. Everything is based on relationships. That's what they thought."

Were they right?

"I don't know. This isn't old Korea anymore. But if I got sick, I'd be too scared to find out. I'd do the same thing. I'd feel embarrassed about it. I'm a rational scientist. But I'd act just like my poor relatives."

Globalization will likely free Koreans from their obsession with the fleshy human web. They can go to rational hospitals and get treated by rational doctors. Bureaucracies will work like bureaucracies should, becoming more "transparent" and "rational," as the jargon has it (Koreans frequently use the English words, even when speaking Korean). In many ways, Koreans will be the poorer for it. In their hearts they know it.

It is only from within the human web that one can appreciate the plaintive question of one observant Korean: "Why do Koreans always say 'we' but do 'I'?" Americans do not face this conflict in quite the same way. It is more acceptable to say I as well as do I. Americans often have the opposite problem, trying to find a reason to say we. Americans, argues Robert Bellah (1985), lack the language or concepts to explain to themselves why they want to sacrifice for the commonweal. They frequently do, but because they lack the public language of mutual commitment and sharing, they do not do it as much or as well as they might.

Janelli (1993, 229–241) writes about young Korean executives who act as if they adhere to Confucian, or collective, values. They work hard, stay late, don't smoke, sit on the edge of their chairs when seniors are present, and generally accept a corporate hierarchy as stratified and ossified as the most traditional Confucian family. Seniors frequently compare their leadership to that of fathers, and the younger workers nod and act like dutiful sons, and occasionally daughters. Everyone pretends that the chaebŏl is like a family, but no one believes it anymore. Juniors do it because it gets them where they want to go, and because they cannot imagine an alternative. Seniors do it because it is in their interest. All increasingly sense that they are like actors in a play whose run is over, but they do not know it yet.

The advantage of Janelli's perspective is that it captures something of the individualism behind the apparent collectivism. The last section of his book is titled "Free Riders, Cultural Dopes, and Rational Fools," putting the lie to the stereotype of the groupish Korean, who supposedly identifies himself with his company as though it were his family, and with his family as though it were himself. Koreans mock the Japanese for acting like this, and they mock each other when one takes it all too seriously (Janelli 1993, 231). At the headquarters of Lucky Goldstar, group calisthenics were unpopular, being widely regarded as too Japanese.

It would be easier for the psyche of Koreans if Janelli's analysis were the whole truth, if Korean family values, extended to society, were only an increasingly transparent ideology. The tribute that vice pays to virtue, hypocrisy rarely seems to consume individuals or societies, at least when practiced within broad limits. Beyond a certain point it may, as with the Catholic church during the Middle Ages, though one might well cite the church's longevity to make the opposite point.

In hypocrisy one knows one set of values to be false, and so the conflict between two sets of values is mitigated: one is observed in practice but not highly valued, the other valued but practiced discreetly. Conflict may emerge, but it is tempered, as superficial as the false values. More catastrophic for both individual and society is when two deeply held sets of values conflict, as in the ambivalence one feels when forced to exploit valued relationships in order to survive and advance, as well as the ambivalence one feels when exploited by people one cares about.

Actually, the term "ambivalence" is too mild, too abstract. Better to talk about the wrenching conflict between the desperate need to assert oneself in the world and the desperate desire to belong with and to others. Better to talk about the rage and hate one feels when one is used by another who one truly cares about, and with whom one wants to continue a valued relationship. Or as Coleridge puts it, "To be wroth with one we love doth work like madness in the brain." One form this madness takes in Korea is *hwabyŏng* disease, discussed later in this chapter.

Janelli writes as if collectivism is today little more than an ideology, at least at the large group level, chaebŏl and nation. "We Koreans" is merely an ideology to which no one has found an alternative. One might argue that this is the inevitable result of applying a Foucauldian framework to Asian relationships. Every relationship becomes a practice of mastery and control, every encounter defined by the parameters of domination and submission. It is true, but it is not the whole truth. It is also true that what Koreans find most satisfying is the harmony, good feeling, chŏng, and satisfaction that stems from belonging to a familylike group engaged in the common pursuit of ideal goals. It is these same terms that Aristotle used to define the highest form of friendship (*N. Ethics* 1156b5–30).

Not even the satisfaction of belonging is the whole truth. The whole truth, if there were such a thing, would be the ambivalence and confusion that result when Foucault and Aristotle are both right. Koreans worry less than Westerners about the intrusion of relationships of domination and control into every aspect of life, including those supposedly regulated by affection and mutuality, such as the family. As members of a traditional, patriarchal society, they know that domination and control are everywhere. Far from idealizing the family as a haven from domination, they know the family to be its home. Many of the Korean short stories referred to earlier have this as their theme, their protagonists trapped not because they lack the courage to leave their families, but because they do not want to; they want to be recognized within their families, not to be free outside of them. They fight to be human, which in practice means that they wait to be recognized. They may wait quietly, but they do not wait happily, or peacefully.

What Koreans worry about most is that domination will become separated from human relationships. One way this happens is when the dominator becomes a beast, the subjects little more than prey. Another way is when domination becomes heartless, merely rational and objective. This, we should not forget, is the real choice in most of the modern world: not between hypocritical collectivism and genuine mutuality, but between hypocritical collectivism and the icy polar darkness of a world circumscribed by bureaucratic formalism and market exchange. For most Koreans the choice is clear.

"Chŏngish Individualism?"

Like shame, honor is not always a superficial value. Honor may run deep, uniting the individual self with the values of the society. For some people in some societies, such as the Japanese samurai culture, honor and shame cut to the bone. It is hard for Westerners to see this because we tend to divide the self in two: the pure, pristine real self and the social self, concerned with ephemera such as honor, which is somehow superficial, less real.[2] In Japanese culture, honor mediates individual and society, providing the individual a private, personal motive to live up to the highest values of society. In so doing, honor acts to unify the individual psyche, giving one a rudder in a sea of change (Ikegami 1995, 371). I made a similar argument about Confucius and jen.

Ruth Benedict (1946) wrongly assumed that the self must be organized by one of two ruling principles: individual or community. Honor is neither, or both, joining individual and community while sometimes directing the individual away from the values of the community toward a higher value, an abstract sense of honor: the values of an ideal community.

What happens when the highest value is not honor, but chŏng, belonging and affection? Chŏng is, in fact, the highest value in Korea, not because Koreans are unconcerned with honor. Honor may become a fierce obsession. I met several Koreans who had been driven virtually mad by the failure of society to bestow the honor due them. The result was lives devoted to the infinitely frustrating search for something that cannot be taken, but only given (though sometimes I wondered if what they really wanted was love, honor serving as a poor substitute).

In general, however, it is not honor but chŏng that motivates Koreans. The result is an even more intense conflict, for although "honorific individualism" as Ikegami calls it, is not necessarily illogical, "chŏngish individualism" is. The question, of course, is whether "chŏngish individualism" might have a psycho-logic of its own.

It does, and the best exemplar is Eunyoung, who returned to Korea when her friends couldn't understand why Daniel Day Lewis didn't marry the woman of his dreams in *Age of Innocence*. Nevertheless, the conflict between individualism and chŏng is more intense, or at least not as readily harmonized, as the conflict between honor and individualism. If we understand honor as Confucius understood shame, honor is not the opposite of individualism. Honor is the values of a particular society (including ideal ones that never existed) made abstract and universal. Pursuit of these values may set the individual against society at any time.

Chŏng does not lend itself to such abstraction. One cannot pursue chŏng in the abstract like one can pursue honor in the abstract—that is, independently of the actual community. Chŏng is an ideal that is realized only in real relationships with others. Chŏng requires that certain expressions of individuality be kept in check. One must make one's edges round, the shape that Koreans most esteem, whether in a woman's face, or in a vase.

This suppression of certain aspects of individuality is not the same as sacrificing one's individuality, as Eunyoung reveals. But it is a starker choice than with honor. Chŏng is no mediation of individuality and society, but a state of we-ness that is neither. Combine Koreans' esteem for chŏng with their esteem for individualism, and one has a recipe for a stronger conflict than in Japan.

Still, it is possible for a Westerner, particularly, to overestimate the conflict, or rather its insolubility. Benedict (1946, 10) assumes that either self or the culture must be a unity. People "integrate [their values] no matter what the difficulties." In the West the self is the unity, in Japan the culture. But what if there isn't any unity? What if the self is a conflict, a conflict that is capable of manifold and complex resolutions in the real world? From this perspective, the self is neither a unity nor a collection of fragments; it is a pattern of conflicts. A culture like Korea will have characteristic or modal conflicts, but the resolution will vary among the members of the society.

What we must most avoid is making the conflict disappear in our theories. If we do this, we make the world simpler than it is, and ourselves more prosaic. There are several ways to make the conflict disappear. One is to say that the "real Korean" resides at the collective end of the continuum. Another is to argue that collective values are now no more than Confucian ideology, just one more form in which power masquerades as knowledge, and everyone knows it. Koreans just have not thought of an alternative.

Contrasting positions, both share the strategy of transforming a rich but conflicted self into a less conflicted but less interesting one. Still another way to make the conflict disappear is to declare the self a fiction, every self marked not so much by conflict as fragmentation. If the self was nothing but fragments, there would be no need to look at how selves residing in different cultures put the pieces together differently—or fall apart differently. Everyone would be the same, a collection of fragments.

It is hard to overestimate the importance of affection in Korea. Not only is it what makes life meaningful for most Koreans, but it the leading principle of social organization. Unlike honor, chŏng is in many ways antithetical to public life, drawing the circle of intimates tightly together, setting them against society, "just we two." But there is another respect in which chŏng takes on a public quality, or at least stands in dialectic (that is, dialogue) with the public. Hahm Pyong-choon (1986) has made this argument with special force. "Affection was made an 'idol' in old Korea," he says, by which he means the Chosŏn (Yi) Dynasty, 1392–1910. For more than five hundred years, the goal was to personalize the impersonal. Formalism was equivalent to coldness. It still is. Old Korea is deeply present in the new.

If a choice is to be made between law and affection as an agency for maintaining the culture, the Koreans would clearly prefer the latter as they have done in the past. The importance of affection in Korea lies in its function as a source of social stability and order. It was an important means of social control. [Traditional wisdom] stressed the fact that as long as the family remained cohesive and stable the country and the world also remained orderly and peaceful. (Hahm 1986, 67–78)

In the West we understand something of the terrible dangers of making affection for leaders the basis of social stability. Hahm, who knows something of the Western view (he wrote this essay while at Yale Law School), is equally impressed with the dangers of a lack of affection in politics. The risk is not just the creation of an iron cage, as Max Weber characterized the regime of bureaucratic formalism, but the potential for greater manipulation of the citizens by a totalitarian regime, which substitutes state-mediated relationships for private ones. In the West we think this is best avoided by separating private and public. Affection is the realm of the former, responsibility and social contract the realm of the latter. Tocqueville understands that this strategy carries its own risks. Isolated and lonely citizens are more, not less, amenable to certain types of totalitarianism.

Both strategies, affection and formalism, are risky, as is anything to do with governing humans. Lest we be too sanguine about the Western separation of affection and social contract, we should remember that the most awesome and terrible consequence of mixing affection for leaders and politics occurred not in the East, but in the West in this century. At the very least, Mao, Hitler, and Stalin are on a par, West no more immune than East to charismatic leaders who treat their willing followers as children.

Confucianism identifies the ruler with the father, using idealized family relationships to justify obedience. To no small degree the political theory of Confucianism is feudalism. But Confucius (unlike the legalists and neo-Confucians) creates a tension between family and ruler. If the two values ever come into conflict, family comes first. The *Analects* (13.18) tells of a man called "Straight Body" whose father stole a sheep. Straight Body testified against his father, and the governor reported the case to Confucius, proud of the boy's uprightness. Confucius disagrees, saying that in his country the son who covered up for his father would be the true straight body.

Confucius assumes not merely that parents and children will be close, but that they will mutually possess each other's bodies. One should be careful not to get killed or maimed in warfare, says Confucius, not for one's own sake, but because one owes a nonmutilated body to one's parents. One should not travel far from home while one's parents are alive, and one should mourn for three years because one was cared for totally for three years by one's parents. Only in mourning for one's parents, says Confucius, may one realize oneself fully (*Analects*, 8.3, 4.19, 17.21, 19.17).

It is hard to know if Koreans experience more family closeness than Americans, or whether they just experience it differently. Americans are not so prone to generalize from family to society and are more likely to regard family closeness as sui generis. I'm inclined to think that Koreans experience family closeness differently.

> What money is to the son of the west, marriage is to the Korean: every man
> is after it. . . . He wants to be married, not for selfish pleasure, nor because a
> little sugar-coated heart longs to rest in his love and be looked after. Not a
> bit of it: he wants a son, a son of his very own. He wants him wildly, unreasonably; anything for a son. (quoted in Cumings 1997, 50)

Certainly a caricature, this anonymous statement from the 1920s is not misconceived. The two most common questions asked of me by Korean taxi drivers, almost all of whom are men, were "Where are you from?" and "Do you have sons?"

The romantic union of husband and wife is in many ways opposed to the claims of society, accounting says Freud for the discontent of civilization. The father-son relationship is much more readily generalizable, much more readily read onto an entire society. A society based on families in which the father-son relationship is primary is likely more amenable to patriarchal authority. On the other hand, Confucius creates a permanent conflict between real families and symbolic ones, such as the state. This conflict too is a resource for resistance, and not such a lonely one. Tocqueville tells us why this resource is needed.

Weber (1951, 235) wrote that Confucianism does not support an ideal of a "unified personality," because under Confucianism "life remained a series of recurrences. It did not become a whole placed methodically under a transcendental goal." Only now we see that it is precisely this lack of a unified personality that may be a moral virtue, fostering a tension that need not be resolved. Not the lack of unity, but the attempt to achieve unity by fitting everything under a single principle, is the danger. (The other danger is to idealize fragmentation, finding not selves in conflict but just pieces.) The danger is not just in psychology, but in politics as well.

Yi Mun-yol characterizes the conflict this way in his novel *The Poet:*

> The great admiral Yi Sun Shin quit a battle on which the nation's whole destiny depended in order to attend his mother's funeral, and no one criticized

him. . . . If once the two principles of state and family loyalty come into direct confrontation within an individual, such a system of priorities can make the haemorrhage in that person's conscience all the deeper and more deadly. (Yi Mun-yol 1995, 51)

Every different way of organizing society causes psychological conflict, what Yi Mun-yol calls hemorrhages. The trick is to see where the bleeding comes from, its locus unique to every society, but not necessarily in order to staunch it. The wound is, for many Koreans, preferable to its only possible cure, bureaucratic formalism. Better to bleed for old Korea in the new.

Hwabyŏng Disease

What happens when the conflict between individualism and collectivism becomes too intense, when the self does not just bleed but begins to disintegrate? The outcome depends on the culture, even though the conflict is evidently universal. It is not just Koreans who "long for independence, but do not want alienation; they want to belong to a group but hate to be confined" (Kim Tae-kil 1990, 86). Everyone wants these things, though what people mean by "independence," "alienation," "belonging," and "confinement" varies among individuals, and across cultures. We all live between agoraphobia and claustrophobia; the difference is how we define too open and too tight.

Various too are the ways in which people in different cultures go mad when they cannot find the balance anymore. It is through the characteristic social pathologies of a culture that we see aspects of the culture most clearly (Devereux 1980). Cultural syndromes are a magnifying mirror, showing us in heightened and unmodulated form what the cultural reality looks like when it goes to extremes. Cultural syndromes are idioms of distress, as the medical anthropologist puts it.

Koreans get *hwabyŏng* disease. Americans get borderline personality disorders. Not every emotionally disturbed Korean or American gets these disorders, of course, but they are the modal disorders of particular places and times. Until now I have stressed the complex similarities between Koreans and Americans, or at least how the differences are more subtle and convoluted than the individualism-versus-collectivism continuum suggests. In the modal disorders we see the differences exaggerated. Sometimes exaggeration is helpful, as long as we remember what it is.

Hwa means fire, and *byŏng* means disease, so hwabyŏng means literally fire disease, but it is often translated as anger disease. Sometimes it is called *ul hwabyŏng*, especially when referring to the depressive phase of the illness. Hwabyŏng is recognized in the *Diagnostic and Statistic Manual* of the American Psychiatric Association (*DSM-IV*) as a unique Korean folk syndrome, "attributed to the suppression of anger." Symptoms include anxiety, panic, and a feeling of a lump in the throat (American Psychiatric Association 1994, 847) Interestingly, the attribution of hwabyŏng to the suppression of anger is itself part of the folk syndrome. Patients generally come to the hwabyŏng clinic after diagnosing their own illness and its cause, "swallowing all this anger." Not cause but relief remains elusive.

There is only one hwabyŏng clinic in Korea, at the College of Oriental Medicine at the Kyung Hee University Medical Center. But many Western-oriented psychiatrists and mental health professionals recognize the syndrome, though they disagree on whether it is anything more than an anxiety conversion disorder. For many, the value of the designation hwabyŏng is that it gives a name to a disorder whose symptoms and causes are comprehensible to patient and doctor alike. In other words, it gives them a common vocabulary.[3]

The doctor of Oriental medicine (O.M.D.) who directs the hwabyŏng clinic at Kyung Hee explains the origins and path of hwabyŏng in terms of blocked chi, the life energy that gets trapped in the chest, which is why it feels hot, as though it is on fire. The fire of "fire disease" is not just a metaphor for anger, or a description of the burning tightness in the chest. It expresses the principles of Oriental medicine, in which disease is explained in terms of the imbalance of fire and water energy in various parts of the body.

The doctor discusses a recent case in some detail, a thirty-four-year-old woman who was an inpatient at Kyung Hee and knew her disorder to be hwabyŏng (Lee Seung-Gi, Kim Jong-Woo, and Whang Wei-Wan 1996). The patient's father had another woman. The patient's mother had gone through hard times to raise her. After marriage she discovered that her father-in-law had a second wife, which she found disgusting. Her mother-in-law was a cleanliness fanatic, always cleaning something, never speaking to anyone. Whenever there was a conflict with her mother-in-law, which was frequent, the patient's husband, a pleasant but weak and unambitious man, took his mother's side.

The patient, a middle-aged woman from a lower middle-class background, was admitted to the hospital with headache, a disorder of the digestive system, insomnia, and vomiting. She was depressed, anxious, and easily startled. Occasionally she would explode with anger, only to retreat into passivity. She knew that her feelings were making her ill, but could not talk about them. She is, says the doctor, a typical hwabyŏng patient, a generalization confirmed by another study of more than one hundred patients seeking treatment at the clinic (Kim Jong-Woo 1996).

The woman's disease took more than a decade to emerge after the first apparent sources of stress. The usual cause is conflict with family members. Conflict with the mother-in-law is the second most frequently mentioned source of stress. An abusive or adulterous husband is the first. For constitutional reasons, and because they have fewer social outlets through which to express their anger, women are more likely to suffer from hwabyŏng. So says the doctor, who along with his colleagues traces the disorder to Korean culture, which does not allow people to express their feelings. In his account, hwabyŏng has as much to do with poverty, injustice, and social discrimination against woman as it does with the psychological problems of individuals. He writes a column for several women's magazines advising women on how better to manage their stress.

The patient was treated with a combination of Oriental medicine (herbs, acupuncture, and breathing therapy) and counseling. She left the hospital, but it would be difficult to say that she had fully recovered, because the environment in which she lives, and which is the source of her illness, has not changed. Once daughters-in-law were the modal victims of the disease. Now they give it to their mothers-in-law. Or so the saying goes. Plus ça change, plus c'est la même chose.

Western-trained and -oriented psychiatrists (M.D.s), including the one who wrote the DSM-IV description of hwabyŏng, use a somewhat different language in describing the disorder, not referring to chi or liver energy, for example. Nor do they use acupuncture or moxibustion in its treatment. Nevertheless, the similarity between their understanding of the disease

and that of the doctors at the hwabyŏng clinic is striking. Western and Eastern doctors describe the psychosocial origins of the disease in virtually identical terms, sharing modest pessimism regarding the ability of treatment to do more than alleviate the worst symptoms.

For both Oriental and Western-oriented physicians, counseling is generally aimed at fostering acceptance, transforming the han of resentment into the han of bitter acceptance. A Korean psychiatrist talks of trying to convince a woman to give up all expectations of her daughter-in-law, so she might develop an attitude of active resignation, the give-up mind (chenyŏm). One is reminded of Freud's assertion that the goal of analysis was to transform hysterical misery into ordinary human unhappiness.

For Western-oriented physicians just as much as Eastern ones, hwabyŏng is a uniquely Korean disorder, its symptoms reflecting the constraints of the culture: not just on the expression of emotion, but the lack of opportunity many Koreans have to change their lives. Striking is the way Korean physicians, both O.M.D.s and M.D.s, mix social and psychological diagnoses, one minute referring to the patient's family, the next to the constraints of Korean culture and history, as though they were continuous, one long chain of suffering, or "slimy rope."

"Han" is the term used by Koreans to characterize the anger that results from living under such constraint. The term evokes not just individual resentment, but the suffering of the Korean people, who have been forced to live, and suffer, under the dominion of three great powers, as well as their own ruling class, the yangban, and more recently the military dictators. "Koreans are born from the womb of han, grew up in the bosom of han, and live out han, die leaving han behind," says the well-known poet Ko Un, whose own tortured existence testifies to the truth of his claim (Luke Kim 1996, 10). Many Buddhist temples have a small "Washing the Han" building, often right next to the Gate of Non-Duality.

Hwabyŏng is probably not the most common form of psychological disorder in Korea, if these things can be measured. In addition, there are other cultural syndromes, such as taein kongp'o (literally anthrophobia), a social phobia characterized by fear of blushing, fear of offending with bad breath or body odor, and fear that one's gaze might be seen as too sharp, fierce, or threatening to others (Luke Kim 1996, 15–16). Taein kongp'o seems not so frequent, however, nor is it uniquely Korean. Taijin-kyofu is its Japanese equivalent. Like taein kongp'o, it is a form anxiety takes in cultures that place enormous influence on reading the nonverbal reactions of others, what Koreans call *nunch'i*. But if hwabyŏng is not the most common psychological disorder, it is the disorder that most Koreans seem to believe is characteristic and evocative of their culture. Almost every Korean I spoke with was familiar with the disorder, and most talked about it as distinctly Korean in some way.

Containers That Crush or Drop

One could compare hwabyŏng with Western psychological disorders by noticing its similarity to traumatic stress disorder and hysterical conversion. It may be more useful to step back and find another comparative framework, one a little more abstract, allowing us to capture the differences as well as the similarities. Wilfred Bion's (1970) concept of the container and the contained is useful in this regard. A psychoanalyst who devoted much attention to group psychology, Bion argues that relationships can best be understood in terms of the play of container and contained. The model is the mother's holding or containing of the infant, in which she bears her securely without dropping or crushing her, allowing the infant room to breath and move around without allowing so much room that she falls to pieces (compare with Winnicott 1986).

A recent advertisement for British Airways shows a passenger securely supported in a roomy seat, no doubt in business or first class. Supporting the seat is a giant stewardess, while the executive, the size of a baby, dozes secure in the knowledge that he will be neither dropped nor crushed. This is a representation of containment, what we all want and need from the day we are born until the day we die. (It is interesting, in this regard, to observe how tightly Korean babies are bound to their mothers when out and about, usually with layers of fabric.)

Bion applied the concepts of container and contained to social relationships, regarding the social group as functioning like mother to contain the individual. Unlike the ideal mother (or flight attendant), the social group has great difficulty holding without crushing. To hold its members well, the social group would have to provide them with emotional support—a sense of belonging, purpose, and security—without crushing their individuality and spontaneity. Similarly, the members of the social group must learn to stretch the container without exploding it, learning to temper their demands on society, which include demands for meaning, above all the meaning of life, not expecting the society to meet every demand perfectly. As an example of the individual struggling to contain himself, Bion cites the stammerer attempting to contain his emotions within the containers that are words (1970, 94). Bion cites Jesus as an example of an individual struggling with a social container that threatened to crush him.

One might equally well cite the struggles of Ko Un, the poet quoted earlier, who was a Buddhist monk and acting head of Haein Temple when he resigned in 1962 to become a spokesman for Korean nihilism, or so he was generally regarded. A decade later he was spokesman for a militant Korean nationalism. In 1983 he retired to the countryside with a new wife and young children. One might argue that this is merely a personal odyssey, and of course it is that too. Those who know Korean history will recognize in him something of what Bion calls the mystic, who traces the inside of the container, poking and pushing at its weak points, where the society is most repressive as well as most vulnerable to being penetrated (Ko Un 1993). Kim Sakkat, the real-life poet whose life is fictionalized in Yi Mun-yol's *The Poet*, is another such mystic challenger of the container that is Korea.

Korean culture, the culture that produces and understands hwabyŏng disease, is a culture at risk of crushing its members, leaving them no way out. The director of the hwabyŏng clinic explains this experience in terms of a series of walls surrounding his patients, walls that include limited education, limited resources, limited experience in verbalizing emotion, limited options. He then goes on to include the more distant walls of frequent foreign invasions suffered by Korea, as well as the tension between North and South Korea.

What's that have to do with hwabyŏng, I asked?

His answer was that all are sources of han. As another physician puts it, "Han is a symbol, a sign-language of the Korean psyche and Korean history" (Luke Kim 1996, 10).

Why don't men get hwabyŏng, I asked?

"Oh, they do," the doctor replied. "Then they give it to their wives. They drink, they go out with the wind [a euphemism for adultery], they abuse their wives. Even if he is a peasant (*sangnom;* pronounced more strongly, "*ssangnom,*" it is derogatory) at work, he can be a king at home. So he gives his han to his wife, and she suffers for him. But it is still their disease." And an eminently social one at that.

There is no hwabyŏng disease in the United States, even though there are patients with almost identical symptoms. There is no hwabyŏng because hwabyŏng has a cultural meaning, both to those who suffer from it and to those who treat it, a meaning that runs together the experience of Korea in the world with the experience of women (though not just women) in society. Although there is no hwabyŏng disease in the United States, there is a disorder that might be regarded as similarly culture bound, though the term "culture expressive" (that is, expressive of the culture) would be more accurate. This is a disorder characteristic of a culture more likely to drop its members than crush them.

Christopher Lasch (1979) called ours the culture of narcissism. Instead of hwabyŏng, the dropped American, abandoned by his wife and downsized out of his job by his employer, might devote himself to learning to pleasure himself, soothing his wounded self-esteem through plastic surgery, diet, and exercise, practicing his capacity for self-love, "the greatest love of all," as the popular song puts it. Less facetiously expressed, we may say that the dropped one likely suffers from what clinicians would call a disorder of the self or personality, probably not a full-blown borderline personality disorder, but the schizoid, schizotypical, and histrionic personality disorders so often associated with narcissism, understood as withdrawal from genuine relatedness with others. Heinz Kohut (1984) simply calls them disorders of the self, as good a term as any.

It is not possible here to go into the theory of these disorders, though one should probably say theories, since different schools explain them in disparate ways. Nor is it necessary to enter into the very difficult debate over whether these disorders have actually increased dramatically in recent years in the West, or whether the apparent increase is due to a change in theoretical perspective, the theory creating the disorder it observes. Suffice to say that many therapists, and not just psychoanalysts, hold that the type of patient they see in the United States has changed.

Freud saw women suffering from hysteria, and hysterical conversion symptoms, not unlike the symptoms of hwabyŏng. Most patients entering treatment today complain of vague feelings of unease, emptiness and un-fulfillment, an inability to feel as happy, secure, and fulfilled as they believe they are entitled. Low-level chronic depression is common, as is an in-ability to concentrate, once regarded as a failure of will. Together, these symptoms seem made for Prozac, or perhaps it would be more accurate to put it the other way around. The symptoms are made for a class of drug that provides "chemical containment," as one Western psychiatrist puts it, holding together a self that feels more fragmented than crushed, more ragged than hysterical, more empty than deeply depressed.

These are not truly psychological disorders, you might respond. They are marks of a culture in which people feel entitled to perpetual fulfill-ment, turning to therapy, including drug therapy, as people once turned to religion and philosophy in order to deal with problems more closely asso-ciated with lack of meaning and purpose in their lives than genuine emo-tional illness. Yours would be a harsh response, but far from mistaken, though it would underestimate the suffering involved when the culture no longer contains.

Some of this failure is social, about the failure of our economy and soci-ety to contain the fear of unemployment, poverty, and illness without treat-ment. The failure of containment is above all spiritual, about the failure of the culture to provide adequate meaning by which its members might ex-plain and understand their lives: their suffering, losses, and lack of fulfill-ment—that is, their human condition. In the West we are at risk of being dropped by our culture, provided an inadequate and superficial repertoire of stories and values by which we might make sense of our lives.

In the United States the modal psychiatric disorder reflects a society more likely to drop than crush its members, abandoning them not just to their own resources but to a life whose meaning must forever recede be-fore their grasp. This is the story told by F. Scott Fitzgerald in *The Great Gatsby*, the quintessential American novel. As though meaning could be seized like any other material thing, rather than through the only way it ever has: giving oneself over to relationships with others, including such ideal others as gods, saints, and *bodhisattvas*.

What are we to conclude? Not that the selves of Americans are more in-dividualistic than Koreans, just as the prevalence of hwabyŏng does not make the Korean self more collective. The self is a reservoir in which all human possibilities are contained. In understanding the ways in which cultures form psyches, we should seek to grasp not the poles, but the different patterns of conflict between them. From the conflict perspective, the most important pole is that which is undervalued in the culture, for it is the pole most likely to exert an attraction that the culture is organized to deny: individualism and self-assertion in Korea, collectivism and belonging in the United States.

The best evidence for this claim is the frequent, indeed almost universal assertion by Koreans that the Korean psyche is "collective." Such a statement is true, but it is not true as the speaker often intends. It is a true statement about a value that Koreans hold dear that makes it more difficult for Koreans to say the "I" with which they so often act. It is a true statement about one half of a psychological conflict built into the culture. That one-sidedness is enough to make Koreans different from Americans, who emphasize the other half. And it is enough to make them similar.

Conclusion

Let us return for a moment to the Korean short stories referred to in Chapter 2. Filled with existential angst, their protagonists are not so terribly different from the postmodern characters who populate contemporary American short stories. Mostly, of course, this similarity has to do with the fact that angst is angst, the difference between its existential and postmodern varieties more theoretical than practical, especially if you are living it.

This similarity does, however, raise the question of whether the characters in the Korean short stories are being crushed by their society, the source of hwabyŏng, or dropped, the source of the borderline personality disorders. In fact, most of the characters are being crushed and dropped at the same time, which is what it means to be isolated in a "uri" world. This state of being simultaneously crushed and dropped is important, lest my argument be read as replacing one false dichotomy, individualism versus collectivism, with another, crushed versus dropped.

My argument is intended to illuminate modal disorders—that is, the extremes. Characterizing modal disorders is not the same as summarizing societies, which, like selves, contain every extreme. Most of the short story protagonists are like Mr. Chi, enmeshed in a web of relationships with people with whom he cannot connect, and from whom he cannot separate. The result is too much of too little, too many people with whom he feels too little real connection. Here is the source of han, and hwabyŏng.

The Korean situation is not the same as that faced by the average protagonist in a novel by Roth, Updike, or Frederick Barthelme, whose characters are generally confronted with too few people with too little empathy, but their predicament is not the exact opposite of the Korean one either. When we compare idioms of distress, they seldom are.

CHAPTER FOUR

Evil Is Unrelatedness

Koreans are not less individualistic than Westerners. They are, however, differently individualistic, more inclined to use the ideology of collectivism to ease the conflict between individualism and collectivism that is at the heart of every psyche. Resolving the conflict between self and world in this way makes it difficult for Koreans to know evil. There is not enough space between self and others for evil to appear. Or at least this lack of space makes it difficult for Koreans to say evil. This is quite an "at least." Can one know evil without saying it? Koreans sometimes present themselves as more collectivistic than they are, or at least as more simply collectivistic. Could Koreans denial of evil have a similar quality, aimed as much at convincing themselves as others? This is one of the issues I set out to examine.

"Names are guests of realities," says *Chuang-tzu*, a Taoist classic. Chuang Chou is designating a position between nominalism and essentialism: names are words, but they are not just words. Words must be invited by experience and get along well enough to stay awhile. Does the absence of a particular concept of "evil" mean that the corresponding reality does not exist? If we deny "evil" have we abolished its reality? The question does not seem quite so easy, and so one might be inclined to argue the opposite: words are just words, their relationship to reality strictly nominal. Yet, to hold this position, which many do, is not without cost. One does not have to go as far as Samuel Huntington to hold that humans share certain common experiences that give meaning to their words.

Actually, Huntington's (1996, 56) position is ambiguous. On the one hand, he holds that "human beings in virtually all societies share certain basic values, such as murder is evil." On the other hand, he finds such commonalities trivial. The real action is with the clash of civilizations. It is ironic that the man who sees fundamental conflict and fault lines everywhere misses the fact that people in all societies do not agree that murder is evil, not just because they do not agree about the definition of murder, but because they do not agree about whether evil exists. Perhaps it is subtle differences like these that are the real fault lines. But how shall we know them?[1]

Common experiences using slightly different words is what I expected to find, based on my preliminary interviews with a small number of Korean Americans (see the Research Appendix). I expected the Korean denial of evil to be relatively superficial, a nominalist defense against an essential experience. Push Koreans a little bit, and I would find many of the same elements of evil I summarized under Evil West in Chapter 1. Koreans would not have the word "evil" (except, perhaps, the approximately 25 percent who are Christian), but they would have experiences that could readily be translated by the English term "evil." The Korean linguistic organization of badness would be different, but their experiences not so different. Or so I thought.

What I found was vastly more complex, a world in which it hardly made sense to say that Koreans deny evil, as the term "deny" presumes an experience to be denied in the first place. Rather, Koreans organize experience in such a way that evil does not have the possibility of appearing, possibly not even as an experience. "You learned the *concept* 'pain' when you learned the language," says Wittgenstein (1967, para. 384). But you don't need language to *experience* pain, or else why do babies cry? Is evil like that, or is it a more elaborate concept, about which we have a choice of whether to experience it or not? Or rather, about which cultures have a choice?

"If Koreans don't believe in evil," said a Western colleague, "then they must be relativists."

No, I replied, you can't be a relativist about nothing. Koreans aren't relativistic about evil. They don't believe it exists. It's not the same thing.

"What do they mean 'evil doesn't exist'?" continued my colleague. "Lots of things don't exist in Korea. Say windsurfing doesn't exist. That doesn't make it not real."

It's different, I replied. Windsurfing could exist; it just contingently doesn't (it does, but of course that is hardly the point). Evil couldn't exist because Koreans have created a universe in which there is no place for it.

Understanding evil is a complicated business. Not only must we consider the possibility that members of another culture experience evil without possessing the concept, but we must also consider the possibility that words easily and readily translated as "evil," like the Korean *ak* and *choe*, are not really about evil at all. In addition, we must consider the possibility that both these things are true: Koreans have an experience of evil they cannot or do not put into words, and this experience has only a little to do with the words they do use, like "ak" and "choe," that are readily translated as "evil."

A Nonworking Hypothesis

In order to get a grant to study something, it is necessary to pretend that one knows what one is actually setting out to discover. This pretense is known as a working hypothesis. My working hypothesis was that the Korean denial of evil would proceed by means of division and fragmentation, breaking up the concept into less terrifying pieces, a little evil here, a little there. This would be functional not just psychologically but culturally. Or rather, the two defenses would mesh, the psychological defense reinforced by a culture marked by eclecticism and syncretism in things religious.

Evil, I hypothesized, would be divided into different areas of life governed by different religious principles. About family relationships, most Koreans (not just Confucians) would define evil in Confucian terms, such as lack of filial piety. About metaphysical issues, most Koreans (not just Buddhists) would define evil in Buddhist terms, such as the ignorant clinging to things and people. About other matters, such as evil as the caprice of the world, most Koreans (not just shamanists) would define evil in shamanistic terms, illness and bad luck resulting from not paying proper attention to the spirit world.

I did not confirm my working hypothesis, and I did not disconfirm it either. Nor did it become irrelevant, just too categorical. Koreans are too creative for my hypothesis to do them justice. I was made aware of this early in my research, when a Korean informant told the story of his brother's funerals. In the morning the family went to the Confucian shrine. Later, two shamans came to the house to purify it. In the evening they all went to the Buddhist temple, so the monks might say prayers for his spirit. While spending a couple of days at home before returning, the informant noticed a pair of his underwear was missing. His mother had taken them to the shaman to be blessed. She was worried he was working too hard.

My working hypothesis was correct insofar as it suggests something of how the elements of the Western concept of evil are redistributed in Korea, but it is incorrect insofar as it suggests that the sectors have boundaries. It would be more accurate to say that about family relationships and evil, most Koreans draw upon Confucian, Buddhist, and shamanistic elements, and more besides, leading to a mix that is all of the above and then some. Nor does it make much difference what religion the informant belonged to. Koreans said remarkably similar things about evil, no matter what their religion, including Christianity.

Since the early 1960s, when the number of Christians in South Korea was little more than 1 million, the number of Christians, particularly Protestants, has increased faster than in any other country in the world, doubling every decade. Today approximately one-fourth of Koreans are Christians, and some would set the figure higher (Andrew Kim 1995, 34). (See the Research Appendix for more on how slippery estimates of religious membership truly are in Korea. The *Korean Christian Yearbook* for 1990 gives a figure for all religions of 49 million believers out of a population of 41 million!)

Landing at night at Kimpo Airport in Seoul, it is easy to count more than a hundred red neon crosses in the city. One wants to be able to say, indeed one feels almost compelled to say, that such a dynamic social force is having a significant influence on the Korean view of evil, but to the contrary, the Korean view appears unchanged. About evil, at least, Christianity is being indigenized.

The situation is similar with shamanism. Must not such a colorful and dramatic belief and practice, to which most Koreans adhere at some level, deeply affect the Korean view of evil? The answer is yes, and no. Because the spirit world is so similar to the world of the living, it would be at least as accurate to put it the other way around. Shamanism is a projection of everyday Korean beliefs about things we call evil onto a not very different or distant world. In shamanism one can see aspects of the Korean non-belief in evil more clearly, but only because shamanism holds them at a little distance from where they originate in everyday life.

There is, however, an important caveat to this claim. We may understand Taoism as a type of philosophical shamanism (Taoism originated in Chinese shamanism). Although there is no single master rule or principle by which to understand and explain the Korean nonbelief in evil, the Tao's denial of dualism comes closest. The ideal of "more than one, less than two" explains much, not just about the Korean nonbelief in evil, but about human relations overall, including the tension between individualism and collectivism that is at the heart of Korean culture.

Although I call it a Taoist principle, this is a conceptual rather than historical claim. The transitional location of the Korean self can as readily be explained in Confucian terms, as my comparison of jen and arete in Chapter 2 reveals. The transitional location of the Korean self is "overdetermined," the term Freud used to explain the origins of neurosis. Like neurosis, the origins of culture (any culture) are overdetermined. Although the Taoist influence is apparent in the *Analects* and is frequently overinterpreted, one might almost put it the other way around, that aspects of the Tao are a Confucian poem.

Throughout this book I use philosophy, be it Taoist, Confucian, or any other, as a cultural trope, not to explain the origin of anything but to bring aspects of the culture into relief. Most Westerners, including myself, are more familiar with the broad outlines of Eastern philosophy than the day-to-day details of particular Eastern cultures. There is a risk in interpreting culture in terms of philosophy (it makes everything too neat, as neat as philosophy itself), but awareness of these risks may help to minimize them.

Kohlberg at the Coffeehouse

One research technique was to visit coffeehouses (Seoul must have thousands) and strike up conversations with people there. Denizens of the coffeehouses were no random sample of Koreans, but they were not just students either. Korean apartments are small, and much meeting and entertaining is done in coffeehouses by Koreans from all walks of life.

My colleague, a distinguished university professor, struck up a conversation with two young women in a Shinchon coffeehouse. One was majoring in Chinese studies, another in education. Both began by saying that they could not define "evil." Both knew the Western term. The term they used was "ak" and its variants, such as "saak," which might be translated as wickedness, or very ak. Occasionally they employed the term "choe," which might better be rendered as crime or sin.

Although they cannot define evil, they are willing to agree that certain acts, like murder and rape, may be evil. This is, of course, a terrible situation for an interviewer. The last thing one wants to do is to be in the position of getting people to reluctantly agree with what they think the interviewer wants to hear.

Most of their examples were drawn from Western images and movies, though with a little prodding they were able to think of Korean examples, such as the fox with nine tails who turns into a beautiful, destructive temptress. Like so many Westerners, they seem torn between an intuitive feeling that certain acts deserve to be called evil and a type of sociological relativism: evil is defined by the culture. Or so I thought.

"How do *you* define evil?" they ask.

"Pleasure in hurting and lack of remorse," I reply. It is what most Western subjects say. The young women felt tricked, like I knew all the time and wouldn't tell them. I felt tricked too, like they had an answer of their own but wouldn't give it. Instead, they said what they thought they should, what students should say to their professors. But that was not quite right either.

One student referred to Lawrence Kohlberg's (1983) study of moral reasoning. This is the most well known study of its type, in which Kohlberg developed a series of questions to measure the level of moral development, from fear of punishment at one end, to universal moral principles on the other. One question concerns Heinz and whether he should steal a drug he cannot afford to save his wife's life.

"You know the story of Heinz?" she asked. "The one where a man steals a drug to save his mother's life." (She misremembers the story, changing wife to mother, a point I shall return to.) "That proves that morality is relative. It depends on your value system. The Japanese colonialist didn't think he was evil, because his value system said it was okay. I can say he's wrong, but I can't say his value system is wrong, can I?"

You might argue that the student is so out to impress the interviewer, or at least to engage in what she thinks is an appropriate professor-student discourse, that nothing true can be learned here. Perhaps, but generally there is something true to be learned from every exchange, as long as one does not take everything at face value.

Two things stand out. First, she gets Kohlberg's point just backward. That it was right for Heinz to steal the drug shows, says Kohlberg, the existence of universal moral principles that transcend the laws of particular societies. Far from supporting a type of moral relativism, Heinz's theft demonstrates the existence of universal principles all can refer to. Second, she sounds almost exactly like Western students, who intuitively feel that certain things are evil but believe they lack any grounds for saying so.

In fact, she only sounds like Western students. The similarity is misleading, the convergence thesis, as it is called, dubious. The convergence thesis argues that modernization and urbanization have certain basic structural requirements, particularly the substitution of secondary relationships for primary ones, the weakening of large traditional families, and the rise of nuclear families living in cities. The result is individuals who identify less closely with their societies, feeling themselves thrown back on their own resources, questioning everything, everybody, and every value that does not serve their interests. Wherever there is modernization, these changes will occur, even as some societies, such as Japan, seem able to resist them longer than others.

From one perspective, the coffeehouse women are instances of the convergence thesis, caught in the vortex of modernity as my colleague puts it, himself a scholar of the changes wrought by Western influences on Korea. The women have lost their traditional beliefs and values and are about as confused and confusing as most Westerners about the topic of evil. Perhaps they are more confused, as they lack a cultural tradition that once, at least, believed in evil.

These university women were among the first Koreans I interviewed. More than two hundred interviews later, I understand what they were saying quite differently than I did at first. All understanding takes place as we reinterpret what we thought we knew in light of subsequent experience. For the West, the relativism of evil is a metaphysical problem: the lack of sufficient grounds by which to say that one practice or belief is better than another. The problem is the lack of an independent standpoint, a verified God's-eye view by which to compare two beliefs or practices and find one, or both, wanting.

The university women sounded like they were discussing the relativism of evil the way a Westerner would, but they were not. Their position (which became clearer as the conversation progressed) was that one can only know right and wrong from within the perspective of a relationship. The problem is not the lack of independent grounds but the difficulty of placing oneself within the proper framework of relationship. The Western version of the problem is the lack of an external, third-party standpoint from which to judge.

Although it would have been easy to hear these woman saying that they lacked an objective perspective from which to judge, it is not what they were saying. They were saying that *the relationship is itself the standpoint of judgment,* and one cannot judge without knowing much more about the relationship. For those familiar with Western debates on the topic, it would not be misleading to say that the women were taking a position closer to that of Carol Gilligan (1982), who in her book *In a Different Voice* argues that the ethical dilemmas posed by Kohlberg are too abstractly formulated. To understand them one must understand how the participants conceive of the obligations inherent in the relationships involved.

This interpretation of the coffeehouse women's viewpoint, though, would not be quite right either. For Gilligan the issue is care: how do the partners in the relationship care for each other? For the coffeehouse women, the issue is not so much the partners in the relationship as the relationship itself, as though it were a third entity. Here the operative question is whether the relationship contains within itself an obligation, and of what kind? This question became clear when the other student said, "It doesn't have anything to do with the law. It all depends on who Heinz was stealing the medicine for. If it was for his friend, that would be one thing, for his mother another." She might seem to be talking about the partners in the relationship, but she is actually talking about the relationship as it is defined by the partners in it, a subtle but important distinction.

The Choe-Pŏl Cycle

As the term is used by most Koreans, "choe," does not seem an obvious candidate to translate "evil." Choe has more the quality of sin, except that it is concrete whereas sin is often a state of mind. "Choe" and "Pŏl" render the Korean title of *Crime and Punishment*, by Fyodor Dostoyevsky. "Crime" is perhaps the best sense of the term "choe," except that the crime to which choe refers may be a violation of norms or rules, not just laws.

Although "choe" does not seem the most likely term to translate "evil," it has the most important thing going for it. A great many Koreans use the term "choe" rather than "ak," when translating "evil," or giving examples of the worst thing there is. They do so because choe does not stand alone, a violation without consequence, but rather it is part of an essentially human relationship, the choe-pŏl cycle, within whose framework Koreans understand what the West calls evil.

Understanding another culture's use (or nonuse) of a term is not always about finding the perfect linguistic fit. Sometimes it is about following what at first seems like a rather poor fit to its extralogical conclusion. If encountering a foreign culture is like two ships passing in the night, then an anomalous term is like a flare, a point of contact between two self-contained worlds.

"If you commit choe, you or your children will get it back."

Why, I asked over and over to this most frequent of responses.

> Look around you. If you do something bad, your friends will stop speaking to you. If it is really bad, the person you do it to will take revenge, or his family will. Maybe your grandchild will be born handicapped. Why do you keep asking why? It just is.

The most articulate defenders of this reality were the older women who worked in the restaurants of Shinchon, but it was by far the most common answer, almost exactly the same as the answer Korean Americans gave in my preliminary interviews in the United States (see the Research Appendix). "Practical karma" is the term one Korean American used to describe it.[2]

The term "karma" is a little misleading, not just because of the Buddhist connotations but because of the metaphysical ones. The principle is really social induction, to coin an ugly but useful term: the pattern of social relationships generalized into an abstract principle. Though no one put it quite this way, this is the reasoning involved. "Look, you can see all around you that when someone does choe there are consequences to pay. The one you hurt takes revenge, or his family will. Even if you don't go to jail, everyone one will know, and your children will be excluded. Even if you kill him, his spirit may make you sick." It is but a small step from this observation to the general principle.

The principle originates in the face-to-face group, the extended family and village. There one can see the results, including the fact that some sicken and die after committing choe. It takes an act of faith to generalize this principle to the larger society, but it is not an act of religious faith. It is an act of social piety: the hope and belief that the cycle of choe and pŏl that gives meaning to life in the face-to-face community can be generalized to society at large. It is, in other words, an act of hope: that beyond the face-to-face society the world has not, and will not, become meaningless.

Choe and pŏl give meaning not just, or even primarily, because people want to know that the wicked are punished. On the contrary, they want to know that there is meaning and purpose to human suffering. Better to suffer for having committed choe than to suffer for no reason at all. The meaning is not necessarily moral. It is a belief in a roughly balanced universe, what the ancient Greeks called "dike," only misleadingly translated as "justice." Dike is not justice. It is more akin to physics. For every action there is an equal and opposite reaction. When a child suffers for a parent's misdeeds, it is not justice. But it is dike, a comprehensible rebalancing of the universe.

Although most Koreans hold that the choe-pŏl cycle is inexorable, belief in it is strongest among the older women of Shinchon and younger Korean Americans living in the United States. Why Korean American students are so conventional in their beliefs is interesting and invites further study. Perhaps it is a way of holding onto the homeland of their youth, the Korea of almost a generation ago. The youth of Korea today have not even this to hold onto.

Belief in the choe-pŏl cycle is weakest among Korean students, a number of whom are cynical about the ability of political power to intervene in the natural cycle. Conversely, they are more troubled by the fact that some seem to get pŏl without having committed choe. In other words, they lack confidence that the universe is in balance.

Some Koreans referred to "heavenly" (*ch'ŏn* and *hanŭl*) retribution, terms whose meaning harkens back to ways of thinking that precede Confucius. During the Chou Dynasty in China (1027?–256 B.C.), heaven was an impersonal ethical force, a cosmic guarantee that virtue would be rewarded and vice punished. Because it is impersonal, this heavenly force cannot be called "god." Nor does it control the destiny of men and women. It does, however, act to enforce and legitimate moral order (Chai and Chai 1973, 25–26). Although contemporary Koreans refer to heavenly retribution in a way that sometimes seems to invoke a universal principle, the reasoning is hardly metaphysical. It is social—even when, as is sometimes the case, Koreans refer to the intervention of supernatural entities, like the ghosts of the departed (*kwisin*).

The world of the Korean supernatural is not a higher (or lower) universe, but a parallel one, where almost every aspect of human relationships is faithfully reflected. Han Mahlsook's *Hymn of the Spirit* (1983), a popular novel of the 1980s, has the dead and living doing everything with and to each other but making love. More prone to feelings of abandonment and loneliness than the living, kwisin want most of all to be remembered. This, though, only makes them more human.

To be sure, social induction requires an act of faith, but it is cultural, not theological, faith: that society at large will continue to operate as it does in the family and in the village. This faith might be called faith in society as an abstraction, faith that in this world things balance out in the end. It is on this faith that traditions rest, and it is about this faith that Korean university students are most skeptical. They are, in other words, most skeptical about the continued influence of a pattern of human relationships that has defined choe and pŏl, and so made them real, for thousands of years.

A Western student put it this way: "If you believe in an all-powerful God who can change your life in an instant, then you won't do evil."

A middle-aged Korean restaurant worker put it this way: "If you can feel how your acts affect others, then you won't do ak."

One might argue that the difference is that the Korean woman has substituted society for God. But what if we look at it the other way around, with God as the projection of the originally sacred community into the cosmos? Much is gained in this God projection, above all a more abstract, principled view of morality. We should also ask what is lost. What is lost is a vivid connection between morality and empathy and the conviction that all goodness stems from a sense of human connectedness. To be sure, the echo of empathy remains in the God construct. The "Golden Rule" (Matthew 7.12 and much earlier in *Analects*, 5.12) is that echo, but it is a rule, not a relationship. What if this relationship, and with it a morality based on empathy, cannot tolerate the concept of evil?

"Tell Me the Relationship and I'll Tell You What's Evil"

"Tell me the relationship and I will tell you what's evil." In one way or another, this is what most Koreans said, including the coffeehouse women. One said it in just these words. Occasionally the "tell me the relationship . . ." answer was expressed in terms of the five Confucian relationships. Evil is to violate the expectation inherent in the relationship, such as to fail to practice filial piety. Most, however, did not put it in strictly Confucian terms. It would be a mistaken to see the "tell me the relationship . . ." response as part of the "Confucian legacy," the term that is still used to explain all too much about Korea.

What does it mean to see the world, and everything in it, in terms of relationships? One informant explained it this way, but the problem is universal: "It is through my relationships with my parents, and my brothers, that I first experienced evil, and everything else too."

What he meant is not that his parents and brothers were especially evil, but that his parents and brothers were everything, his whole world, the source of all meaning. When the world is so close at hand, when everything one knows about evil, and everything else, is learned and practiced in the family, and relationships modeled on the family, how can one ever call something, or someone, evil? One may call someone, or some act, bad, even terrible. To call it evil is to make an accusation of generalized malevolence, directed not at the world at large but against those to whom one is closest. To say "evil" is tantamount to calling the whole world and everything one loves evil.

It is surprising how many informants talked about how much they hated those with whom they had chŏng. Surprising to this observer, that is, but not to Koreans, who even have a word for it: "bad chŏng" (*miun chŏng*) it is sometimes called, but it is still chŏng.

"He's been my friend for years, but every time I'm with him he does something mean. I really hate him, but what can I do? We've got chŏng. It's like what you call fate."

It is an interesting perspective, attachment more like fate than choice. Once again we confront the slimy rope. When the other is tied to the same rope, what my informant calls fate, it is both impossible, and impossibly threatening, to conceive of the hated one as evil. What is remarkable is how far this impossibility extends, even to anonymous others outside the web of family and chŏng. The impossibility of evil in Korea stems not just from the closeness of actual relationships, but the idea of relationships overall.

The situation is analogous to the problem of the Oedipus conflict, as posed by Sigmund Freud. Whether the Oedipus conflict is a cultural universal, or whether it is as problematic in Korea as in the West, is unimportant. I am drawing an analogy, not making a cross-cultural diagnosis. The Oedipus conflict arises because mother is also a woman. Its resolution depends on the young boy's ability to distinguish other women from mother. Most do. Similarly, one cannot generalize about evil until one has distinguished family relationships from other relationships. When the social world is one big family, when every relationship is modeled on family relationships, so that even strangers are called by terms that refer to family members, such as *harabŏji* or *ajumŏni*, evil is unthinkable. It would be tantamount to saying that one's family is evil.

It is, incidentally, not my argument that the inability to see evil is a neurosis, akin to the Oedipus complex. On the contrary, to see every relationship in terms of family relationships is a value choice, a decision that makes the world meaningful, a richly woven human web. No one has grasped this more clearly than Hahm Pyong-choon (1986, 282–317, 318–345). A world of overlapping egos, of constant conjunction with other humans, the ubiquitous chŏng, is not a neurosis. Nor is it "merely" a tradition, though it is that too. It is a choice Koreans have made about what makes life meaningful and worthwhile. It is, however, like all choices, not without consequences, one of which is the inability to see evil. Or should one say choice?

Evil Does Not Add Up

After a certain point it becomes misleading to translate choe, ak, and their variants as "evil." Even though it is Koreans who are saying "Tell me the relationship and I'll tell you what's evil," they are taking the Western perspective, evidently for the researcher's benefit. Seen from the Korean point of view, evil is not defined by the relationship; evil is the relationship, or rather its betrayal.

If the content of the Western concept of evil is itself defined strictly in terms of the violation of expectations inherent in the relationship, then the very concept of evil has shifted: from an act of an individual to a quality of the relationship. If the relationship is the moral unit, then the individual cannot be truly immoral. Immorality does not apply to individuals. The individual may be ignorant, greedy, selfish, and unsocialized. He or she may be arrogant and thoughtless. But he or she cannot be evil. Ignorance, greed, selfishness, arrogance, and thoughtlessness are, from this perspective, not so much categories of immorality as categories of unsociability. People who are this way do not understand what it is to belong to human society. In their ignorance they are amoral, living in self-imposed exile where morality does not apply. Nor does evil.

Inapplicable to the individual, evil is no more readily applicable to the group. Groups may do terrible things, but they lack the quality of moral actors. Satan is not a group; neither is the soul he is said to tempt. The principles of responsibility established by the Nuremberg Tribunal do not apply to groups, nor do the principles established by the Tribunal's counterpart in Tokyo two years later. Once evil becomes an attribute of relationships, it loses its moral force, becoming applicable to everyone and no one. Some in the West have accepted this logic, concluding that evil applies to everyone because it refers to everyone's failed relationship to God. Absent a conception of God as a contracting third party, the transformation of evil into a failed relationship is tantamount to its disappearance.

Disappearance is not bad. There is no reason that the Eastern view of the worst thing there is should correspond to the Western view of evil. It is just not evil. The situation is similar, but more extreme, to that discussed earlier regarding Kohlberg. The coffeehouse women only appeared to be talking about evil in Western terms. In fact, the whole perspective had shifted, so that the translation of "ak" and "choe" as "evil" is more misleading than helpful.

In "Buddhism and Evil," Martin Southwold makes the good point that "evil is a special quality of badness" (1985, 131–132). It is misleading to translate Buddhist terms such as *"dukkha"* as "evil," a common rendering. Similarly, it is misleading to translate Mara as Satan, as J. W. Boyd does in *Satan and Mara: Christian and Buddhist Symbols of Evil* (1975). Dukkha refers to the grasping desire for things and persons. Although Mara is a tempter like Satan, he has more the quality of a pimp than a destroyer. Whatever evil is, it must refer to more than ordinary human failings and desires if it is to be a meaningful category of experience.

Evil must also refer to more than a single category of actions, such as the failure to respect the obligations inherent in a relationship. In response it might be argued that the failure to respect the obligations inherent in relationships is not a single category in Korea. It is the whole world. Perhaps, but in this whole world of relationships, evil is no longer a meaningful category. It will pay to search for other categories that better render the Korean understanding. The ancient Greek terms *hubris* and *moira* actually better render what many Koreans regard as the worst thing, as discussed shortly, just as "dike" better captures the choe-pŏl cycle.

This approach is, in any case, how best to understand the incommensurable concepts of another culture. Focus not on verbal equivalence, concluding that "the worst thing" in Korea must be tantamount to evil, our "worst thing." Instead, focus on how Koreans are actually using the term (not translating it, but *using* it), and what other terms and concepts this might suggest to an English speaker. My limited abilities in the Korean language may have been helpful in highlighting this problem. Most Koreans who could spoke English with me, even those whose English was imperfect. This halting communication required the frequent questioning of terms on both sides, and I was struck by how strangely Koreans used the term "evil," where I would have chosen another word, such as "irresponsible." Had all the interviews been conducted in Korean, which is its own self-contained (but not hermetically sealed) worldview, this anomaly would not have emerged in such sharp contrast.[3]

One of the interesting things about Korans' discussion of ak and choe is how concretely the terms are employed, even ak, which is sometimes used to refer to a disposition rather than an act. But the disposition is almost always concrete, a disposition to a particular act, not an overall trait. Even when ak is employed to represent an abstraction, which might be rendered as bad-ness, or evil-ness, the term lacked scope, referring to occurrences, events, or people, not universals like human nature or history. I frequently asked, must ak as disposition always result in choe? No, most replied, because the evil-minded one might be stopped before he could commit choe. That ak might live an independent mental or ideational existence occurred to few.

When Koreans talk among themselves, rather than to the Western researcher, they frequently use the term *saak-han haengwi* (which I learned from the "evil dinners"). The term means saak behavior, such as a son striking his father. The way the term is used suggests that the term saak does not so much modify the behavior as become behavior. It is not evil for the son to strike the father. Nor has an evil son done such a deed. A piece of evil behavior has occurred, almost as if the act were independent of the actors. This distinction does not mean that the son is not held responsible; he is. It does mean that he is not considered evil. Saak is absorbed into the behavior, so that there is nothing left over for mind, or to general malevolence. Saak-han haengwi is the behavior with no remainder, which is why Koreans do not add up acts of evil behavior and draw conclusions about human nature from them.

Evil does not add up for Koreans because evil never adds up. The concept does not work like that. Westerners do not add this, this, and this instance of evil, and conclude that Evil exists. Evil is not a conclusion; it is a premise, a deduction, not an induction. If names are guests of realities, as the *Chuang-tzu* tells us, then concepts like evil are hosts for a category of experience that becomes real only when we invite it into being. It is, however, interesting to consider why Korea has been so inhospitable to the idea of evil.

Almost a quarter of the respondents were Christian (roughly mirroring the percentage in the population). They were no more likely to do the addition, from evils to Evil, than other Koreans. Though some Christians responded to questions about evil in ways that were obviously and identifiably Christian (for example, evil means to substitute personal pride for the love of God), these were a minority of Christians, about one-quarter. (I follow Western practice and include Catholics among Christians.) The rest reasoned in ways no different than other respondents.

"Do you have a religion?" was generally my last question, so that I might spend the interview guessing. Generally I guessed wrong, especially with Christians. To be sure, there are Christians and Christians, and while I also asked about parents' religion, certainly some of the Christians were recent converts. Nonetheless, it is my strong impression that the answer to the absence of the concept of evil in Korea among Christians lies not in the recentness of conversion (it was actually the more recent converts who were more likely to hold to a recognizably Christian view), but the absence of "cultural receptors" for evil, as they might be called. Foreign teachings do not take, they do not become entrenched, unless there is something in the indigenous culture that can recognize the foreign concept—that is, play host to it. There are few cultural hosts for the Western concept of evil in Korea.[4]

Evil Is Not Alienated in the Other

One of the most remarkable aspects of the Korean experience of evil is that it is not attributed to the infamous "Other." To be sure, Koreans experience hostile others, North Korea above all, whose mendacity and duplicity is fodder for countless stories. Nevertheless, what Hahm Pyong-choon says about Korean history is basically correct. Strong family relationships in Korea are not built on the demonization of the other.

> More remarkable is the fact that positive sentiments of [family] affection were never politically diverted against the external enemy. On the other hand, the first thing that modern totalitarianism had to accomplish before it could function effectively in the communist North Korea was to destroy the networks of familial affection. (Hahm 1986, 68)

It is, of course, ironic that Hahm is creating an external enemy without family ties (that is, not fully human) even as he writes that Koreans do not do this. But ironic does not mean untrue; it just refers to how the truth sometimes turns back on itself.

Why does the tightly knit web of Korean family relationships, a web that makes the concept of evil impossibly terrifying, not depend on an evil outsider? To be sure, the human web depends on outsiders, or at least it generates them. Between the "we" of family ties (*hyŏryŏn*), school ties (*hagyŏn*), and regional ties (*chiyŏn*) and the "we" of "we Koreans" (*uri han'guk saram*) lies an enormous gulf. To be outside the human web in Korea is to be nowhere and no one, a theme developed in Chapter 3. There is no need for the evil outsider because being outside is itself so terrifying. For the same reason, there is no ability to name the evil outsider.

Outside *is* evil. Outside is also nothing. Therefore, evil is nothing, the dread that does not exist because it is nonexistence. A "presentiment of something which is nothing" is how Kierkegaard (1957, 38) defines dread (*Angst*). In a related fashion, Ricoeur writes in *The Symbolism of Evil* (1969, 30, 347) of ethical dread, terror at the inability to connect with the human world, the loss of root and bond. This ethical dread characterizes how Koreans experience evil, only they do not call it that, partly because it is too terrifying and partly because it is an experience that is by its very nature beyond words, something that is nothing. Instead, they say that to be alone and friendless is the worst thing, as discussed in Chapter 3. This definition is as close as Koreans get to the concept of evil. Maybe it is close enough.

We cannot truly fear death, because death is nothingness. Instead, we fear its correlates, experiences that symbolize death, such as night and loss (Lifton 1983). Or as Charles Ryder puts it about the dying Lord Marchmain in Evelyn Waugh's *Brideshead Revisited*, "perhaps because they are like death, he feared darkness and loneliness." Similarly, Koreans do not fear evil. They fear its symbolic correlates, alienation and aloneness. So do Westerners, of course. The question is why Koreans do not do the abstraction, from dread to evil, as most Westerners do. The simple answer is that Koreans are so enmeshed in actual relationships that the abstraction creates and requires a distance from these relationships that is itself experienced as dreadful.

In the West, an evil other is frequently experienced as a relief, the other safely out there somewhere where it can be fought. Many Americans were relieved, not threatened, when Ronald Reagan referred to the Soviet Union as an "evil empire." An evil other is a welcome idea in the West, giving our dread a face and a place. But such an idea is not welcome in Korea. To call North Korea evil would be impossibly terrifying for most

Koreans, because Koreans cannot create the type of distance from the North that would allow them to alienate evil there. North Korea is quite literally still family. (Some estimates of South Koreans with relatives in the North run as high as 10 million families—that is, most of the 45 million people in South Korea.)[5]

North Korea is not unique in this regard. Recall the Buddhist quoted in Chapter 1, who regarded even the Japanese occupation as a type of family relationship, assimilation in the larger Asian family of nations headed by Japanese big brothers. It was an argument aimed at denying that Easterners could be dualistic, treating others as mere objects. Otherness itself is such a terrifying category that Koreans cannot get the distance on anyone to call them evil.

Consider the following argument by way of analogy. The ancient Greeks, it has been said, were sufficiently advanced to have created simple machines to do their work, such as steam engines. They did not; it did not even occur to them to do so, because the human body was such an overriding aesthetic and moral value that to have worked alongside machines would have been experienced as deeply alienating. To have lived in a world of machines would have been to become and feel less human, as though the world itself was no longer a human place. The truth of this argument about the ancient Greeks is not at issue here. At issue is whether Koreans experience something similar, not about machines but about a world of otherness. Too much otherness and difference is itself terrifying, making the world an impossibly inhuman place.

Heinz Kohut (1984), a psychoanalyst, writes about self-objects: others whom we treat as part of ourselves, finding support for our sense of self in our relationships with them. The need for self-objects is not a sign of illness, only of being human. Most well known are the two classes of self-objects that he came to call narcissistic and idealizing. Narcissistic self-objects are like mirrors, in which we see ourselves reflected as we would like to be, loved and cherished, big and strong. Mothers are generally the first narcissistic self-objects, a term that for Kohut is not pejorative, but only a compliment. Idealizing self-objects are those that represent high ideals, distant enough to be worth striving for, but not so distant as to be impossible. Fathers are generally the first idealizing self-objects, though Kohut is quick to point out that mothers and fathers generally fulfill both roles.

Only late in his career did Kohut (1984, 192–201) posit a third self-object, and a third self-object relationship. The alter-ego or twinship transference he called it, in which we sustain our sense of self by being around familiar others. It is my argument, developed more fully in the next chapter, that Koreans rely heavily upon the twinship transference, so heavily that a world that lacks this quality is impossibly terrifying to contemplate. By "twinship transference" I mean not something obscure and deep, but profound and simple. As Kohut puts it about one woman, "her self was sustained simply by the presence of someone she knew was sufficiently like her to understand her and be understood by her" (Kohut 1984, 196). She did not have to talk; she did not want to talk, for that would mean an effort to understand, an acknowledgment of difference. She just wanted to be with. Those who are familiar with Koreans will know how much closeness they can find in silence between friends.

Consider the opposite of the twinship transference, the experience that one is not human among humans. "Some of the most painful feelings to which man is exposed, unforgettably described by Kafka in *The Metamorphosis* . . . relate to the sense of not being human" among other humans: the dread that one is not living in a human world (Kohut 1984, 200). It is this we all dread, and Koreans dread it more. Or perhaps Koreans are just more aware of their dread of absolute otherness, of living in a world in which others are not part of the fleshy human web, but mere others. When there are no others, when otherness is itself too terrifying to contemplate, then so is evil.

Why Koreans feel this dread so acutely is difficult to determine. One could refer to "cultural factors," such as the way Korean children are raised, bundled so closely to their mothers, never spending a night alone, but this would not really be an explanation, just as the all too frequently invoked "Confucian heritage" explains nothing. Child rearing is no independent variable but is itself part of the culture. Child rearing perpetuates the culture. It is probably the single most profound institution of socialization. But it is no cause.

Beliefs Are Not Behavior

The nonbelief in evil does not mean that Korea acts differently, for example more benevolently, toward others, including North Korea. We are used to thinking that ideas like good and evil are causally effective:

if we believe someone is evil, we will act differently toward him or her. But this belief is not necessarily so. Even if it is, it is by no means clear that believing someone to be evil sponsors more aggression and hostility toward them. Koreans do not believe North Koreans are not evil for the benefit of North Korea but for their own benefit, so that their world will not become filled with dread. Believing that North Koreans are not evil might actually make it easier to act aggressively toward the North, as violence between North and South would be just that: a terrible family conflict, not the release of an alien evil into the world.

"Would it be evil if North Korea had nuclear weapons?" was one of my questions. (The term "evil" was used in interviews conducted in English, "saak," which might best be rendered as "wicked" or "vicious," in interviews conducted in Korean.) Almost all Koreans said no, which is not surprising, though it would be a mistake to assume that because Koreans do not believe in evil in the abstract, they do not believe in it in particular cases. Slightly over half said things like "the North Koreans would never use nuclear weapons against us. We're Koreans too." A number elaborated along the following lines. "It is an American problem, not a Korean problem. You Americans worry about it because you do not want Koreans to have power. If the North Koreans had nuclear weapons, they would be ours too."

Such beliefs, while touching, do not necessarily translate into more peaceful relations with North Korea, a point that bears repeating. These beliefs could translate into more dangerous relationships, as Koreans fail to take responsibility for the conflict, blaming it on Americans for example. Conversely, it could make it easier for North and South Korea to settle their differences eventually. Or both. It makes a difference whether people believe in evil, but it would be simplistic to conclude that when people deny evil they are more pacifistic or humane toward others. One does not need to believe in evil to hate and fear others. The connection between belief and act is more complex, a contingent empirical connection, rather than a logical one.

In May 1980, in the midst of the demonstrations that would eventually drive the South Korean military dictators from power, an insurrection broke out in Kwangju in South Chŏlla province. Eventually regular troops from the ROK Twentieth Division invaded the city and reimposed martial law. Within a few days they shot and killed more than two thousand Koreans, according to Asia Watch figures (Eckert et al. 1990, 375). Asked whether these particular South Korean soldiers were "evil" or "saak," every Korean respondent said no. A surprising number referred to rumors, rife at the time, that the Korean soldiers had been deprived of sleep and had taken stimulant drugs. "Koreans do not kill Koreans," said one informant. "Not like that. They were on drugs; they were crazy. That's the only thing that explains it."

What If the Thief Were Your Father?

What if the thief in the night were your father? "If it is my father who has come to steal, I should pretend to be sleeping. It would make me weep with pity."

It was not a Korean who said this; it was Mahatma Gandhi (1997, 82). But the reasoning is similar to a Korean's, perhaps because traditional societies share much in this regard, above all the use of family relationships as a model not just for every relationship but as the framework within which everything in the world is allowed to exist.

In the West in recent years, the question of whether the thief in the night is your father takes on a new meaning, conjuring up an image of the incestuous father who robs his children of their innocence. One reason such acts are so traumatic is that the young child cannot know both: that the father who loves and protects her is the beast who sexually exploits her. Many who are abused in this way split themselves, denying what they know. In extreme cases the result is multiple personality syndrome or extreme dissociation.

Koreans are just beginning to confront incest as a social problem.[6] But incest is a useful model for the problem of evil in Korean society. When it is so close, when "it is through my relationships with my parents, and my brothers, that I first experienced evil, and everything else too," then it is hard to get the distance on evil.

Evil takes distance. When a society does not want or value that distance, and the otherness it implies, then evil becomes an almost impossible concept. When "the family is god," as one Korean put it while explaining the contemporary legacy of Confucianism, then there is no room for the devil, and no room for evil either, not just in the family, but in every relationship modeled on the family, that is, virtually every relationship.

There is, however, a partial exception to the argument that Koreans cannot see evil. Although they are reluctant to see it in North Korea, or in their own troops, many saw it in the *chijon-p'a*, a group of alienated young Koreans in the early 1990s who kidnapped and killed rich people, not for the money evidently, but for the hatred. Giving themselves a kingly name (chijon-p'a means "Extremely Noble Gang"),[7] they showed no remorse upon arrest, saying they had lost belief in society and humans. For those Koreans who thought evil might exist, this gang was the leading example, because its motivations could not be explained away.

Greed, selfishness, jealousy, rage—these are motivations Koreans can understand, the motivations that are familiar in families. The young man who said everything he learned about evil he learned in his family was saying that the greed, selfishness, jealousy, and rage he experienced there were natural, emotions that weave the human web. The "Extremely Noble Gang" killed, it seemed, out of sheer envy and hatred, emotions almost as difficult to acknowledge in the family as incest.

About this gang one Korean, not a Christian, said simply "with them the end of the world is here." Others found comfort in knowing that shortly before their execution several gang members showed remorse, "not toward God, but toward parents and family bondage." One must evaluate Freudian slips differently when the speaker is not a native speaker. Nevertheless, "family bondage," instead of bonds, suggests an insight into why more Koreans mentioned this case as a possible example of evil than any other. The gang's assault was not just on rich people, or even on society, but on the belief in "family bondage"—that bad things will always be explicable, and hence contained, in terms of motivations and relationships that are familiar in families. (I am not arguing that sheer envy, hate, and sadism are not present in families, but only that they are much more difficult to acknowledge there.)

Pagoda Park: "The Last Place Old Men Go"

"Evil is greed for more than one's share: of money, of power, and of honor." This is how one of the old men in Pagoda Park in downtown Seoul answered my question, but it was a view echoed by almost all the old, and by most Koreans. It is an instance of the "tell me the relationship . . ." view of evil, although it would be better to say that it is a culmination of that view.

Site of the reading of the March 1, 1919, Declaration of Independence against Japan, Pagoda (T'apkol) Park has its own political aura, not just of national self-assertion, but of disappointment in the West, which showed itself unwilling to live up to Woodrow Wilson's famous fourteen points. Korea appealed to the world powers for support against Japan, and the world was silent. Possessing its own colonies, the Western world did not want to rock the boat.

If Korea was disappointed in the West, it was also disillusioned with itself. "This disillusionment is reflected in the literature of the 1920s which is full of escapism and hopelessness" (O'Rourke 1981, 6). Many of the old men in Pagoda Park are disillusioned still, but the tone is not one of passive withdrawal but populist resentment.

On the broad sidewalk in front of the park is a display by the *min'ga hyŏp*, the Democratic Family Association, which represents the families of men and women jailed under the national security laws. Members of the association come here every Thursday, like clockwork. Pictures of many of those jailed are displayed, and the mothers, wives, or sisters of some are there to talk about their family members' plight. No one hurrying along Chongno 2-ga stopped.

The protest is the Korean version of the Mothers of the Plaza de Mayos in Argentina, who visited their Korean counterparts recently, standing with them in front of Pagoda Park. It is worth noticing the difference between the two situations: the Argentine "disappeared" were tortured and killed. The Korean "disappeared" have not been truly disappeared. Some have been tortured, and all are being held under law, albeit a law that makes it illegal to wonder (on the Internet) if the North Korean submarine that washed ashore in South Korea was really carrying North Korean spies.

Inside the park, the Seoul city government has a booth promoting the "more efficient use of burial space"—that is, cremation. It is a sensitive subject in Pagoda Park, the "last place old men go" before they die, as the local saying has it. Here the men play Go, smoke cigarettes, talk with each other, and gather around even the faintest novelty. A few were out on the street, looking at the display of the disappeared. None were hectoring the protestors; a few were asking questions. Lots were hectoring the representatives of the Seoul city government.

"Take the exhibit to the professors and rich people, not here," said one. "The rich will always have money for large family burial plots," said another. Still another said that he worked in a cemetery and knew what happened. "The rich get buried, and the poor get burned." "Burn the rich first!" chimed in his friend.

Some Koreans believe that the bones of buried ancestors accumulate power over generations. It was not clear to me that this is what some of the old men were referring to when they said that cremation was one more government plot to weaken the poor, but if it was, the government's plan must have seemed particularly nefarious. It was, in any case, bizarre. The fancy colored brochure promoting cremation showed a happy Korean nuclear family in colorful *hanbok* (traditional loose fitting clothing), standing before the cemetery plot, which looked like something out of Star Trek: a circular dome about eight feet across with room for the urns of a dozen family members.

The populist tone of the crowd was familiar from the United States, only one would never find Americans arguing over cremation. Note too how the selfishness of the rich is seen in terms of the way they foster the fortunes of their own families, by better respecting their dead. It is the extended family, not the individual, that is the competitive unit. But that does not make it any less competitive. A few years ago the Korean government passed sumptuary laws, restricting the number of large flower arrangements that could be displayed at a funeral, for example. Such extravagance was diverting money that could have been better used to build Korea's industrial base. Now wealthy families rotate the flower arrangements between the front door and a back room.

It is in this context that the claim that "evil is greed" should be understood. It is a political statement, though as the anger at the government's promotion of cremation reveals, it is a politics that is hardly separated from family. On the contrary, the political model is the extended family. In the extended family, everyone depends on everyone else for survival. In a sense, everyone exploits everyone else—and has to—but when it works well it does not feel like exploitation. It feels like cooperation. Evil is when someone does not respect the limits, taking more than his portion of money, power, honor—or burial space in a densely populated city.

The group is terribly vulnerable to such persons, but they are not easy to identify. If it were a simple question of equality, it would be easy: everyone gets the same. But it is not, which is why the first question many ask about evil is "Tell me the relationship, and I'll tell you what's evil." Tell me who the persons in this relationship are, and I will tell you if someone has exceeded his portion. Only this puts it too individualistically. It is actually the relationship that is being assessed, which is why the informant said "Tell me the relationship, and I'll tell you the evil." He did not need to know the people involved, only the relationship.

Evil is a corrupted relationship, made impure by one who steps outside the bounds of what the relationship properly allots him or her. One might argue that the difference between the Western view of evil and the Korean view is that there is no third party, no God, no stance outside the relationship to judge it, and no contract or covenant that is separate from the relationship. That is true, but it risks assimilating the Korean view into postmodernism. For postmodernism, the absence of an outside relativizes the inside. Nothing is relativized in Korea, in part because the East has never been as intererested in the project of philosophical fundamental grounding and thus is not as disappointed and thrilled by its absence. The inside remains everything, all that matters.

East Is East and West Is . . .

What the old men are talking about comes remarkably close to what the ancient Greeks called *hubris*. The Eastern and Western traditions appear to merge for a moment (conceptually, if not historically; only in metaphor does history resemble a river), only to head off in directions one would not have originally anticipated. Just as "dike," rather than "justice," best captures the choe-pŏl cycle, so the Greek "hubris" and "moira" better translate what the old men of Pagoda Park were talking about than the English "evil" or "greed."

Hubris is not just "overweening pride," the arrogance that destroys Greek tragic heroes. Hubris is the desire to exceed one's portion or lot in life, to possess more than the share of money, power, and honor that is properly allotted to humans. Moira is this portion, what the Fates distribute to each person. But moira might be equally well employed to render the terms "fate," "good," and "evil," as is widely recognized (Greene 1964).

How could one word cover so much territory? The elements are inextricably bound, good and evil concerned with how we come to terms with the fate that allots us so much and no more, including the fate that ties us to others in good chŏng and bad. To be sure, the men in Pagoda Park recognize something that many ancient Greeks did not: the difference between social and natural inequality. This recognition makes evil more difficult to determine, for it is not just what some men take too much of, but what others give too little of, their share in the social product. This recognition also makes evil more difficult to accept, the old men angry not just at the rich, but at their own inability to do anything about it but suffer. Here is the source of han.

The Korean view is similar to the Greek in another respect as well. "No one does wrong knowingly," says Socrates (Plato, *Meno* 77b–78b; *Protagoras* 353d–58e). We do wrong only out of ignorance, not knowing how doing right will benefit us and make us happier and more eudaimon (fulfilled). "No one does evil knowingly" was also the position of most Korean informants. Some argued in terms that were recognizably Confucian, such as "people do evil because they were not brought up to feel shame at the right things."[8] Most argued that the ignorance was emotional, a failure to practice empathy—that is, the failure to recognize a connection that already exists.

"If people who do evil really knew what the other person was feeling, they wouldn't do it." As is the case with Socrates, the intelligence required is emotional and relational, not psychological and intellectual. Furthermore, the result of intelligence for most Koreans is not so much individual excellence as a restored relationship with humanity, one broken by emotional ignorance: ignorance of the fact that men and women are always and already connected. Or as Confucius says, "men are close to one another by nature. It is by practice they become far apart" (*Analects*, 17.2).

Almost a year later I returned to Pagoda Park. The economic crisis was well under way, and some younger men had joined the crowd. All the younger men were unemployed. Most had been employed in the construction trades, a sector that has been hit especially hard. It was raining heavily this time, but that did not seem to reduce the park population. Together we stood, my assistant and I, under our umbrellas, creating a tent under which we might interview our informant, who as often as not had no umbrella.

The themes were similar to those we had encountered a year earlier, but with an interesting variation, a variation that was even more pronounced at Seoul Station, the railroad station where the homeless congregate. "The rich should share with the poor," said a dozen informants, one in just these words. It is a simple sentiment, and what surprised me was precisely that. It was so personal, as though they were talking about a rich relative. There was little class consciousness, and less populist resentment than one might have expected under the difficult circumstances, no more resentment than a year earlier.

Instead, the emphasis was on sharing, which many equated with nationalism (*minjok- chuŭi*), or rather, with what several called *Tangunism* (*tan'gun sasang* means Tangun ideology). The mythical founder of Korea, born of a god and a she-bear, Tangun made the lives of the people better by providing food and shelter. Not freedom or national glory, but *hongik in'gan*, the provision of widespread benefit, is the mark of true nationalism—Tangunism.

Not that Tangunism originated in a doctrine of sharing. Tangun may have been born in the mists of time, but Tangunism stems from the *Taejonggyo*, the Religion of Tangun Worshipers, founded in 1909, which was more about chauvinism than sharing (Eckert et al. 1990, 250). The denizens of Pagoda Park and Seoul Station were self-consciously struggling to create a new nationalism, one that through sharing would eliminate the need for class conflict. Sharing is, of course, the opposite of taking more than one's portion, the mark of hubris.

While there was little class consciousness as it is usually understood in the West, there was widespread awareness of the possibility of its emergence. "We are one nation, one people, Tangun. I fear the rise of class divisions if this goes on," said the former driver for a construction magnate gone bankrupt. Here is what class consciousness looks like in contemporary Korea: not so much awareness of one's class interest, but fear and regret that one might have to really begin to think in these terms, if, that is, the rich won't share their portion.

Why don't the rich share, I asked?

"Some are arrogant and egoistic," replied the only woman I interviewed at Seoul Station, one of the few homeless women I observed. "But most do not understand. I was like that. When I had a job I didn't even think about the unemployed and homeless. Now I'm one. Now I think the most important thing is for the rich to know. If they knew, they would share." Her sentiment is strictly Socratic, or should I say Confucian? No one does wrong knowingly. They do wrong because their practices, their ways of life, have driven them far apart from those who suffer.

Against this interpretation one might refer to Korea's recent history of militant unionism, arguing that the denizens of Pagoda Park and Seoul Station have more in common with the *lumpenproletariat*. The issue is too big to take up here, except to note that many have held that Korean trade unions, tied so closely to the chaebŏl whose workers they represent, have little to do with class consciousness. Kim Byung-kook puts it this way:

> The workers of the chaebŏl were, in a sense, free from class responsibility. Lacking a sense of class solidarity, they aggressively pushed for a wage hike without seriously considering its adverse impact on the livelihood of less advantaged workers in other declining industries. Strikes, in fact, became a war *within* the working class. (1998, 23)

When Korean unions do think in national terms, the language often comes closer to that of Pagoda Park and Seoul Station. The KCTU, the more radical federation of Korean trade unions, refused for a short while to negotiate about "restructuring" (that is, layoffs) until the families who own the chaebŏl donated their personal fortunes to the state. In response, the editors of the *Korea Herald* (June 6, 1998, p. 4) encouraged the unions to push for "transparency" and unemployment insurance. In other words, the newspaper editors had more class consciousness than the union, whose thinking was more in line with Tangunism.

Mine is not an argument about Korean politics, though it touches upon it. Mine is an argument about the attractions of an "amorphous sentiment of belonging." Though Kim Byung-kook (1998, 43) does not intend this phrase as a compliment, its potential as resource for a new nationalism should not be overlooked. Above all, it is a reality that touches on almost every aspect of Korean life, including Koreans' beliefs about evil.

CHAPTER FIVE

Should Koreans Believe in Evil?

A noted Korean scholar argues that the original meaning of "ak" is "ugly."[1] Evil is whatever is destructive of beauty, above all disharmony. Truth is a narrow category, applicable to certain scientific endeavors. Keats, the scholar continues, got it wrong. Beauty isn't the same as truth. Beauty is what truth looks like when it is applied to human relationships. All humans naturally seek the beautiful unless corrupted by bad experience. This is, he continues an implication of the teachings of Mencius, a Confucian who is widely believed to have taught that human nature is originally good. What else is Confucianism, he asks, but the moralization of aesthetic categories, above all harmony?

In the West we generally put it the other way around, Nietzsche and Foucault among those who would aestheticize moral categories. They would make morals a matter of individual sensibility, locating morality not beyond argument, but beyond reason, in much the same sense that the beauty of a painting is located there. The Korean scholar's position is only deceptively similar. For Foucault (1984, 42), an aesthetic of self-creation must, in the end, be irrelevant to social life.

To see beauty as a social category, harmonious relationships, changes everything. Not because society decides what beauty is, but because a harmonious society is beautiful. Beauty depends on harmony; it is harmony. Evil is whatever disrupts the harmony of human relationships, harmony defined not primarily in terms of getting along, but in terms of the proprieties inherent in the relationship—that is, what properly belongs to the relationship. The Confucian five relationships exemplify propriety, the highest Confucian ideal. Man realizes his nature when he acts in accord with his obligations as son, father, subject, husband, and friend. In a word, evil is ugly relationships, relationships that violate the expectations of harmony inherent in them. This is similar to the view held by the coffeehouse women.

It is a view is not without risk, for it is readily perverted to mean that what is ethical is whatever preserves harmony. Conversely, harmonious relationships are ethical. Without doubt this is perversion: if someone violates the expectations inherent in a relationship, the maintenance of superficial harmony—agreement—would only make the fundamental disharmony more profound. "The gentleman is harmonious but not conformist," says Confucius (*Analects*, 13.23). Harmony is not just in the eyes of the beholder. Nevertheless, some views invite cross-cultural misunderstanding, and ethics as harmony is one. Was it unethical for Blacks in the United States to protest segregation because it upset the harmony of the community?

One might save the scheme by arguing, much as Juergen Habermas does regarding ideal speech, that the definition of harmony must be extended to include all who are affected, all who are within the frame. If the harmony of some depends on the disharmony of others, if it involves treating them ugly, then it is not really harmony. True enough, but this would be a Western gloss, or at least not what the respondents, and the scholar, are talking about. For both, the harmony at issue is already inherent in the relationship, its Confucian telos so to speak. Evil is ugliness because it distorts what is in effect natural beauty, natural harmony.

Evil as ugliness would seem to be a strictly conventional category, as in "It's evil because it offends my sensibility." In fact, evil as ugliness is experienced by most Koreans as a natural category, a violation of natural harmony. It is, however, precisely because it is experienced as natural that evil as ugliness is unavailable as a moral category—that is, unavailable for moral reflection. What we call evil just is, much as a hurricane or other disruptive natural force is.[2]

Unlike other instances of the "tell me the relationship" view, evil as ugliness does not cause the concept of evil to disappear. On the contrary, evil as ugliness highlights evil, finding it everywhere human relationships turn base. Evil as ugliness does, however, complete the de-moralization of evil. Humans may still be charged with causing disharmony, the charge leveled by the old men of Pagoda Park. But the disharmony men cause is no longer connected to the evil that men do. Not because morality and aesthetics are alien categories (since Plato, the West has known their connection), but because ugliness is not a category of action, but sensibility. Evil as ugliness exists without evil having been done.

More than One, Less than Two

One of the informants was a judge in a district court in South Kyŏngsang Province (an effort was made to conduct interviews throughout South Korea). When asked whether he had ever confronted evil in his courtroom, he told a story. Several years ago a man was arrested for attacking his neighbor and breaking his neighbor's nose. Two hours later, the victim persuaded his attacker, who was even more drunk than the victim, to box. Because the original victim had some experience as a boxer, he beat the man who broke his nose severely. The next day the boxer with the broken nose brought charges against his neighbor.

When the two men came before the judge, only one was in handcuffs. After hearing the story, the judge decided that both were guilty, and so arrested the plaintiff, the former boxer. Then he put both on probation. It was, he said, his finest moment as a judge. He does not believe that he is a very good judge, but in this case he says he was brilliant, comparing himself to Solomon, a frequent image of wisdom among Koreans (especially Buddhists), at least when speaking with me.

In Korea the judge generally acts as jury and must determine the facts as well as pass judgment. This judge is overwhelmed by the complexity of the cases that appear before him. Not only does he have difficulty determining the facts, but even when he knows what happened he generally does not know why or who is really to blame. "Some people don't think; some are brought up wrong. Even when you don't want to do something bad, fate takes over. You can't always help yourself."

You still have not answered my question, I continued. Has anyone ever appeared before you whom you would call evil?

Finally he became angry. "How could I call someone evil? I'd have to know their whole life history. And if I did, then I'd have to sentence them to death. What else could I do?"

Does the judge see so much complexity because he does not want to divide the people who come before him into good and evil? Or does he not want to divide the people who come before him into good and evil because he sees so much complexity? Both perhaps. Which came first seems impossible to determine. What is clear is that Koreans hate dualism, and it is this hatred that lies behind the reluctance to see evil—or rather, the refusal to allot it a category of existence. This hatred of dualism is shared by most Koreans, not just Buddhists.

The judge was interviewed with others present. They were students in an adult English language class with which I spent several days, transforming their classes into seminars on evil and their nights into informal discussions of evil at coffeehouses and restaurants. It was in response to the judge's story that another woman told the Solomon story with which I began Chapter 1, concluding that "A Korean Solomon would have found a compromise. He would have made the two women sisters, so they could have cared for the child together."

A Western Solomon would try to divine guilt and innocence, dividing the world and the parties in it accordingly. A Korean Solomon would create a binding relationship between the parties, so that such a division could never occur in the first place. Or rather, he would create a relationship in which past differences are reinterpreted in terms of the present relationship, leading to the discovery of a hidden and neglected, but always present, mutuality. It is in the discovery of hidden mutuality that true wisdom resides.

Taoism

Sometimes it is argued that shamanism is the basis of Korean thought. A Western missionary put it this way in 1906 (his mot is reprinted in a contemporary guidebook to Korea).

As a general rule we may say that the all around Korean will be a Confucianist when in society, a Buddhist when he philosophizes, and a spirit worshiper (shamanist) when he is in trouble. Now when you want to know what a man's religion is, you must watch him when he is in trouble. It is for this reason that I conclude that the underlying religion of the Korean, the foundation upon which all else is mere superstructure, is his original spirit worship. (Tomasz 1993, 51)

I would not want to practice a contemporary version of this arrogant insight (it is both, I believe), substituting Taoism for shamanism. My point is, I hope, more subtle.

According to newspaper surveys and my experience, most Korean women visit fortune-tellers. It is also my experience that most Korean men do too, though many men arrange for their wives to do the actual visiting. Many visit a shaman. One Western lawyer who worked for many years in Seoul complained, "It's not unusual for me to do a lot of detailed work on a client proposal and then have the client go and consult a fortune-teller. He will always take the fortune-teller's advice over mine" (Clifford 1994, 161). Certainly the living and dead keep company in Korea as they do not in the United States, the topic of *Hymn of the Spirit* (Mahlsook 1983), which is about a world in which the dead mingle with the living and the different religions blend, frequently within the same person.

If Koreans are superstitious, it does not profoundly affect their views of evil. To be sure, many less educated people (and not only the less educated) talk about revenge from beyond the grave, but the model—the reasoning—is strictly human, the dead taking their revenge for much the same reason as the living do, but perhaps more effectively.

It is easy to overestimate the importance of superstitious and spiritual beliefs (*misin*—the term is not derogatory), particularly in Korea where figures such as the shaman are so dramatic. In many ways the Korean view of *kwisin*, ghosts of the departed who remain in this world to trouble their relatives and enemies, is less superstitious (or at least requires less of an act of spiritual and metaphysical imagination and faith) than belief in an omniscient and omnipotent God. Certainly kwisin operate according to principles that are virtually human, denizens of a world that mirrors our own. The world of the supernatural is not a higher (or lower) universe, but a parallel one, where almost every aspect of human relationships is faithfully reflected.

This parallel quality includes the ability to negotiate with evil, which means that it is no longer what the West would call evil. If one can enter into a discourse with kwisin, if they can be bribed, placated, and persuaded, then evil loses its quality of absolute otherness. At issue is no longer evil, but moderate malevolence, though moderate otherness puts it better, as demonstrated by those kwisin whose touch causes living people to sicken, not because the kwisin mean to do harm but because to do so is their nature as ghosts of the departed.

To be sure, Westerners try to negotiate with evil. The story of Faust is exemplary in this respect. But in the West the human bargainer is always defeated. Goethe's Faust, for example, can have anything he wants, as long as it never lasts. Once he wants a pleasure to linger, his soul is lost forever. Unless, that is, God should intervene, changing the terms of the contract forever. Kwisin negotiate their own terms: "Feed us, respect us, and remember us, for we are more alone and lonely than humans can know. If you do, we shall leave you to yourselves." Though many bargains are struck with kwisin, this one is the most common, hardly a compact with the devil.

One wants to say that it is not shamanism but Taoism that most profoundly affects the Korean view (or nonview) of evil, except that putting it this way would ignore the origins of Taoism in shamanism. More accurate is the statement that the Korean view of evil is most profoundly affected by a type of philosophical shamanism captured by the *Tao Te Ching*, and *Chuang-tzu*, in which oneness (or at least "not two-ness") is the highest value. The sacredness of nature, the ecstatic union of the shaman with the spirits of nature, and his flight into the celestial sphere are leading themes of these works (Wong 1997, 9).

Although to distinguish between Taoism and philosophical shamanism is perhaps tendentious, doing so is useful insofar as it recalls the connection between the shamanism of everyday Korean life and the more abstract teachings of the Tao. Because shamanism is so dramatic, because a visit to the colorful shaman is on the agenda of every tour group, it is easy to miss the more subtle but important point.

Although stories of kwisin, and the shaman who speaks in their voice, are dramatic, it is actually the more subtle and abstract teachings of the Tao that most deeply influence everyday views of evil in Korea. In shamanism, the spirits inhabit a world remarkably porous to our own, as the dead go back and forth freely between them. The world of everyday life and the spirit world are not one, but neither are they two. The Taoist term "not two" comes closest to the mark. This view of "not two," rendered abstract, transformed into a worldview rather than a superstition, best explains (at least insofar as the best explanation is most general) the Korean nonview of evil.[3]

Does the Tao best explain the Korean nonview of evil to Koreans—or to me? In giving such explanations, the danger of "essentializing" Korean culture is most acute, except that I am not really writing about the essence of Korean culture, but rather I am writing about an interpretation of Korean thought put to me by a number of Koreans, in bits and pieces, that I have filled out with a Westerner's reading of Eastern philosophy. Furthermore, Taoism is a philosophy not usually claimed by Koreans as their own. I have constructed the link via the category of philosophical shamanism, though I do not believe it takes much stretching to do so.

No Korean said to me "I do not believe in evil *because* of the Tao's rejection of dualism." People don't talk like this. If they did, I would be suspicious, as I was with the coffeehouse women who enlisted Kohlberg. Rather, many Koreans said things like "I don't believe in evil because divisions like that destroy natural harmony." If one were truly a Taoist, one might not even know it. The Taoist interpretation of the Korean nonview of evil is my reconstruction, designed not so much to crystalize the Korean view as to distinguish it from Western perspectives—that is, to make it knowable to a Westerner. Some Koreans have found this reconstruction useful, not so much because they recognize themselves in it, but because it operates at a distance that renders their experience strangely familiar, the term "strangely" as important as "familiar."[4]

In the West, the model of birth and creativity is dualistic, God working on formless matter to create the world. In this dualistic model there is a place for evil, perhaps even a need for it: it is one of the oppositions that must be overcome. Only through the conflict of good and evil is progress possible.

In the East, the model of birth and creativity is singular, though even that way of putting it is not quite right, as it assumes a dual against which singular takes its meaning. The model is the Tao, a oneness that has the quality of nothingness, insofar as it is so vast and capacious it has room for all things without contradiction. From this perspective, creation comes not from conflict, but from the generation of unities out of dualities, unities being understood not so much as fusion as "more than one, less than two." (The same term is sometimes used to characterize relationships marked by chŏng.) In creating unities out of conflict, one comes closer to the original simplicity of nature, and to what the Korean Solomon would do, transforming two women fighting over a single child into sisters.

If God working on formless matter is the Western ideal of creativity and generativity, the *Tao Te Ching* says simply "the great fashioner does no splitting" (no. 28). It is this ideal that the Korean judge tries to uphold, finding guilt where there is innocence and vice-versa, not in order to reverse dualities, thus creating new polarities. To do so would reflect the ideal of the Western dialectic, each apparent synthesis becoming the motive for a new conflict. But rather, the Korean judge applies the Taoist ideal in order to find the underlying natural unity behind the apparent opposition. Here, the Korean says, is real creativity, finding a natural harmony out of apparent conflict. The judge means to restore something of humanity's original nature, finding a deeper unity in two men's conflict. That this deeper unity has to do with their shared badness, or perhaps just humanness, is ironic, but hardly contradictory.

Koreans hate boundaries, above all the boundaries that divide one into two. One sees this hatred in even something so simple and notorious as Korean drivers, who not only refuse to drive in traffic lanes but drive as if they refuse to recognize the laws of physics—that two bodies cannot occupy the same space at the same time. Drivers drive as close as they possibly can to each other, relying not on horns and gestures but on *nunch'i*, which literally means eye measurement but implies an acute sensitivity to the mood (*kibun*) and intentions of others. To be without nunch'i is to be less than human. To be blessed with nunch'i is to know without saying or telling, which is tantamount to knowing differences without having to speak or recognize them—the ideal.

Do Koreans Deny Evil?

The question can no longer be postponed. Do Koreans deny evil, and dualism, in the psychological sense of denial, in which an individual repudiates what he or she knows to be the *meaning* of an event? In most cases, the denied event is not itself disavowed. What is disavowed is its emotional significance. "The ego thus avoids awareness of some painful aspect of reality and so diminishes anxiety and other unpleasurable affects" (Moore and Fine 1990, 50–51). Denial, it should be noted, is entirely normal. Without some denial we could not function as humans in a threatening and painful world. The question is one of degree. Blanchot's advice, "keep watch over absent meaning," should be understood in this sense. The absence of the term "evil" is not so important as whether the absence of the meaning of evil amounts to denial.

Could it be that Koreans deny evil out of rage at the separateness and disappointment that come with the recognition of boundaries? Evil is unknowable because it is the ultimate boundary, the ultimate other. From this perspective, it is not so much that Koreans need separation to know evil, but that separation is itself the evil they cannot know. This interpretation finds resonance in the Christian view that evil is separation from God. It finds a different resonance in the conception of the Tao as perfect nothingness: perfect because only nothing is without boundaries.

In Chapter 4 I argued that above all Koreans fear nothingness; now I argue that they idealize it. This juxtaposition of fear and idealization is no contradiction. Idealization is the most common form of denial, recognizing the dreaded entity's existence, but transforming—even reversing—its meaning. And perhaps this reversal is not mere denial. Perhaps all creativity has this quality, transforming what we most dread into something we can live with, even worship. The sublimation of denial it might be called. Or as Rainer Maria Rilke (1981, first elegy) puts it, "Beauty is nothing but the beginning of terror that we are still just able to bear." We bear terror by making it beautiful, like the Tao, yet another meaning of aesthetics.

One might hypothesize that Korean resentment at separation stems from Korean child-rearing practices. A close relationship with mother, during which the young child is in almost constant contact with mother's body, even at night, is followed at the age of about two years by separation and the demand that the child conform to the standards of society.

Infants and toddlers are seldom separated from their mothers and never left unattended. No crib or cradle deprives the child of physical contact with its mother, with whom it sleeps and on whose back it travels. . . . During these early years, children are hardly punished at all. . . . Children do not receive such indulgent treatment after their second year. . . . Children over two are often left in the care of older siblings or occasionally older cousins. (Janelli and Janelli 1982, 31–32)

A similar pattern, up to a point, has been identified in Japan, this one based on *amae* and what is called skinship. Amae is an intense relationship of mutual dependence, skinship the close physical contact between mother and child that fuels amae. Mothers and children spend most hours of the day in close physical contact, sleeping together, bathing together, and nursing. In the Japanese view, the mother's job is to erase the gap between the infant and herself, drawing the child into a social relationship so rewarding it will encourage the child to seek out social relationships for the rest of his or her life. Referring to the Japanese ideal, Benjamin states that "one of my favorite articles of Japanese material culture is the winter coat that fits over both mother and baby" (G. Benjamin 1997, 107–108). It is one of my favorite articles of Korean material culture as well, seen everywhere on the winter streets of Seoul.

The difference between Japan and Korea in this respect seems to be what happens after the first years, when Japanese children are nudged more gently from the nest.[5] This difference, though, like so many cultural differences across Eastern countries, may be less significant than the cultural transformation taking place within Korean society itself. Having smaller families gives mothers more time to devote to their young children, unless the mothers work outside the home, an increasingly common practice resulting in the dilution of skinship. What impact this will have on rage at separateness remains to be seen, but it appears as if both intense closeness and sharp separation are being attenuated. Fewer children are receiving more attention from busier mothers. Go figure.

The causes of Koreans' disappointment and rage at separation must, in any case, remain speculation. What is clear is that Koreans do not just deny separateness. They hate it in a way that supports the supposition that this hatred has its origins in psychological denial. Here is yet another meaning of "tell me the relationship, and I'll tell you what's evil." "Tell me the relationship . . ." and I'll weave a web among the people in it so tight that evil cannot force its way in—either because the relationship is tight to begin with or because it is modeled on such relationships. If every older man is "father" (*abŏji*), then how can there be a thief in the night? Or rather, since there most assuredly are thieves, how can the thief be evil?

Let us not let the West off the hook either. The most common form of Orientalism is not the exaggeration of the flaws of another culture but blindness to the mirror-image derelictions of one's own. It is possible that the Western propensity to see evil is also a denial of humanity's separateness, above all our terrible dependence on circumstance: that even the worst among us are not so much agents as victims of the forces that compel them. Or as "The Enlightened One," a character in *Hymn of the Spirit* puts it, "to sin when evil moves one to do so is also karma" (Mahlsook 1983, 205).

Perhaps the Western concept of evil is little more than an attempt to give grand cosmological meaning to mere human vulnerability. The fate of the human species is to know its vulnerability while being unable to justify it. If there were no evil, we would have to invent it. Or deny it. Is this the difference between West and East? One invents to deny, the other denies to invent?

Perhaps all knowledge has the quality of denial, in which our deepest insights, because they are and must be partial, act to deny a reality whose complexity we cannot bear—not just because reality is so intricate, but because manifold reality challenges our ambivalence beyond limit. Here is a good reason to compare Eastern and Western views of evil, two halves that don't make a whole.

Hsün Tzu

I approach the difficult question of whether Koreans deny evil by a circuitous route, comparing Hsün Tzu's view of evil with that represented in Korean fairy tales. Hsün Tzu, whose name was K'uang, followed Confucius by several hundred years, and Mencius by two generations. He was, and is, considered a Confucian. This is what Hsün Tzu said about human nature:

> Man's nature is evil (*hsing-o*); goodness is the result of conscious activity. . . .
> He is born with feelings of envy and hate, and if he indulges these, they will
> lead him into violence and crime, and all sense of loyalty and good faith will
> disappear. . . . Hence, any man who follows his nature and indulges his emo-
> tions will inevitably become involved in wrangling and strife, will violate the
> forms and rules of society, and will end as criminal. (1963, 157)

Greed and selfishness, terms frequently rendered by the more literal "ego-mind," are not evil in the Western sense: they lack the delight in destruction and the lack of remorse that give the Western concept of evil its weight. But the introduction of hatred and envy mark Hsün Tzu's argument as possibly being about what the West calls evil. In *Canterbury Tales*, Chaucer said this about envy:

> It is certain that envy is the worst sin that is; for all other sins are sins only against one virtue, whereas envy is against all virtue and against all goodness. ("Parson's Tale")

Envy wants to destroy goodness itself, precisely because it is good, beyond the possession and control of the envious one. "Whatever a man lacks in himself he will seek outside" (Hsün Tzu, 161). This characterization, though, sounds more like jealousy. But perhaps fine distinctions like this do not translate very well: not just across languages, but across cultures.

It is evident that a relatively sophisticated debate exists within Confucianism, one that is often couched as a dispute between Mencius and Hsün Tzu, over whether human nature is originally good or evil. Mencius says that "the great man is he who does not lose his child's-heart" (Book IV, Part B, 12). Rather than rejecting outright Mencius's view that the child's-heart is originally good, Hsün Tzu holds that humanity's original innocence ("original naïveté and simplicity") is corrupted almost from birth by the harsh demands of his environment. "If I understand Hsün Tzu correctly," says Burton Watson, "he is arguing that . . . the simplicity and naiveté of the baby will inevitably be lost by all men simply in the process of growing up, and therefore it cannot be regarded as the source of goodness" (Watson 1963, 159).

It is not clear that Hsün Tzu holds a doctrine comparable to original sin, the Bible's teaching that humanity's heart is evil from youth (Genesis 6.5–6, Psalm 51.5). What Hsün Tzu seems to be doing is contrasting man's instinctual nature, which is "prejudiced, irresponsible, and chaotic," with his conscious life, which may be subject to ritual and education and so become good.

One is reminded of the distinction between Hobbes and Locke in Western political philosophy. Some emphasize the great difference between them, but C. B. Macpherson (1971, 74–75) points out the essential similarity. If Locke really thinks human nature is so good, then why are humans always getting into wars and conflict? Why do they need government? Similarly, Hsün Tzu says, "If the nature of man were good, we could dispense with sage kings and forget about ritual principles" (Hsün Tzu 1963, 163). When Hsün Tzu says, "It is clear that man's nature is evil, that his goodness is the result of conscious activity," we should remember that for Hsün Tzu conscious activity is natural too, though not instinctual. Conscious activity needs something to work on and with, the resources provided by education, culture, and ritual.

It is not necessary to reach a conclusion about Hsün Tzu's teaching and whether it is truly the opposite of Mencius's. My point is that questions about humanity's evil nature, and a debate comparable to that one found in the West between Hobbes and Locke, are present in the Korean tradition. Koreans could at least imagine that human nature is evil from youth, because a famous Confucian philosopher has broached the issue, which has since become part of the Confucian tradition with which Koreans are familiar and to which Koreans remain loyal. Korea became "the most Neo-Confucian of all East Asian societies," says Michael Kalton (Cumings 1997, 49). It still is.

A number of Koreans, not necessarily those with the greatest formal education, referred to Hsün Tzu's teaching, understanding it to represent a different, darker view of human nature. Were Koreans inclined to see evil, they would not lack the traditional resources to do so. Not just the terms, but a teaching, a tradition, and a well-known dispute are available.

It makes no difference in this regard whether Hsün Tzu is the actual author of "Man's Nature Is Evil." Some, like Kim Sung-Hae (1985), argue that section 23 is not genuine Hsün Tzu but the product of a legalist disciple, such as Han Fei Tzu. Although she disagrees that the evil nature of humanity is genuine Hsün Tzu, Sr. Kim recognizes that this teaching is itself a part of the Confucian tradition, what she calls "the well-known theory of the evil nature of man" (1985, 123–125; interview). That recognition is enough to make my point. Koreans do not lack a tradition to give voice to the frightening suspicion that man's nature might itself be evil. They choose not to take it up, quite a different matter.

Korean Folktales

Inchoate threat and impending disaster are everywhere in Korean folktales. Protagonists may be destroyed by it or escape from it. Rarely do they triumph over it. Almost never do they confront it. The fantastic characters who inhabit these tales should not mislead us into thinking that we have entered another world. Korean folktales resemble shamanism in that both tell colorful and fantastic stories about another world that, upon closer examination, seems remarkably similar to this one, a parallel universe in which different characters play by the same rules as we. Although evil is personified in Korean folktales, the characters behave toward it much as Koreans do in the real world.

In "Dealing with Evil in Korean Fairytales," psychiatrist Rhi Bou-yong states that "evil is still something like sensation—an object or exciting participation which leaves horror but not an object which is personally related to the individual" (1980, 19).[6] Expanding on this point in an interview, the psychiatrist explained that when evil is not seen as something that can be confronted or fought, it tends to disappear as an ethical problem. If we cannot even speak evil, how can we know to fight it?

One exception might be a story called "The Fox Girl", in which the young boy who is the protagonist finally destroys his evil sister. He first learns of her nature by hiding at night in the stable, where the animals had been mysteriously dying.

> The boy watched her roll up her sleeves and rub her hands and forearms with sesame oil. Then, to his horror, she stuck her arm into a horse's anus, pulled out its liver, and ate it. The boy was petrified. He dared not move until she went into the house. (Han 1991, 83–87)

His parents do not believe him and send him packing. Finally he comes upon a monk, to whom he tells his story. The monk gives him a magic potion in three little bottles and tells him to return home quickly. By the time he gets there, the fox girl has killed their parents. The young boy would have been next, had he not quickly taken to his horse.

> The boy looked back and saw the fox girl grabbing at his horse's tail. . . . The boy looked at the last bottle and, praying that it would work, threw it at the fox girl. It broke and a large lake formed before his eyes. He watched the fox girl struggle in the water and sink. Then, to his relief, the dead body of a fox with nine tails floated to the surface. (Han 1991, 87)

But this story is not actually a confrontation with evil either. The young boy is not seeking to destroy the fox girl to save the land from her evil. Nor he is seeking to save his soul. He is seeking only to escape by any means possible from the evil that is so closely related.

There are thousands of Korean folktales. In surveying half a dozen collections, I found only three in which a confrontation, as opposed to clever escape or defeat, occurs. In addition, a number of informants recounted folktales. Many had to do with kwisin, and *tokkaebi*, mischievous horned goblins that are more temperamental than malicious. The pattern was the same, none involving a genuine contest with evil.

More truly an exception is "The Fortuneteller and the Demons," in which a blind fortune-teller exorcises the demons who have taken the life of a princess. Driving them from her body, he restores her to life. But her father becomes suspicious of the fortune-teller and decides to execute him. At the last minute the nobleman learns that he is an honest soothsayer, but the demons prevent his message from reaching the executioner, and the fortune-teller is beheaded (Han 1991, 91–96).

This story is as close as one gets to a confrontation with evil in Korean folk tales. It is an authentic agon, but it is not Faust. One major difference is that the demons never battle humans for their immortal souls. All they want is human life, just as any mortal enemy might.

You may reply that it is unfair to contrast Korean folktales with the Western Faust, who after succumbing to the temptations of evil finally confronts it, losing his life but regaining his soul. But the comparison is not out of place. Although we know it as a work of literature, the story of Faust was originally a folktale, told for centuries before it was finally set down in the *Faustbuch* (1587). Only then did it become the stuff of literature, first by Christopher Marlowe and then by Goethe.

Nothing like the Faust legends occur in Korean folk tales. The pattern is that identified by Rhi. Evil, understood as forces of dread, doom, and destruction, exists but cannot be confronted. From time to time men and women may escape from it, often by an act of spontaneous emotion involving music or dance. The result is that "Koreans admit the existence of absolute evil. One sees it in our folktales. It's there. But it is so frightening Koreans are paralyzed, unable to confront it. So they ignore relative evil as well" (Rhi Bou-yong, interview).

Illustrations of Denial?

Does this admission mean that Koreans deny evil? Sir George Sansom, quoted by Benedict in Chapter 1, believes Asians deny evil and soften dualisms, although of course Sansom is writing about Japan. Many Westerners are even more critical, holding that Koreans are deeply dualistic in their thinking and practices while denying it in their theory. Koreans will not admit to their own tendency to frame issues in terms of black and white, good and evil. If it were true, then this tendency would fit the psychological concept of denial precisely, revealing that Koreans are unable to know the meaning of their own dualistic tendencies.

Following are some illustrations of this denial. Most are from Westerners who know Korea well. But as Said reminds us, Orientalism is above all the product of Westerners who know and love the East.

"Koreans have been accustomed to framing issues in terms of absolute good or evil rather than as a series of imperfect choices," says Mark Clifford, author of *Troubled Tiger: Businessmen, Bureaucrats, and Generals in South Korea* (1994, 281).

Koreans would rather surrender than compromise, says David Steinberg in his "Stone Mirror" column in *The Korea Times* (1997). Koreans do not know the meaning of compromise, which is why they formulate issues so vaguely. Once positions are set, there is no going back, no room for maneuver, no give and take.

When Koreans talk about harmony, it often seems ironic and hypocritical to Westerners.

> Orientals possess a mysterious, unified and harmonious spiritual culture that can scarcely be understood completely by Westerners, who have different ways of thinking and different systems of logic. Although it is risky to generalize, it is clear that Oriental cultures have a certain gentle, mild, rhythm and harmony. (Clifford 1994, 76)

And

> The East's Confucian culture emphasizes harmony and the Golden Mean, rather than confrontation. Based on agrarian culture, it features moderation,

reconciliation and harmony while human relations are shaped by traditional ethics rather than rights under the law. (Clifford 1994, 143)

Park Chung Hee made the first statement, Chun Doo Hwan made the second. Both were military dictators. Park was assassinated by his chief of security. Chun Doo Hwan was recently released from being jailed for corruption and for staging the Kwangju massacre.

Immediately after making the distinction between Western obliteration of the Indians and Japanese absorption of the Koreans, the young Buddhist mentioned in Chapter 1 said, "There is no similarity between Eastern and Western thought about these issues. How could you even compare them?"

Two generations ago, storytellers narrated silent movies, speaking the parts to the audience. Today a few still entertain in Pagoda Park. One old teller of tales was recounting a story about a daughter-in-law who made a mistake. The father-in-law said that he didn't notice what it was, and peace was restored to the family. The moral, another old man explained, was that we keep peace best by feigning ignorance.

The most heavily fortified border in the world runs through Korea, surely an instance of "dualism." When I said this to Koreans, many replied that the border is really a Western imposition, the product of a fight for global hegemony between the Soviet Union and the United States. Left to themselves, Koreans would have worked things out.

"If We Can't Be Subtle about Evil, We Just Won't Admit It"

Several informants responded to my question about evil along the same lines as a student at Inha University: "Evil is a dangerous concept. Maybe you have studied it so much that you can be subtle about it. We can't. It you call someone evil, there's no compromise, no going back. So we don't even think about it. If we can't be subtle about evil, then we won't admit it." The judge said much the same thing. If he thought any of the criminals who appeared before him was evil, he would have had no choice but to sentence them to death.

Although most Koreans deny evil, only a few, like the Inha University student, could put the reason into words. Korean culture does not allow or foster complex feelings of ambivalence, a willingness to tolerate good and evil all mixed up together in every person's heart. The emotional burden is too great, especially when one recalls the dilemma of the student who said that everything he knows about evil he learned in his family.

In these circumstances, the tendency to resolve the dilemma by splitting the world into good and evil is insistent. Do this, however, and one has crossed the Rubicon. There is no turning back, no compromise, no relationship left. Better not to see the evil in the first place. This viewpoint can easily segue into the belief that to see evil is to create it. In an important respect, that belief is true.

One might, however, take a slightly different perspective, which is an especially good idea in those cases in which a researcher's conclusions are based on a subject's compliment (Maybe you who are so clever can be subtle about evil.). Recall the student who referred to how much hatred he felt toward a friend with whom he had chŏng. Perhaps Koreans are actually more tolerant of ambivalence, better able to manage the love and hate that are found at the heart of every intense emotional relationship. Koreans would refrain from seeing evil not out of a dearth of ambivalence, but an abundance, leading to an appreciation, generally nonverbal, of how every close relationship breeds and breathes ambivalence.

In order to maintain close relationships, one must learn to live with the ambivalence; naming evil is not helpful in this regard. About evil it is hard to be ambivalent. Seen from this perspective, Koreans would overlook evil in order to be close to those who embody it (the thief in the night who is one's father), while Westerners would create evil in order to locate it outside our most intimate relationships. From this perspective, it is Westerners who are more heavily defended, less able to tolerate ambivalence.

I asked a Korean professor of sociology who denied the relevance of the concept of evil, How do you explain something like the Holocaust? "Events like the Holocaust are outside of history," she replied. "They are irruptions; they have nothing to do with ordinary life. It is a specialized field of study." Beliefs like hers are dangerous, at least as dangerous as the belief in evil. They constitute the denial of the connection between extraordinary and ordinary evil that Rhi talks about. Or so I had thought.

Westerners, at least a large group of Westerners who have thought seriously about historical horrors such as the Holocaust, believe it is important to bring those horrors under the horizon of history. In *Modernity and the Holocaust*, Zygmunt Bauman (1989) argues that we understand the Holocaust only when we see it as an instance of modernity, Weberian rationalization taken to its extralogical conclusion. Similarly, George Ritzer (1996) argues that the rational process that can produce a Holocaust also produces McDonald's hamburgers. The Holocaust is not unique; nor are the malicious motives of the men who caused it. If we are not to have more historical horrors, we must be forever on our guard against them, and the evil they represent.

The Holocaust lacks resonance in Korea. It is truly outside of history. Certainly it is outside of Eastern history, but most Koreans talk about it as though it had nothing to do with evil, nothing to do with them, nothing to do with ordinary human life. The sociologist with whom I spoke was not unique. For her, as for so many Koreans, to be ever on our guard against evil is only likely to create evil, polarity, and conflict.

Earlier I argued that the denial of evil does not necessarily lead to more benevolence among humans . . . or nations. Koreans seem no less likely to respond aggressively to North Korea because they do not believe in evil. Aggression and hatred are not the products of a concept such as evil. Evil is one way we make sense of experiences of intense aggression and hatred, experiences that originate not from a concept but from (dare I say it) human nature. The denial of evil might actually lead to more irresponsible behavior, as though one could not possibly act with malice for its own sake if these categories do not exist.

While the denial of evil may contribute to aggression, hatred, and destruction, it is hard to refuse the conclusion that during this century the greatest evils, or at least the evils on the largest scale, have been committed in the West, not in the East. As malicious and destructive as Japanese aggression was during World War II, the greatest acts of destruction in this century have been Western: the Holocaust, Stalin's purges, World War I, World War II in Europe.

The East has done its share. The Pol Pot regime in Cambodia ranks among the worst horrors of history. Mao killed millions. The Rape of Nanking is comparable in horror, if not scope, to the Holocaust. What we cannot say in the West is that our vigilance against evil has somehow mitigated evil. Or if it has, then one would have to conclude that the belief in evil has mitigated the evil that the belief in evil creates. That, or the West is more evil in the first place. Otherwise, we should have to equate modernity with evil, arguing merely that the West has a head start. Neither Bauman (1991) nor Ritzer (1996) would argue anything that simple. In any case, Pol Pot, Rwanda, (and to a lesser degree) Stalin contradict that conclusion: mass murder does not require the techniques of mass production. It is, tragically, essentially a cottage industry.

Reading Elaine Pagels's account of the origins of the concept of evil in Christian thought, *The Origin of Satan* (1995), one is struck by how the creation of the other, and the dualism on which this creation is based, not only constitutes the phenomenon of evil but creates what it deems to be actual evil: an other who must be fought, above all the Jew. Pagels's answer is tolerance of diversity and otherness, the postmodern answer to everything, but only because postmodernism presumes a world of vast heterogeneity to begin with, so different from the Tao, which presumes an underlying sameness.

A Korean would respond, "How can I be tolerant of evil? Better not to see it in the first place. Better not to create a world torn in two, from which evil can emerge." In fact, this response is essentially what the Inha University student said. It seems an inadequate response, but does history bear that out? Or does not history suggest that the evil that culminates in the Holocaust begins with the creation of evil to which Pagels refers?

Bombing the Fish

Catherine Lewis tells a story about several boys gathered around a fish tank at a Japanese preschool. Each time one dropped a small clay pellet into the tank, they would cry out in unison, "Bombs away!" The teacher told them that this behavior might harm the fish, but she did not stop them, and they continued to bomb the fish. Later she raised the issue in class discussion. What does everyone think about this behavior? Several students said it sounded like fun; most were worried about the fish. The teacher guided the discussion in such a way that the boys' bad motives never came up (Lewis 1995, 125–126; G. Benjamin 1997, 176–179).

The boys might have mistaken the clay for food, or they might have not thought about what they were doing, but the possibility that the boys might have wanted to hurt the fish was never confronted, and the teacher never referred to the boys' repeated "Bombs away!" Interviewed at the end of the day, the teacher denied that she even privately thought the boys meant to hurt the fish. They were deficient in empathy for other living things. Once it was explained to them that they might really hurt the fish, they would not want to do it again.

For one with a background in psychoanalytic theory, the teacher seems misguided. If we ignore children's aggression, we only heighten their tendency to deny it while they continue to behave aggressively. We only increase children's inclination to split good and evil, fostering their tendency to attribute their own malevolence to others. Better to gently interpret the aggression, so the child might come to own that part of him- or herself rather than alienating it in others. Such an interpretation might also bring to light the unconscious identification with the victim that lies behind much aggression. No people have suffered more from the consequences of "Bombs Away!" than the Japanese.

The Japanese teacher saw the boys' behavior differently, in much the same way Koreans do. If we recognize the existence of malevolent motives, we actually make it more difficult for people to feel empathy and connection with others, as we create a world in which others are indeed like we know ourselves to be: frequently malicious and destructive, or at least filled with malicious and destructive impulses. Better not to hold up that mirror in the first place.

One might respond that the Koreans, and perhaps the Japanese, create their web of empathy only by demonizing the other: we are good people, they are malicious. It is a fine theory, but the practice of the Koreans, at least, does not support it. Koreans are almost as reluctant to demonize others. Doing so would open the door of the world to an intrusion of otherness so alien, dreadful, and inhuman that it must herald the end of the world, precisely what the Korean woman said about the *chijon-p'a* (Extremely Noble Gang).

Perhaps there is no answer; perhaps the discovery of evil is as filled with tragedy as its denial is. Certainly it is not only the East that has failed to be sufficiently subtle about evil. With such a dangerous concept we should at least consider the possibility that its denial serves humanity better in the long run than its discovery. Once again I use the term "denial" in its strict sense, in which the meaning of an experience is rejected. In this case, the experience is the apparently natural tendency to divide the world in two. Koreans do this, as demonstrated by my "illustrations of denial," but Koreans do not acknowledge that they are doing it. This denial is, I am suggesting, not as bad a strategy as one might suppose.

Ruth Benedict writes of Japanese god characters who, unlike the Judeo-Christian God, are two-sided, having both good and bad qualities. Against such dualistic "god characters . . . common in world mythologies," Benedict sets the "higher ethical religions," which exclude them. Dualistic god characters "have been excluded because a philosophy of cosmic conflict between good and evil makes it more congenial to separate supernatural beings into groups as different as black and white" (Benedict 1946, 191).

Taken in the context of her book as a whole, Benedict's reference to "higher ethical religions" is mere nominalism, just one more name like "protestant." Still, she makes an important point. Eastern thought, including Korean thought, does not so much deny dualism as move it, relocating it within the larger whole represented by god characters, who represent not just humans but cosmos. The Tao performs much the same function of relocating dualism, teaching that what appears to be a fundamental opposition to humans who stand one on side or another is actually part of the whole. This insight is, I have suggested, not necessarily a sign of a restricted capacity for ambivalence, but of a heightened one.

A friend to whom I put my suspicion that Koreans were more dualistic than they knew put it this way: "You say we are dualistic. Of course we are. That's human nature, to think you are right and the other is wrong. The difference is that we try to remember that humans are part of a larger nature, and within this larger nature there is no good and evil. There just is." By larger nature, I think he meant Tao.

What about the Holocaust? I might have asked. Is that the same as a mother's love? Only at some point the argument becomes circular, pointless. The Tao is not an ethical category nor a judgment. It is a container, an empty space within an infinite vase, with room enough for all things and heaven and earth besides. Humans cannot model their societies after it, because like heaven and earth the Tao cares nothing for humans.

> Heaven and earth are not humane;
> they regard all beings as straw dogs.

Sages are not humane;

they see all people as straw dogs.

The space between heaven and earth is like bellows and pipes,

empty yet inexhaustible. *(Tao Te Ching, number 5)*[7]

Humans can, however, seek not to flout the Tao's principles, which means not positing what my friend would surely regard as another Western dualism such as that between the Holocaust and mother love.

Silence

Until now I have argued about terms, and whether a particular term, "evil," may meaningfully be said to exist in Korea. In important ways, in the most important ways (that is, the ways in which the term resonates most deeply in Western culture), the concept of evil does not exist in Korea. But perhaps this approach is the wrong way to address the issue. Could it be that the most important experiences are the ones for which we have no names? For Wittgenstein (1961, 6.53–7), as for so much of Western philosophy, my language is the limit of my world. "What we cannot speak about we must pass over in silence." Perhaps, but possibly we can know something about the silence by encircling it, so to speak, as we know the shape of the dark emptiness that is the interior of a vase by knowing the shape of the vessel.

Buddhists believe that the most important form is emptiness itself, nonbeing. The Tao is nonbeing. From the nonbeing of evil in Korea we can learn much. After much has been said, most important is what remains unsaid, what all that was said acts to deny, or rather makes impossible to exist in the first place.

I have suggested what the nonexistence of evil acts to deny in Korea: the possibility that evil is so close we can reach out and touch it, as we touch the ones we love. In the end they are one—one's family, the world.

But what does the *existence* of evil serve to deny in the West? Here I make an assumption about words and silence. A word (again, I make no distinction among words, terms, and concepts) brings something into being, the something that it represents. At the same time, a word allows other things to fall out of existence, their potential denied by the word that in creating one reality annihilates a million more. Otherwise expressed, the principle of silence cuts both ways. Koreans are silent about evil, their silence serving to deny certain awesome possibilities, above all that the thief in the night is one's father. Westerners are not silent about evil. This silence does not mean that the West does not deny anything. It just means that the West denies something different, whatever the word "evil" keeps from being born into existence.

Above all, evil keeps a thought from being born, the terrifying thought that the world is one, the God who makes and rules it a malevolent being who cares nothing for the happiness of His creatures, except perhaps to thwart them. In a word, evil solves the problem of theodicy, which haunts the West: how could an all-good and all-powerful God allow the suffering of innocents? Evil solves the problem by splitting, attributing malevolence to a realm, and experience, of the one opposite of God.[8] In other words, evil serves to deny the possibility that the thief in the night is "Our Father who is in heaven."

From this perspective, it is no accident that there is an affinity between the way the ancient Greeks thought about evil, what they called "moira," and the way the Koreans do, which is why the old men in Pagoda Park sounded like they were talking about *hubris*. This affinity occurs not because East and West once converged—as Edward Said (1994, 58) points out, Orientalism began with Herodotus' stories about the exotic East—but because the Greeks knew the malevolent carelessness of their gods. Moira was fate, good and evil rolled into one, mark of a universe that cares nothing for human happiness. In such a world, hubris is the mark of transgression because it is human pride and arrogance that most denies the natural order represented by moira (Greene 1964). Only when we posit that God is good, and that He cares about humans, do we need evil.

A recent article in the *International Herald Tribune* (1997) told of Governor Mike Huckabee of Arkansas, a Baptist minister, who introduced legislation that would change the practice of referring to tornados and violent storms as "acts of God," a traditional Western designation. We must not allow, he said, a destructive and deadly force to be attributed to God. But if God is all-powerful, then to whom but Him do we attribute such devastation? Here we see the dilemma of Judeo-Christian monotheism in a nutshell. If God were all-powerful, we would need to call him Bad. Since this is impossible, we need evil, or else we could not sleep at night.

And now we see that the problem of the young Korean, who could not know evil because it was too close, part of his family, and the problem the West calls theodicy, the justice of God, are one: how to know the malevolence of what we value most in the whole world. The answers are two, denial and division, but the problem is one.

CHAPTER SIX

Globalization Is Evil

"**G**lobalization is learning about other cultures so we can dominate them economically." So said a Korean student of naive virtuosity, one of almost 250 Koreans with whom I spoke about globalization, the same group with whom I talked about evil.

Implicit in the student's statement is a profound and far-reaching fantasy: that Koreans could learn about other cultures at a distance and not be touched by them, establishing factories in other countries and exporting to still others, but remaining free of their influence.[1] It is a widely held fantasy among Koreans, and a destructive one. It is worth considering why it is so influential.

The term "globalization" is everywhere in Korea. The word used by President Kim Young Sam was *"segyehwa." "Segye"* means world. *"Hwa"* is Korean for the process we render with the suffix "-ization." *"Kukchehwa"* is a more sophisticated synonym, "internationalization" being probably the best translation. Some academics draw a distinction between the two words: internationalization is about opening up to the international community; globalization is about becoming part of it. For most, however, the terms are synonymous. Since it is "segyehwa" that is in common use, it is the term I used. Not a single Korean, no matter how old or ill-educated, was unfamiliar with the term.

"Restructuring" (*kujojojŏng*), the code word of the Kim Dae Jung administration, is giving "globalization" a run for its money these days as far as its frequency in popular discourse is concerned. For many Koreans, restructuring is tantamount to layoffs. It is striking that few informants saw the connection between globalization and restructuring. There are at least two reasons why this connection is often missed. First, seeing the connection requires a minimal level of theoretical understanding, unavailable to all informants. Second, seeing the connection requires a recognition of the degree to which Korea has already been penetrated by the larger world. Koreans are still not keen to do so, and the lack of connection may have the quality of denial, though it was difficult to tell in any particular case. I focus on globalization, as it represents the larger and more abstract threat—and promise. Restructuring is a response to globalization, not vice-versa.

Koreans do not have not a word for evil. For globalization, Koreans have a word that is one everyone's lips. In the end it amounts to much the same thing; globalization is an empty word, used to connote the fantasies and nightmares of a nation without having to speak them. In this regard, globalization too is a silence waiting to be filled—not with words, but meaning.

I asked every Korean I spoke with about globalization. It was the first question I asked, originally intended as no more than a conversation starter, so that I could establish rapport before delving into the more difficult territory of evil. The question took on a life of its own, however; the tone of Korean responses to questions about globalization was remarkably similar to their responses to questions about evil. (Soon I began to ask other questions, thinking that perhaps *everything* Koreans said had the quality of their responses about evil. This was not the case, and soon I trimmed my questions. See the Research Appendix.)

Koreans did not say that globalization is evil, but of course Koreans did not say that anything was evil. That Koreans experience globalization as though it were evil is my interpretation. To call something "evil" means to objectify one's dread, granting someone or something that is terrible and awesome the quality of other. One may feel oneself to be evil, but only to the degree that one's own evil shares the quality of otherness, an alien presence in self and world (Alford 1997c, 35–49).

What if it is not otherness that one most fears? What if what one fears is the quality of being the other, alienated, isolated, and alone, bereft of attachment? Then evil may become unspeakable, too close to home. The experience of evil cannot be projected into an other because it is the very experience of otherness that is so terrifying. This, as I have argued at some length, is the situation for almost all Koreans.

One might argue that with a concept of evil Koreans might better know their experience of globalization. I don't think so, and in any case it hardly matters. "Evil" is not available to Koreans. If it were, aspects of experience the West associates with dread and terror might be more accessible to them, and these aspects might also be more readily projected into others. For all the trauma of globalization, the International Money Fund bailout, and the national humiliation that followed, Koreans have not done a great deal of enemy making, which is not to say this is an easy time to be an American there.

In the end it matters not a lot whether one calls globalization evil. I say this not because I am a nominalist. My position is closer to that of *Chuang-tzu*. "Names are guests of realities"—realities that are ambiguous enough to admit of several interpretations: not any, but several. The trick will be to find an interpretation of "globalization" that is close enough for me to understand it as evil, for this is how I believe Koreans experience globalization, and close enough to other, related categories of Korean experience for them to know what I call evil. Then we shall be able to communicate. We might even enlighten each other.

Koreans experience globalization as evil because they quite rightly experience it as the intrusion of the standards of the market and the bureaucracy—instrumental reason—into every aspect of life. On the one hand, globalization promises that Koreans need not be poor. On the other hand, globalization promises the dissolution of human ties, a prospect that fills Koreans with dread. Much like Satan, globalization tempts those it would destroy, asking Koreans to sell their Korean souls for a bauble.

Globalization is the conjunction of Max Weber and Adam Smith. It represents the dangers of atomization, isolation, fragmentation, and loss, turning Koreans into strangers in their own land. "We are becoming strangers to ourselves," said one middle-aged informant. "We don't recognize each other unless we are making money." In a word, globalization destroys chŏng, which for many Koreans remains the highest value.

For most Koreans, globalization is an idea more terrifying than North Korea. North Koreans are related. With North Korea, the South Koreans have chŏng. It is miun chŏng (bad chŏng), but it is better than no chŏng at all, which is precisely what globalization threatens. Globalization represents the transformation of warm human ties, including ties whose warmth stems from hatred rather than love, into strictly instrumental encounters. Miun chŏng, warmth through friction, is better than no human warmth at all.

Globalization also promises. It promises freedom. If hwabyŏng disease is the Korean malady, then globalization is its solution, the opening of Korean society. For all the attractions of chŏng, Korea can be a tight, closed, and claustrophobic world. Many Koreans are isolated in their uri world, the world of we Koreans, alienated and crushed at the same time. For many, like Mr. Chi, who loves to meet foreigners, globalization is a promise of freedom and new connections. It sounds wonderful, and it can be. At the same time, freedom may stand only inches away from dread.

The sudden experience of freedom can seem like the law of gravity has been rescinded. Liberation turns into terror. In psychoanalytic jargon, this experience is called borderline, the problem of living between losing and fusing (Lewin and Schulz 1992). Unable to live in this space, those suffering from borderline experience exchange crushing connection for no connection at all—that is, terror. For those constrained too tightly and too long, the freedom to experiment can be the freedom to fragment. Claustrophobia turns into agoraphobia. The problem is not unique to individuals. Hwabyŏng disease is a disorder of claustrophobic cultures, borderline personality disorder mark of agoraphobic ones. Chapters 6 and 7 concern the conditions under which opportunities for cultural experimentation created by globalization may be liberating, as opposed to being merely fragmenting. In other words, they concern the circumstances in which evil may lead to enlightenment.

In approaching globalization as a source of dread and wonder, I am treating it as a cultural phenomenon. Some, such as Wallerstein (1990a), disagree with this treatment. Culture is derivative of the world economic system. Boyne (1990) responds that globalization is an emergent phenomenon, living a life of its own. It does not seem necessary to draw the distinction so sharply, a strategy reminiscent of old Marxian debates about the autonomy of the social and cultural superstructure. One can acknowledge that globalization is part and parcel of global capitalism coupled with Weberian rationalization and still hold that aspects of globalization are inexplicable in strictly economic terms, all that explanatory emergence means (Brodbeck 1968). One can agree that globalization is what colonialism and imperialism look like in the waning days of the twentieth century, and the question still remains—what do they really look like? Strangely familiar, and like nothing we have ever seen.

Beeper as Fetish, Theory as Fetish

Consider the ubiquitous beeper and cellular telephone, prized possessions of half the population of Seoul, or so it sometimes seems. Walking down a crowded street in Seoul, one is constantly hearing phones ringing and beepers beeping. Everyone who isn't accompanied looks like he is talking to himself. He is talking into his tiny cell phone. One young man, referring to his friend, took out his beeper, holding it in the palm of his hand, while pointing to it. "See, my friend is right here, right now. He's with me right now, while I'm talking with you." It sounded like he was holding his friend in his hand, as though the beeper were his friend.

Had his beeper become a fetish, a postmodern medium to take the place of a genuine relationship? Or was his beeper a transitional object, representing not just mother but a traditional community spread out in space, all over Seoul? Did it ease the pangs of separation? The beeper is not, after all, a pair of expensive sneakers. It represents, at least potentially, a real linkage with another human.

The greater the distance at which the study is done, the more difficult it will be to know the answer, because we will not know what the young man is thinking. To know this, we must ask him and his friends. What matters is not what he is doing, pointing at the beeper as though it were his friend, but what he is thinking and feeling as he does it. There is no way around it, no theory to take the place of talking and listening. If we fail to talk and listen, not only are we less likely to know whether he is suffering from illusion, but we are more likely to reproduce his illusion in our theory in the guise of understanding it: the illusion that everything new and distant is really familiar and close at hand.

Consider those academics who write about globalization as though it were not merely interaction across boundaries but the elimination of boundaries of time and space. "To invoke Roland Robertson's felicitous phrase, the world has in many respects become a single place," says one critic quoting yet another (Scholte 1996, 45). Soon the globe will be encircled in texts referring to texts, or replaced by them. But the world has not become a single place, and what needs to be understood is why the illusion is so powerful.[2]

Behind the powerful illusion is reasoning similar to that of the young man and his beeper. When the world that is close at hand suddenly becomes attenuated and unfamiliar, a phenomenon rendered more dramatic by the end of the Cold War, the tendency is to say that everything is really the same, only more so. "My friend is really closer than ever before, right here in my hand," says the young man. In an analogous fashion, academics treat diversity as though it were the same diversity everywhere.

If diversity has no content, if we do not look closely enough to know its stories, then more diversity is not very different from more homogeneity. Particularity and diversity are the way otherness and difference are valued from the perspective of homogenization. Globalization itself becomes a transitional object, but a flattening one, making something new and frightening more familiar than it really is by looking at the world from such a vast distance that everything looks the same, even difference.

What if it only appears that everything is the same? What if behind the apparent sameness lie great differences—not abstract differences, but real ones? Benjamin Barber quotes an MTV executive: "Kids on the streets in Tokyo have more in common with kids on the streets in London than they do with their parents" (Barber 1995, 105). No, the kids, as well as the coffeehouse women who talked about Kohlberg, only think they do. Or perhaps we only think they do. Even Westerners who despise their own contemporary culture often believe in its global omnipotence, as though the icons of consumer capitalism in other lands must mean the same thing elsewhere as here.[3]

Young Americans and young Koreans both love their beepers, though young Koreans love them more. What if they love them in different ways, for different reasons? We will never know unless we ask, not just about their beepers but about their worlds. Beepers are, after all, just things. Their status as cultural sign is what counts, and we cannot know what it signifies from a distance. Otherwise expressed, the theory of globalization is no substitute for anthropology. And when we do the anthropology, we may not need the theory of globalization anymore. Or at least we will not confuse the theory with the phenomenon.[4]

Globalization and Evil

Most discussion of globalization in Korea is surrounded by an aura of fear. The $60 million bailout by the IMF only intensified that fear. A few days after the agreement with the IMF was signed, an informant expressed the fear this way: "It has been quite chilly for a few days, and people are identifying the weather with the current economic situation. Everyone is afraid." Weather is emotion at a distance, out of our control, but still able to affect us—like the world itself.

Koreans are constantly reminded that once before they failed to cope with a changing world. *The Korea Times* compared December 3, 1997, the day the IMF agreement was signed, to August 29, 1910, the "Day of National Disgrace," when Korea was annexed by Japan. Koreans have been making similar comparisons for some time. Several years ago, former president Kim Young Sam put it this way:

> About 100 years ago, we faced a similar global tide of change. At that time, Korea failed to cope with it wisely despite the Kabo reform effort and, in consequence, lost its sovereignty and suffered humiliation and hardship for decades. . . . Thus, our first attempt at national modernization ended in failure. (Kim Young Sam 1995b, 269)

President Kim Young Sam went on to say that it must not happen again, that Koreans must meet the globalizers with their own weapons, globalizing before they are globalized.

In Korea, globalization is the imperialism of the formerly colonized, imperium always at risk of reverting to colony. As the former president said in his 1994 New Year's Address, "Only those countries that thrive in the increasingly fierce international competition will be key players in world affairs. As for those countries which fail in the race, even their survival will be at stake" (Kim Young Sam 1995a, 126–127).

Korea is no longer a low-cost producer. Until recently, Korean factory workers earned more than their English counterparts.[5] Pusan's shoe industry, the world's largest in the 1980s, has disappeared, its factories moved to lower-cost producers in China, Vietnam, and Indonesia (Clifford 1994, 331). Korea's strategy of state-directed investment in huge chaebŏl, privately owned conglomerates that dominate the economy, has proven ill suited to the new global economic order. (Sales of the two largest chaebŏl, Hyundai and Samsung, alone accounted for almost 20 percent of the Korean GDP in 1994; the top four accounted for 50 percent [Thurow 1998, 25]).

Koreans fear that they will go the way of Argentina, which appeared as a major player in the world economy for a few years before it slipped back into second-world status. "I'm scared that our moment in history is over," said one informant who declined to give his name. "Just call me an average salary man," invoking a term that was once a source of pride but is now more closely associated with anxiety.

Koreans have an almost untranslatable word, *sadae-juŭi*, loving and admiring the great and powerful. One of the interviewees for an international educational administrator grant said that "Koreans are good at putting things together from parts made elsewhere." It was said with a mixture of pride and disparagement; she meant that Koreans were creative with other people's ideas. Like many people in small countries subject to a series of national humiliations, Koreans are both arrogant and self-deprecating about their nation's abilities. This apparent contradiction is one of the "but also's" to which Ruth Benedict refers.

In fact, Koreans frequently combine *sadae-juŭi* with great confidence in their ability to only apparently adopt other people's ideas, while in fact transforming them into genuine indigenous products, such as that marvelous image of Christ crucified on an A-frame, a device used for centuries by Korean laborers to carry heavy loads on their backs. Will Koreans be able to indigenize globalization? Must this be an oxymoron, a contradiction in terms?

Koreans overestimate their integrative powers. That overestimation is part of the fantasy of not being touched by what they must become in order to survive. "Korean body, Western utensils" is not just a cliché; it is a telling metaphor, as though the Korean body can ingest foreign ideas without altering the basic structure of the Korean body. The cliché is an illusion, the narcissistic defense against sadae-juŭi, as though Koreans could admire and adopt the ways of the powerful without really being affected by them.

Introduced from the top down in Koryŏ society among the civil aristocrats, Korean Confucianism took several hundred years to spread throughout the body of society. Today it has become thoroughly metabolized, so to speak, present in every part of the social body. Will globalization be metabolized? If it is, it will not take two hundred years, but something like twenty more.

At the core of the Korean discussion of globalization is a collective fantasy: that Koreans can globalize their economy but not themselves, not their relationships. It is such a powerful fantasy because it conceals such a terrible dread: that globalization will transform every relationship based on affection into strictly instrumental encounters. Koreans will become other to themselves.

Koreans had hoped that they might use Western commerce and technology without being deeply affected by it. Their adaptations would be only superficial. The message of the recent economic crisis is that this hope will not be realized. Most Koreans know by now that it will not, but they cannot yet bear that knowledge, which is why Koreans are paralyzed. The ties that bind the chaebŏl to the bureaucracy are not just the ties that weave the web that keeps foreign economic interests at bay. They are the ties that keep Korea Korean. Or so many Koreans believe.

Consider what the West is asking: not just that Korea open its economy to the West but that its economy become like that of the West, market-driven and impersonal. To us it sounds efficient. To Koreans it sounds as if they are being asked to become other to themselves. As one informant said, "If we let the West tell us how to reform our economy, it won't be a Korean economy anymore. It will just be an economy." He sighed.

This informant is not just speaking nationalism, or if he is, then it is the nationalism that uses the same word for the Korean nation and the Korean people (hanminjok): that is, belonging with others, what it means not to be the other. For many Koreans, to be part of a strictly instrumental transaction is to be the other, a means to someone else's end.

"But you benefit too," I said to a Korean merchant who put it this way to me.

"Yes, but if the money we exchange is not part of a relationship, then how am I any different from this dirty thing," he replied, holding up a 10,000 won note.

The merchant is not worried about violating the Kantian categorical imperative, treating someone else as a means to an end. He is worried about becoming an object to himself by engaging in objectifying relationships. Here Korean individualism and collectivism merge in a brilliant synthesis. Better than we, Koreans understand the costs of treating others as objects—to do so is to become an object to oneself. This eventuality still terrifies Koreans. It should.

In the West, we make a distinction between the realms of market and family. One is objective, the other subjective, a haven in a heartless world. Hating dualism in all things, Korea is still fighting this division of the world: the parceling out of the soul, as Weber put it. To many Koreans, this fragmentation is at least as threatening as the recent economic crisis.

In response to the economic crisis, Koreans have embarked on various frugality campaigns, many of which have a nationalistic tone, such as not buying Western products (Korean Air stopped serving Western meals on its flights, but only for a little while). But nationalism is not an explanation; it is a phenomenon in need of an explanation. For many Koreans, sacrifice and frugality are a five-thousand-year-old tradition, a familiar strategy in unfamiliar times. Sacrifice and frugality represent the continued presence of the old Korea in the new. Said one informant, "Koreans have been too proud and avaricious. Ironically, I think, only suffering makes humans more humane." Success divides Koreans; suffering may connect them again.

Sacrifice and frugality have a quality of nostalgia; they represent a welcome and familiar routine, the media through which Koreans have known the world, and each other, for five thousand years. Mixed with nationalism, frugality and sacrifice are what it means to be Korean. They may work in the short run, but not in the long. Smart enough to know that the old approach won't shield them for long, Koreans are not yet able to come up with a better approach. They would have to surrender too much of value.

"Koreans still regard the West with a mixture of awe and disgust," said one Korean. "We go back and forth, because we don't know where to put you." He said this as we ate lunch at a National Grains restaurant, devoted to using only domestically grown grains in its meals. Huge portraits of Cardinal Kim and various television stars, all praising the virtues of domestic grains, covered the walls. Nationalism is one answer, but it is not a very effective one, and Koreans know it. But what will they have to learn, and who will they have to be, in the new world order?

To call Korea the "Hermit Kingdom" is a cliché, but being a cliché does not make it false. "A self-contained, autonomous Korea not besmirched by things foreign remains an ideal for many Koreans," says Cumings (1997, 137). The *chuch'e* ideology of North Korea, until it just fell apart, is about precisely that: autarky in all things. Cumings calls it "the opaque core of North Korean national solipsism" (1997, 404), and he is among the most sympathetic of observers, recognizing the continuity between North and South in this regard. As open as South Korea has become to the world's economy, many Koreans believed until recently that they could fake it, preserving the untouchable core of the old Korea in the new. I think they still can, but not by pretending.

Managed Globalization

Koreans still have a choice as to how to modernize: what aspects of old Korea to keep, what aspects to abandon. Not all the choice in the world, but they have a choice nonetheless. In less than a generation, they will have almost no choice at all. Presidential speeches are probably not the best place to look for this type of choice making, not even when they are titled "Outlining the Blueprint for Globalization" and collected in a book called *Korea's Quest for Reform and Globalization*. But still this source may tell us something.

> Globalization must be underpinned by Koreanization. We cannot be global citizens without a good understanding of our own culture and tradition. Globalization in the proper sense of the word means that we should march out into the world on the strength of our unique culture and traditional values. Only when we maintain our national identity and uphold our intrinsic

national spirit will we be able to successfully globalize. (Kim Young Sam 1995b, 273)

When people talk like this, it is apparent they have not a clue. The former president talks as if choices do not have to be made, as if all of every good thing is possible, as if Korea can have all the old it needs, with all the new it wants.

Managed globalization sounds like the opposite, like it is about making choices. It's not. According to one influential Korean scholar,

> Managed globalization takes place along three dimensions. First is the reconstruction of individuals. Inward-looking and xenophobic individuals cannot cope with the challenges of spontaneous globalization. They need to be re-formed into open-minded, encompassing, and flexible individuals through systematic educational efforts. . . . Secondly, managed globalization also aims at restructuring society and state. . . . There must be radical departure from the past practices by restructuring social norms, ideas, and institutions. In this context, rationalization, liberalization, and deregulation constitute the core of societal restructuring for coping with spontaneous globalization. (Moon 1995, 66)

No wonder Koreans are frightened! Will anything remain the same after globalization is through with Korea? Will Koreans remain? No wonder Koreans sometimes pretend that globalization changes nothing. They fear it changes everything.

Managed globalization requires that Koreans embrace what they most fear, a rational society. " 'Affects,' considered by Weber as typical of irrationality, are precisely the things that render life worth living for Koreans, since they are concrete expressions of interpersonal commitment" (Hahm 1986, 96–97). Globalization threatens to result in a society without affection, something that Koreans not only dislike but dread, for it is affection that binds humans together in society. It is affection that makes society worthwhile. By affection, I mean chǒng.

Think, for a moment, about globalization quite literally—too literally, but fantasy has its place. Korea is spread out to cover the globe, attenuated almost to infinity. Conversely, the rest of the globe intrudes into the landmass that is Korea. Korea becomes a dark star, containing everything alien and different the world over. Koreans will not disappear, but they will become aliens in their own country, and aliens abroad. At home they will be overcome with foreignness, and abroad they will be overcome with isolation. Koreans will be alone in a world of otherness as a world of otherness intrudes on them. It is what Koreans most fear, becoming alien to themselves, living in a world of pure otherness.

Globalization will not happen in this way, of course. The literal scenario is a fantasy, but it is the fantasy that makes it so difficult for Koreans to talk about globalization. They do talk about it, of course, but not about its meaning. Instead, they talk about strategies, managing globalization, becoming globalization in order to defeat it. Occasionally the fantasy slips through, as when an informant said, "Globalization means that the government is preparing us to live with an invasion of foreigners."

Amor fati, said Nietzsche. Love your fate, embrace it, wish that it was never otherwise. "Ignominious adaptation" to one's prison, replies Theodor Adorno (1974, 97–98), and he is just right. Reality must be accepted, but it need not be loved. When Koreans talk about managed globalization, their talk often sounds like Nietzsche-cum-Adorno, Koreans being asked to love their new prison, Weber's iron cage of rationalization. In response, Koreans pretend, embracing globalization with a vengeance, but in the secret hope that they can outglobalize the globalizers. The illusion is one of control, not because aspects of globalization cannot be managed but because so far the "management" aims only to anticipate the inevitable and do it first.

Becoming globalization in order to defeat it and stubborn, recalcitrant, nationalistic resistance to the economic demands of the IMF and the West are two different strategies, but they do not represent two different ways of thinking. They are one, two sides of the same coin, defenses against the dread of invasion, transparency, and loss of self—loss of what it means to be Korean. The complementary strategies are, in other words, defenses against the evil that cannot be spoken. Not planning but rather understanding is the first step. It need not be a Western understanding of evil. That would not help. A Korean understanding is required. In the absence of understanding, every plan will have an "as if" quality.

The Japanese had a plan. The Iwakura mission, as it was called, visited Europe and the United States during 1871 to 1873, primarily to seek out appropriate models for Japan's modernization. (The Japanese were remarkably thoughtful about modernization during the entire Meiji era; it did not just happen, probably accounting for the cultural coherence with which Japan meets the modern world even today.)

The report of the mission was written by Kume Kunitake, a Confucian scholar and samurai. It seemed to the participants that the underlying difference between East and West was the restless, Faustian spirit of Western peoples and their intensely acquisitive attitude. "Our Eastern notions," wrote Kume, "are ultimately derived from virtue and morality, while theirs are based on the need to protect property." Marius Jansen concludes that this distinction "stemmed from the Western conviction of human nature as evil, with the consequent need to regulate competition, and from the Eastern conviction of human nature as fundamentally good" (Jansen 1980, 59–60).

The samurai scholar sounds a little too much like the Korean dictators quoted in Chapter 5, who praised Eastern ideals of harmony, staking out a dichotomy between East and West that the ideal of nondualism seems to deny. A plan predicated on fundamental distinctions between East and West is perhaps better than no plan at all, but it can hardly be the whole story, particularly today. A more subtle reading is necessary. In Korea, particularly, this reading requires an overdue accounting with history.

After years of debate, Koreans recently tore down the building from which the hated Japanese colonial administrators ruled Korea. Built in 1926 in Seoul, it was deliberately designed and placed to block the view of Kyŏngbokkung Palace from Kwanghwamun, the Gate of Radiant Transformation. Bisecting the line of power that flowed from the throne room of the palace through Kwanghwamun gate to a street lined with government ministries, many Koreans think it was designed to destroy the geomancy (*p'ungsu*) of downtown Seoul. Most believe that the building was designed by its German architect to resemble the first character of Nippon when seen from above (Cumings 1997, 213).

Now the colonial administration building is gone, and Koreans say they can see the mountains in the background. They had not noticed them before. They can also see the palace, which they now point to proudly. But what palace? It is a palace built during the Chosŏn dynasty, the most rigidly Confucian era. Feudalism, cultural sterility, the reign of bureaucrats, the suppression of women, and military weakness are some of the practices associated with that time. Is it to this palace that they point with pride?

The great advantage of being conquered is that one does not have to be responsible for one's own history. In almost every case in Korea the reigning tradition was overthrown by outside forces. Chinese Confucianism overthrew Buddhism, and Japanese colonialism overthrew Confucianism. Koreans were not forced to come to terms with their own traditions, not required to sort out their good and bad aspects. The greatest danger Korea now faces is that Koreans will treat globalization as one more conquering power, to be fought with its own weapons. It is a signal danger, because Korea has a good chance of winning this battle, its recent economic setbacks notwithstanding, and so losing the war to know its own history. Korea risks becoming globalization in order to defeat it.

Not that "successful" globalization would look the same in Korea as in the West in any case. In Korea globalization is more likely to foster the refeudalization of social relationships that Max Weber wrote about, rationalization sponsoring the rise of a new political and business elite with even more resources at its disposal to reduce the population to civic serfdom, using the pressure of international competition as the justification. It is a risk not necessarily more severe in East than West, but it is different.

In the West the population is more atomized, each man and woman thinking the same thoughts at a vast distance, as Tocqueville put it. The risk is mass democracy—that is, no real democracy at all. In the East the population is more prone to new forms of patriarchy. In Korea the risk is that the population will move from serf to consumer and producer, having only briefly passed through the realm of citizen. Globalization could accentuate this process. The term "global citizen" is not hyperbole; it is an oxymoron. Citizens of the world are citizens of nowhere. Hannah Arendt made this point a long time ago in *The Human Condition*, and it still stands.

Let's speculate for a moment. What might have happened had Korea become democratic twenty-five years earlier? It could have, as Cumings argues in *Korea's Place in the Sun: A Modern History* (1997). Had the United States acted differently in the years immediately following World War II (by intervening more, not less), Korea might have been spared its dictators. Many argue that Korea was not ready for democracy, that the years of the dictators, above all Park Chung Hee, created the economic precondition for democracy, a stable middle class. Others point out how remarkably unstable Korea was during this era, marked by assassinations, coups, and insurrections. Kim Dae Jung, the new president, stated recently that "if we had true democracy in Korea, then the collusive intimacy between business and government and corruption would not have been as great here." He went on to argue that more democracy sooner might have actually enabled Korea to avoid the economic collapse (Kagan 1998, 39).

Would an earlier and more thoroughgoing democracy also have allowed Koreans to debate the choice of globalization more fully? One wants to say yes, but the answer is far from certain. For many Koreans, globalization was never a choice. Or rather, the choice was between globalization and economic marginalization, winning or losing, all or nothing. As one informant put it, "We are on the information and globalization train. There is no choice except to be marginalized economically and politically." True enough, but there are different tracks to follow, and every stop is not necessarily on the margin. There were choices that were never discussed.

One would like to say that democracy would have helped, but how well have comparable issues been debated in the Western democracies? The bigger the issue, the more difficult it is to bring it under traditional politics. Chapter 7 concerns some less traditional ways of thinking about politics, experiments in living and being they might be called. If politics is ever to meet enlightenment, it is here, at the margins of society.

What If the Chairs Were Not Connected?

Hankuk University of Foreign Studies is the Korean university most committed to globalization, at least in theory.[6] A professor who teaches there pointed out a notice in the faculty lounge, written in Korean of course:

FACULTY MEETING TO DISCUSS IMPLICATIONS OF GOVERN-
MENT'S GLOBALIZATION POLICY FOR KOREAN UNIVERSI-
TIES. Korean faculty only.

The last three words were written in smaller letters, as though the Korean faculty was embarrassed. Like the editor of *Korean Literature Today* (1996, 5), who equates globalization with translating Korean literature into English, the faculty wants to do globalization at a distance, without the bother of dealing with foreigners.

I spoke with 150 students at Hankuk, mostly in small groups. Sookhee told the following story.

"When I went to London I saw the benches in the subways. They were still benches, not chairs, but the benches had dividers, so that each person had his own place to sit, so that you couldn't crowd too many people on a bench."

"I like sitting all together sometimes," said another.

"So do I," replied Sookhee. "See that's my point. I don't want to become English; I just want to know me and Korea better. How could I know that we sit close together if I didn't see a country with its benches made so people can't?"

Sookhee is talking about enlightenment, the only enlightenment there is, seeing one's own in the mirror of another. To learn about different ways of thinking about the relationship between individual and group is not just information, but the creation of new possibilities for what it is to be human, a self in the world, not because one way of arranging interpersonal distance is better than another, but because it is different. If we do not know that there are alternatives, we will not have the possibility of either rearranging, or perhaps just rethinking, the relationships. We will not have any choices in who we are. Above all, we will not know what we are doing.

Peter Winch (1964, 322) calls the knowledge of alternatives wisdom, and he is not far wrong.

> The concept of learning from . . . other cultures is closely linked with the concept of wisdom. We are confronted not just with different techniques, but with new possibilities of good and evil in relation to which men may come to terms with life.

To see a new possibility for good—that is, a richer life—means seeing new possibilities for evil: what the destruction of the meaning of one's life would look like. They go together, and globalization is the icon of their union, the yin and yang of all possibilities. Knowledge of evil, the worst thing in the world, can lead to enlightenment. Perhaps it is the only path to enlightenment—which only makes reality all the more poignant.

The history that makes globalization as enlightenment possible at the same time renders it unattainable. Does this paradox render history as tragedy? No. To see this as tragedy would ignore the spaces in society that are created by individuals, spaces in which diverse histories may emerge. To be able to see those spaces is the best reason of all to get the distance right, so that we do not weave the web of history so tight that individuals disappear, and with them the possibility of enlightenment.

If this diverse history is not tragic, it is nonetheless ironic. Consider that whereas the Seoul subways do not have benches like those in London (for the most part they do not have benches, period), many underground arcades, and some bus stops, have plastic chairs attached to long steel beams, each beam supporting perhaps a dozen chairs. Lacking its own legs, each chair is nonetheless a separate seating place, dividing each sitter from the others even more completely than the subway benches in London. Separate seats but common legs, as good a metaphor for the social self as any. But which self, individual or group? Or is it perhaps the conflict between the two that is best represented by this seating arrangement?

Sookhee could not see the complexity of her culture, including its complex, conflicted selves, until she saw her culture, and herself, mirrored in another—not because Sookhee could only find what she was looking for elsewhere. It was already in her own culture, but she couldn't see it. Sookhee could not see it because it was too close, too familiar.

What would happen if someone took the beam away, the beam that connects all the seats, granting them common ground? Is it possible that Sookhee could not see the connected chairs because to see them as a cultural symbol is already to have begun the separation? She has, of course. Now she has to bring it home. This statement presumes that she has a coherent home, a coherent Korea, to bring it home to.

"We are the *sin sedae* generation," said Kyungsook. "It means the in-between generation, what you call generation-X. Our generation has a big problem: how to tell 'I' from 'we.' "

"Yes," responds another, "especially when everyone says 'we' but does 'I.' " We have met this theme before.

"Exactly," continued Kyungsook. "But we have an opportunity our parents didn't. We can look outside. Globalization means that we can see Korea from the perspective of the world. I can find myself in people with red skin and blond hair."

Like Sookhee, Kyungsook can see herself at a distance. She just needs to bring the mirror closer.

Transparency Is Hell

"When Korea becomes more globalized it will open up more. And when it opens up it will become more organized." A student, Jisu, wrote this in her essay. I supposed she was echoing former president Kim Young Sam (1995a, 126–134), who used terms like "organized" and "rationalized" as synonyms for overcoming corruption and bureaucratic inertia. Only when I talked with her did I understand that she was really talking about interpersonal boundaries.

Koreans, Jisu elaborated, have trouble with I/we boundaries. "Private and public, no one knows the difference, no one respects it." Private and public are not identical with "I" and "we," of course. Much that is private in Korean life is actually the "we" of family. But there remains a question of interpersonal boundaries, about what activities properly belong to what spheres. "Public" actually redefines both "I" and "we," loosening the "we" while including the "I." A traditional society is no more capable of supporting a public realm than is one of strictly autonomous individuals. A public sphere, and hence genuine democracy, not just plebiscitary rule, depends on a delicate balance between tradition and modernity.

Referring to a legislator implicated in the Hambo Steel affair, one of an endless series of money-for-political-favors scandals, Jisu comments, "He says he took the money because he couldn't sell his house because his son committed suicide there. So he takes the money as a private person, votes in favor of Hambo, and acts like it's two different people. And you know the worst part: the public buys it. They were very sympathetic to his plight."

Koreans have an expression: "It's talk only between us." This saying reflects a fantasy that for some purposes only we two exist. This is the fantasy behind chŏng. Or as Choi and Choi (1994, 80) put it in the language of social psychology, "the expression functions to draw the interactants to a contextually constructed intimacy by encapsulating their interaction from others." The saying expresses a romantic ideal absent the sexuality, the warmth of chŏng creating an intimate universe in which a third can only intrude—or rather, in which a third hardly exists at all.

One imagines that the power and attractiveness of the idea of "only between us" stems from the intimacy of mother and baby in Korea, and the deep satisfaction found there, but that must remain speculation. In any case, it is not just Sookhee who found in a society's benches its social ideal. That terrible romantic Herbert Marcuse admired the parks of Hanoi, because even in such a public place the benches were big enough for only two.

At first Jisu sounds naive: when Korea becomes more globalized, Koreans will become more organized about their boundaries, and there will not be so many scandals. Yet perhaps she has a point. The failure to distinguish a public realm means that, in effect, everything is private, albeit the extended private, ruled by the principles of traditional obligation and *pok* (blessings), the great chain of giving and receiving, be it blessings or money.

In one sense Crane is mistaken when he writes in *Korean Patterns* that "where clear-cut responsibility and personal relationships are not delineated, then there is little sense of responsibility. There is little feeling for looking after a public place or community" (1978, 77). Crane is mistaken because the concept of a public does not exist in Korea. There is only the extended private. In another sense Crane is correct. When experiences fall outside of tradition, but not under law, they are nobody's responsibility because nobody recognizes him- or herself as a responsible actor in the situation—that is, as being responsible to others. The public is a nowhere land, an anomic wilderness.

In a world in which one is responsible to so many for so much, many Koreans experience anomie as liberating. Between the "we" of family, school, and regional ties and the "we" of "we Koreans" lies an enormous gulf. In this gulf Koreans often find freedom in behaving irresponsibly, as long as they do not have to account for their actions later. The culture only encourages this irresponsibility, allowing individuals to act as though the self who takes a bribe is not the same as the one who acts in a public capacity.

The culture encourages this split by creating a gulf in which no responsibility exists. Chŏng is not just a connection. It is a separation, a redrawing of boundaries to create a space in which the collective world disappears. That separation is not always good. It depends on whether the partners are exchanging love or money. For many Koreans, it is evidently hard to tell the difference.

Globalization will likely go some way to lessening the type of bribery associated with the Hambo scandal: the distribution of money from private entrepreneurs to private politicians, an oxymoron possible only in a society on the cusp between traditional and modern. Globalization will redefine traditional relationships, making it less defensible for individuals to take money for their vote, while pretending (including to themselves) that the money represents not an instrumental relationship but chŏng.

In this sense, globalization will likely bring a new order to Korea. Unfortunately, the new order is likely to bring with it a more modern, rationalized form of bribery, in which not individuals but parties and other organizations are the beneficiaries of corporate, not individual, largess. In this Korea has yet to catch up with the West. When it does, Koreans will not be mistaken in thinking they have lost something of value.

"Fish thrive best under conditions of moderate eutrophication," said one Korean. Eutrophication is nourishing rot, the algae that darken the water and feed the fish. "Transparency is hell," he continued. "It's the last thing I want. How could I be free?" Many Koreans say the same thing, though they don't always say it in public. Transparency is the vehicle of globalization. Calls for transparency are everywhere. Koreans use the English term, even if no one seems quite sure what it means. One of its aspects is financial statements that tell a more complete story; not taking bribes is another. Although the term is everywhere, no one seems very keen on it, even if few are eager to equate obscurity and darkness with freedom.

The most transparent regime of all is Jeremy Bentham's Pantopticon about which Foucault writes (1980, 146–165), a prison in which everything is open to scrutiny. The transparent society is the disciplined society, everyone accountable to no one for everything. But if Koreans have good intuitions about transparency, they have not yet sorted out its elements.

Koreans value darkness, I believe, because it fosters freedom of feeling—freedom to rely on one's feelings rather than the rules, freedom to be guided by one's feelings. Nunch'i (acute sensitivity to others) is freedom. "Why do you drive through red lights?" I asked one taxi driver. "I feel if they are really red," he replied. He meant, I believe, that some lights were not really red because they were "red" in the middle of the night, or when no one was trying to cross the street, or when no other cars were around. His freedom in a world of boundless constraint was the freedom to use his feeling in this matter. A Westerner might refer to this as the freedom to "exercise one's judgment." A Korean would understand, but would still call it feeling.

Freedom from transparency is the freedom to feel that a gift of 200,000 won is okay, but 500,000 is too much. The trouble is, though, that it is not really freedom when the transaction, the bribery, is driven by anxiety, as it so frequently is—anxiety that traditional relationships cannot be counted on, and that transparent, rational ones cannot be counted on either. It is one thing to ask your cousin to intervene on your behalf with the doctor with whom your cousin went to school. It is another thing to ask your cousin to bribe the doctor because you can no longer count on the traditional relationship but cannot give it up either. Bribery is the commercialization of traditional relationships, the cash nexus in place of the human one. Bribery corrupts traditional relationships by purposefully confusing them with instrumental ones—purposefully because in a changing society no one can tell the difference, and no one dares try.

Lacking in the preceding accounts are fruitful venues for the experimentation that leads to wisdom. The practice of widespread bribery retains a link to traditional relationships while undermining them. The regime of chŏng is too tight, too asocial. The anomic wilderness created by the increasingly wide gap between tradition and law is too alienated and disconnected, not just from others but from culture. Behavior that falls into this gap is likely to be merely irresponsible rather than creatively irresponsible—that is, responsible to unconventional ideas, ideals, and persons.

There is a place for the Foucauldian aesthete in Korea, but he or she is not likely to be found in the gap between tradition and law. There one finds not aesthetic self-assertion but the imitation of the most self-aggrandizing aspects of Western individualism. Koreans are not, I have argued, lacking in individualism. Into the gap between tradition and law rushes the worst aspects of individualism, egoism freed from the bonds of human relationships. (Here is why many Koreans quietly welcome the economic crisis. "Koreans would rather suffer than rationalize," said one informant, "as long as we suffer together.") One must look elsewhere for the experimentation that leads to wisdom, not at the gap between tradition and law but at the margins of tradition, and the sutures that join and separate old and new. Chapter 7 provides some examples.

CHAPTER SEVEN

Globalization as Enlightenment?

This chapter reviews several successful experiments in enlightenment, stories of Koreans who seem to have successfully borrowed from Western culture in order to expand the horizons of their own. Whether my stories are convincing depends not just on what Koreans are doing but on how one understands enlightenment.

I have suggested that enlightenment involves encountering otherness, an encounter that may be experienced as evil. If this experience is not too overwhelming, wisdom may result, the wisdom that stems from seeing one's own in the mirror of another, as well as the wisdom that stems from borrowing from others. In *Beyond Orientalism*, Fred Dallmayr (1996, 62) approvingly quotes Nirmal Verma, who suggests that through the experience of other cultures we seek, and sometimes find, completion.

Two traditions, Indian and European, are seeking a sort of completion in one-another . . . by creating a "common space" within which the voice of the one evokes a responsive echo in the other, feeling the deprivations of one's own through the longings of the other.

With this lovely sentiment I must disagree. I think we should use each other ruthlessly. Not abuse, but use, taking from another whatever we can use, and however we can use it, acknowledging it if we can, denying it if we must. We should take and use any and everything that we can, in any way we can use it. I am talking about nonmaterial things of course, and above all, ideas. When you take my idea, you do not make me poorer; you may even make me richer by giving me another person who understands to talk with.

The image of enlightenment as light is misleading, as though we were enlightened only when we illuminated the furthest dark corners of the world. The better image is Kant's own, enlightenment as speech, or rather, conversation, our thoughts unformed and useless unless they are shared with others. Although we can see alone, we think best "in community with others," as Kant puts it (Schmidt 1996, 29–30). But although enlightenment requires community and culture, it remains an attribute of individuals who live in communities and cultures. It is not the province of ages, civilizations, societies, or cultures. As in the economic realm, globalization is likely to divide the world into winners and losers, in this case between those who are able to use the collision and confusion of cultures to foster enlightenment, and those who become merely confused.

The relationship between globalization and enlightenment is evidently complex. It will be worthwhile to pursue this complexity further before turning to the experiments in enlightenment. In some ways what follows is a philosophical diversion. In other respects it is central. There is no point in talking about globalization as enlightenment if enlightenment is just a code word for all good things, some of which turn out to be incompatible.

Minerva's Owl

Minerva's owl flies at dusk. What reason is there to assume that enlightenment leads to freedom, or even autonomy? "As if truth were proven by the continued existence of man," said Nietzsche (Habermas 1973, 257, my trans.). "As if enlightenment had anything to do with human freedom" is my emendation. Only when we take this possibility seriously will we be prepared to create what freedom there is in the nooks and crannies created by globalization, what I earlier called ruins. *Pathei mathos* the ancient

Greeks called it—the wisdom that comes through suffering, almost always too late to prevent more suffering, but not too late to make us wise.

The view that enlightenment must mean more freedom and autonomy is not so much a Western conceit as a modern one—but not just modern. In spite of all their differences, on this point Kant and Foucault are united. For Kant, enlightenment is reflection on limits, above all, the limits of knowledge. For Foucault, enlightenment is the experience of transgression: not of the formal limits of knowledge but of the limits of being. We know these limits only by attempting to breach them.

> Criticism indeed consists of analyzing and reflecting upon limits. But if the Kantian question was that of knowing what limits knowledge has to renounce transgressing, it seems to me that the critical question today . . . is to transform the critique conducted in the form of necessary limitation into a practical critique that takes the form of a possible transgression. (Foucault 1984, 45)

Kant's study of the limits of knowledge is formal and universal. Foucault's is practical and political. Each, however, assumes that enlightenment is about the expansion of human freedom by confronting its limits. You shall know the truth, and the truth shall make you free. But why? Why could not enlightenment consist of an increasing recognition of the limits of human freedom: that we shall know more than we will ever be able to do, and that the very conditions that enable this knowledge prevent its realization, at least for more than a few. Globalization is, I suggest, one of these conditions, allowing us to know the value of what we are not able to do, at least not on a large scale: combine tradition and modernity in a million creative ways, in order to have the best of both.

For Foucault, transgression is not so much the organon of enlightenment as it is enlightenment itself, not because every transgression succeeds in freedom but because humans realize themselves most fully in the act of transgression, refusing the limits that nature and society (or rather, nature as mediated by society) give to us.

> This critique will be genealogical in the sense that it will not deduce from the form of what we are what is impossible for us to do and to know; but it will separate out, from the contingency that has made us what we are, the

possibility of no longer being, doing, or thinking what we are, do, or think. . . . It is seeking to give new impetus, as far and wide as possible, to the undefined work of freedom. (Foucault 1984, 46)

Today we live in enlightened terror that we will accept limits that are not. There is perhaps an element of metaphysical narcissism at work, a fancy way of saying wounded human pride. If reason can no longer convincingly escape the constraints of human particularity in order to know universals, then at least we have the comfort of knowing that every universal is really particular, a matter of subjective cultural interpretation. If the world is but a text, then we can read it any way we want, including backward. In *Nineteen Eighty-Four*, George Orwell called it "collective solipsism," a lovely oxymoron. If I think I am floating a few inches off the floor, and you think I am floating, then I'm floating. There is no difference because history no longer exists, only ideology, what Foucault calls power/knowledge, a term Orwell would have understood.

The trouble is that this type of knowledge (for collective solipsism is not what Plato calls ignorance, knowledge of nothing; it says something true) may make other types of knowledge, including enlightenment, impossible. Collective solipsism may do so in much the same way that grand theories of globalization make us ignorant: by ignoring the details of real lives that manage to find a moment of freedom amid the terrible unfreedom of the world. Knowing the details means knowing these lives to be real and concrete, and the real and concrete is always situated and hence unfree. In a word, the intentional ignorance of details is but one more strategy in the refusal to be pinned down by reality.

Although I have suggested that enlightenment properly has the quality of Greek tragedy, it is the tragedy of pathei mathos, not the grand tragedy of Hegel. Michael Valdez Moses argues that globalization is the "prototypical and recurrent tragedy of Hegel: the conflict between traditional ways of life that have become ingrained and the modes and orders that try to displace and supersede them" (1995, 11). It is hard to imagine a worse perspective on globalization than Hegel's reading of Greek tragedy. No one has missed more of the life of *Antigone*, the play on which he bases his reading, than Hegel, transforming a complex and human conflict between Antigone and her uncle Creon into a battle of Big Ideas.[1]

What if we define enlightenment as regret for what might have been but never will be? History opens up new possibilities for a moment and then closes them forever. Not Hegel but Moses comes closer to the mark, the one who could see the promised land but was not permitted to enter. There are moments in the lives of societies, and perhaps entire civilizations, in which we can see what we cannot have. We become sadder but wiser, as the cliché has it, as good a definition of enlightenment as any, what the Greeks meant by pathei mathos.

What if Wallerstein (1990b) and Boyne (1990) are both correct? The cultural efflorescence and carnage that is globalization lives a life of its own insofar as it creates possibilities for freedom that globalization as economic system will flatten under the steamroller of Weberian rationalization and the weight of markets. This experience too may be enlightenment, one filled with regret that the vehicle spoils the destination.

Enlightenment is not necessarily knowledge we can use, even to make us free. That would be instrumental reason. Enlightenment may have more to do with asking an important question and waiting for the world to answer. The world has not yet answered as far as globalization is concerned, but it looks like the answer will have more to do with Moses than Hegel, suggesting new and richer possibilities for living and being that cannot be grasped because the phenomenon that brings East and West, North and South, the modern and the traditional world, into fruitful contact is the same phenomenon that will level both. Globalization is not, after all, Western culture. Globalization is only the vehicle of its transmission, a vehicle so driven by economic rationality (or perhaps economic rationality is globalization) that it must soon homogenize what it for a moment brings together in eclectic plentitude and wonder.

I do not know that this is true. More important, I do not know how true it is, or in what way it is true. If enlightenment is about asking a question and waiting for the world to answer, it is also about doing something while one is waiting, something that might affect the outcome, at least at the margins. The margins are where the action is as far as enlightenment is concerned. Enlightenment is marginal wisdom: a wisdom of what is possible at the margins of the constraints within which humans live.

My account of enlightenment is not as bold as Foucault's ideal of transgression. Mine is marked not so much by modesty as regret—that what might have been never will be. The very forces that allow us to wonder at the possibilities make their realization impossible. One might call it the irony of globalization, but that would come too close to the stance of ironic detachment that characterizes so much postmodern life. One should rather just call it the way of the world. Only when we mourn its loss will we be in a position to know how much freedom we really have in the small spaces that remain, the freedom to combine old and new to make something better than either.

Enlightenment, says Kant (1949), is the emergence from immaturity, defined as the ability to judge for oneself without relying on others. Enlightenment is, in other words, about being as well as doing, not so much about knowledge as how to live with knowledge. To the knowledge we must live with I would add regret. To be *muendig* (mature) is to be in possession of a richer sense of regrets.

To some the preceding will seem obvious. To others it will seem a great letdown; enlightenment is nothing if it is not the march of human knowledge and freedom. In this, many moderns and postmoderns are united, that transgression is merely the latest version of the truth that will make us free. Against this view I recommend the sober possibility that enlightenment may have nothing to do with human freedom. Only if we know this possibility will we take little experiments seriously, not glossing them over for grand theories of freedom or treating globalization as though it were more than it is—or less.

In what follows I tell several stories about enlightenment, experiments in living that press at the margins of the culture in order to create more room to be. The experiments are real. So too are the constraints under which they operate. They are the constraints of globalization as enlightenment, constraints as empirical and historical as they are epistemological and theoretical. If we have learned anything in the period from Kant to Foucault, it is that we fool ourselves when we treat enlightenment as an abstract, formal quality of thought. Enlightenment is practical and historical. More than ever before, to be enlightened means to know more than we can do. The real sin against knowledge would be to know less in order to do more.

Experiments in Enlightenment

The doctor received his Ph.D. in classical Chinese philosophy from a prestigious American university. Appointed professor at an equally prestigious Korean university, he became legendary for his brilliance. Soon tiring of the restrictions of his field, and wanting to make a gesture of political defiance during the dictatorship, he resigned to pursue a career as a doctor of Oriental medicine.

The doctor's clinic looks like a ballet studio, a large sunny room with polished wood floors, mirrors covering one wall, what looks like an oversized card catalog on another. It contains his herbs and medicines. The other two walls are covered with Chinese calligraphy, his own. It is the most open room outside of a temple that I have seen in Korea, perhaps fifty feet square, filled with light. Mounted on what looks like a small stage is his workbench and examining table. It is also, apparently, a podium. Here he gives intersession classes in Oriental philosophy for college students, taught in the traditional Confucian way. He also teaches Hegel. In one corner is an autoclave, used to sterilize his acupuncture needles.

The doctor, his head closely shaved, is dressed in a long black robe. He looks like Michel Foucault. He must be about fifty. He has a reputation as a wild man, arrogant, rude, a real fauve. With me he is polite, but preoccupied, busy with the mysteries of the universe, how to reconcile Eastern and Western philosophy on the basis of Oriental medicine. He is crazy enough to think he can do it, not so crazy as to think he has. Once or twice he loses the thread of the conversation, but I do not have the sense that he wants me to leave. He wants me to stay so that he can listen to himself think. He might find a clue.

He is trying to prove the power of Oriental medicine in Western terms. His current project is healing certain wasting neurological disorders against which Western medicine is ineffective. "Most of the doctors of Oriental medicine, they have the right idea, but they have no discipline, no standards. The question isn't whether it is Eastern or Western but whether it is true. About that the West is more demanding."

How does "hand acupuncture" work, I ask? (I had been troubled by headaches, and a Korean nurse taught me to apply pressure at the first joint of my index finger, which represents the head. It seemed to work.) The hand represents the human body in miniature, he replied, just like the ear does. See, it looks like a fetus. But "represents" is a misleading term, he continued. The whole is contained in the part, like a hologram. "Every hair has a brain." The human body is a universe, a cosmos. We can't see the universe with the naked eye. Similarly, we can only see a part of the body with the eye. "We see the blood that escapes when we cut our hand, but not the *chi*, or spirit of energy. Who would say that what we see of the universe is all there is? Well, the anatomists commit the same error with the body. Reality is more than it appears."

The doctor says he practices "a Confucianism of the body." He recognizes that about some things Western medicine is more efficient. "If I had a broken arm, I'd go to a Western doctor to fix it." He pauses for effect. "Then I'd come home to my own medicines and heal it." What he refuses to recognize is that Western medicine might reflect a basic split in the universe, between philosophy and science. To his mind, he is still doing classical Chinese philosophy.

For a short while among a small group of Western intellectuals, many associated with the Frankfurt School of Critical Theory, there existed a similar ideal: a new science of a new nature. If approached in a new, more receptive way, nature might finally reveal her human side. Herbert Marcuse is perhaps the best known of this group. Not Francis Bacon, who wanted to hound, torture, and vex nature for her secrets, but Saint Francis would be the model. No longer is such a view compelling, and postmodernism only contributes to its demise, being generally quite uninterested in nontexts.

Today the view of Juergen Habermas prevails. Science and technology operate under different principles (what he once called "cognitive interests") than the lifeworld. If they ever are united, it will be at the expense of the lifeworld, which will be rationalized beyond recognition. The task is to keep science and technology in their place, preventing the colonization of the lifeworld by the instrumental values of science and technology.

Habermas recently spoke in Seoul. Upon finishing his lecture, Habermas remarked that he was surprised that so many Koreans were turning to him for answers. Koreans would, he said, do better to find the answers in their own traditions. Surely he is correct. The only question is whether Eastern tradition too must recognize a fundamental split in the universe. Or is this just one more Western dualism?

The doctor will not be drawn into a naive critique of Western dualism. "We have to be dualistic thinkers in order to make the distinctions upon which thought depends. The mistake the West makes is transforming dualism into a substance, its objects existing as independent entities."

The question we must ask is whether the Oriental doctor is at risk of making a comparable mistake, believing that only if he can cure some otherwise incurable diseases can he demonstrate that the world is really one, that the East had it right all along. Or rather, only if Eastern thought demonstrates its superiority by Western standards—it can do something with the body that the West cannot—will its truth be recognized.

If anyone can do it, he can, but it seems a misguided, or at least unnecessary, project. There are other, less totalistic ways by which East might learn from West, and vice versa. These ways would respect a fundamental split in the world (between nature and culture is one way to put it), without assimilating this split to the distinction between West and East. That is the real danger.

A depressing postscript: the doctor recently closed his clinic-cum-studio and returned to Harvard. He was, he said, spending all his time managing his relationships. He may have also meant that he spent too much time looking for money. He needed to get away for a while. He has not changed his subject of study, just its locus. In this case, however, location is everything.

The Fortune-Telling Therapist and the Yoga Instructor

The fortune-teller worked out of a downscale suite of offices in Seoul. No magazines, but lots of autographed copies of his book, *Write Me an Amulet*, about his successful predictions of oil spills, bridge collapses, fortunes of the rich and famous, and the like. "Light essays on counseling" is how my assistant put it. The waiting room was occupied by several anxious-looking young people, one twenty-something young man, a young woman, and an older couple, belying the stereotype that only older women visit fortune-tellers. The doctor was running a little late this morning, as we say in the States.

Inside his office, three sisters were consulting him. The door to his office was open, in order to let some of the heat from a small gas heater within filter out to the waiting room. The therapist appeared to be about thirty, wearing a dirty blue robe, like a monk's habit, over a sweater. He is scruffy and unkempt, the only young Korean I have seen with a beard. If he were wearing a stethoscope around his neck, I would have taken him for an overworked intern, too dedicated to care about his appearance.

"What you inherit from fortune is 60%," says his book. "Your effort counts for 40%." It is irresponsible to merely predict someone's fortune, as most fortune-tellers do, the book continues. You have to counsel the client, so that the client can develop his or her potential and won't give in to a bad fortune. Consider a famous fighter against the Japanese occupation. His fortune predicted that he would become a beggar, so he tried to kill himself. He failed, and later became a great organizer of the resistance, begging money and support from thousands for his patriotic efforts. The fortune-teller believes this is his task: to combine fortune-telling ("the science of divination" is the literal translation) with therapy and counseling. This task takes time, and repeat visits.

The fortune-teller shares his office suite, and a secretary, with a former student radical who teaches yoga to pregnant women to ease their birth pangs. We can hear the peaceful panting in the waiting room. Hers is a famous story, immortalized in a mural on the wall of Hankuk University of Foreign Studies, her alma mater. Like a number of radical students in the 1980s, she traveled to North Korea on a personal mission of peace and reconciliation. Once there she did not make herself welcome. A Catholic, she refused to bow to the Great Leader during a large public ceremony, and she was eventually placed under house arrest. The Catholic church in South Korea sent a priest to fetch her back. As they traveled back over the demilitarized zone, a risky business, they were arrested, and she was jailed for four years by the South. Soon after her release, she married the newspaper man who covered her story. Eventually they had a child. The yoga she learned before giving birth she now teaches to others.

The juxtaposition of these two lives tells us much about contemporary Korea. The options have become smaller, perhaps, but at least as real for the two former student radicals who now share a suite of offices. There are not a lot of alternative career paths in Korea, and they have found two of them. But these are not just alternative careers; they are alternative intellectual strategies, alternative ways of putting the world together, including East and West.

When we finally get to see the therapist fortune-teller, he is charm itself. Three walls of his office are covered with books, mostly on Oriental medicine and the science of divination. But he has a small section of English-language works on popular psychology. No Freud, but some Fromm, and a number of self-help books, including *If You Meet the Buddha on the Road, Kill Him*. An assistant, actually an apprentice, sat in on our session. A few dozen rolls of toilet paper are stacked in the corner. We can still hear the women panting next door.

As most Koreans do, the fortune-teller began by telling his story. His grandfather was a Chinese herbal healer. The fortune-teller had received his university degree in Chinese literature at Korea University, a good school. Active in the student movement, he could not settle down after graduation. Shoe-shine boy, stationery store manager, billiard parlor manager, postal clerk—these were some of the jobs he had held before becoming a scientist of divination. He told me his story, my translator informed me later, to distinguish himself from a *mudang*, one who is possessed by a spirit and has no choice but to become a healer. He had had a choice.

The fortune-teller's parents have practically disowned him for his choice. " 'We sent you to the university for this?' " they cry. But this is the only job that has ever meant anything to him, a job where he can "counsel people and warm their hearts." Evidently he does just that. The three sisters looked relieved on their way out, but the fortune-teller is unhappy that his clients generally ignore him in the street. They are embarrassed.

The fortune-teller does not claim authority on the basis of education, training, inspiration, or having been taught by a great teacher, though he mentions his grandfather frequently. He says he has studied hard, is honest, and really wants to help people. Several months later, a Buddhist asked an American professor at a Buddhist temple to refer her to a shaman. Instead, I referred her to the fortune counselor.

The fortune counselor does not seem very interested in fortune-telling, for all that. It is the counseling he enjoys, but no one will listen until he makes a few predictions. Actually, they are not predictions at all, but retrodictions—insight into his client's life that he would not normally be presumed to have, so demonstrating his magical powers of intuition. Just as the psychiatrist who treats hwabyŏng disease says, Koreans expect the practitioner to know what ails them without asking, or without their telling. They wish not so much to be saved as to be transparent to power and charisma, to be known by others without (it seems) the pain and bother of knowing themselves.

Both Confucius and Buddha doubted words, and in this respect their influence shows. Confucius doubted words because he worried about whether he could live up to them (*Analects*, 4.22, 4.24, 5.10, 14.27). Buddha doubts words because the truth is ineffable. Koreans doubt words for both reasons. Words acknowledge separation, that you have to explain yourself to another. Silence implies, or at least promises the possibility, of being understood without having to say, thus strengthening and preserving the belief in a type of unspoken connection. It is, perhaps, what we most want in all the world, to be known and understood by another without having to know or speak ourselves. Mothers and babies have this for a little while, or so it is said. Koreans want to have it back. Who wouldn't? The trouble is that silence can also be a cover for irresponsibility. Sometimes we do not talk about what we are thinking or doing because we do not want to know.

I ask the fortune-teller, Why do some people have good fortune, and others have bad? Is it bad karma? It's hard to know why, he replies, but it doesn't really matter. The main point is that bad fortune and good fortune are not always so clearly distinguished. It depends on what you make of things, like the "beggar" who fought the Japanese. It is the fortune counselor's task to help people cope with their fates. Mostly this means helping them make the most of what they've got.

At lunch we got to talking about the student movement, the fortune-telling therapist and my assistant having much to reminisce about. It seems to have worn out a generation, as though nothing they do now can be as important as what they did then, bringing down the dictatorship. "There is much less anti-Americanism now than then," said the therapist, smiling.

"Korea has become a capitalist power," I replied.

No, he countered. "It is because there is no longer a historical alternative, Marxism or socialism, to which we can ally ourselves. What else is left?" My assistant looked ill. The fortune-telling therapist returned to his soup, which dribbled down his robe.

Enlightenment in Small Spaces

What is left is small-scale alternatives, creative combinations. It is merely from a world historical perspective that there are no longer any large-scale alternatives. From the perspective of people's lives, there are thousands of new combinations, creative compromises with unfreedom. In creating new experiments in living, these Koreans are creating enlightenment, the only enlightenment there is. This is not the enlightenment sought by the famous Oriental doctor, the unity of science and culture, East and West, but the enlightenment of small spaces. The doctor's is that too, of course: his large studio is but a small space in the scheme of things, which is why I have included his story here.

Distinctive about these small spaces is the way each is framed by history and tradition. Contained within a history and culture, their experiments in small spaces push at the edges of history and culture, as Kim Sakkat, the real-life poet whose life is fictionalized in Yi Mun-yol's *The Poet*, did. Or as did Hwang Chin-i, the sixteenth-century *kisaeng* (the Korean equivalent of a geisha), whose unconventionality is legend.[2] The experimentation most likely to contribute to enlightenment is the experimentation that is deeply embedded in the traditional culture while pointing beyond it.

The experiment cannot point from another culture to one's own. Nor is experimentation fertile when there are only ruins to play with. Or if it is, it cannot be socially fruitful, an inspiration to others. The transgression about which Foucault writes is not destruction. A culture so fragile that it cannot be transgressed without obliteration cannot support enlightenment. An act of transgression that obliterates all boundaries cannot serve enlightenment. Transgression requires something coherent to transgress, lest it become mere play amid the ruins.

Experimentation must take place within the form and frame of culture, even as it draws from without. Experimentation is eclectic, but it is not mere eclecticism. The form and frame of culture and history are necessary lest the experiment become incommunicable. Enlightenment is not really about light, as Kant reminds us (Schmidt 1996, 29–30). It is about conversation. Such a conversation presumes that one's own culture remains reasonably intact, an assumption that in Korea may soon become unrealistic.

Korea is at a place now where it will never be again, where few countries ever are for more than a moment: the old Korea of fortune-telling, Oriental medicine, even of the student revolution, is still alive, even as it is being replaced by the culture of globalization, a combination of Western influence and structural features common to all modern, urban, industrial societies, be they West or East. The convergence thesis it is called.

For a few years, certainly no more than a generation, there are heightened opportunities to mix and match, heightened opportunities for eclecticism, for learning new combinations, such as that represented by the Oriental doctor, the yoga instructor, and the fortune-telling therapist. These are heightened opportunities for wisdom as well. There are also heightened opportunities to understand wisdom. Globalization theory is generally not much help here.

Globalization theory is not much help precisely because it is a theory, meaning that it operates with high-level abstractions, such as East and West, "globality," and fault lines. When globalization is liberating, it results not in the integration of opposites but in the proliferation of alternatives, which some creative individuals are able to use to enlarge their worlds. In *Against Method*, Paul Feyerabend writes of the "paratactic aggregate," the worldview of so-called primitive man (1975, 240–251). The paratactic aggregate is a loosely coordinated collection of parts, not the forced integration of opposites. It is the original tolerant world, not because people force themselves to tolerate what they dislike, but because alternatives are not connected so tightly in the first place that one must displace another. Syncretism only becomes necessary after one has divided the world in two in the first place.

The ideal of the Tao has the quality of a paratactic aggregate, a container so large that it has room for everything without contradiction. So do the 100 percent + 100 percent cultures written about by many anthropologists, in which, for example, Western medicine does not displace traditional medicine but exists alongside it, one more choice to make the world a little more fit for humans. The connection to the way Koreans think about evil is apparent. Evil does not exist because Koreans do not feel forced to do the addition or to place everything into one of two mutually exclusive categories. The antidualism that makes evil impossible is a way of thinking that allows for greater experimentation with opposites that are not really opposites—just additions that do not have have to be added up.

When globalization works, it does not create new men and women. It gives old men and women new choices. Globalization liberates not by integrating but by providing more "ands." Roland Robertson (1992, 177–178) suggests that it was the syncretism and eclecticism of Japanese religion that prepared Japan to meet the world with the coherence it has. The Japanese were free *not* to integrate everything. If Robertson is right, Korea still has a chance.

Of all the complex predictions of what the new Korea will look like, one stands out for its profound simplicity. "The moral future of Korea is to live in two worlds," is how the informant put it. He did not say that Koreans would ever put them together. This was not the point. The point was that some Koreans would be freer because they could enlarge their menu of choices, moving back and forth between them, much as the informant travels between East and West.

Somewhere inside, the informant—and others—are able to hold the pieces together, making richer lives for themselves. Others will not be so lucky. Their choices will shatter them. Which happens will, for many, depend on whether there exists a coherent culture to form and frame their new choices. It takes an old 100 percent culture to make the new 100 percent culture available for experimentation. In other words, the old culture must be present and real to be available as a transitional object to the new, with which it is never replaced, and rarely even integrated, but added to. Sometimes that is enough.

Zdravko Mlinar writes of a transition from "identity as an island to identity as a crossroad." He continues, it is

increasingly unlikely that a territorial unit can continue to *preserve* its distinctiveness on the basis of . . . "de-linking." . . . There is an increasing possibility that distinctive identity may be *formed* as a unique crossroad in the flow of people, goods and ideas. (Mlinar 1992, 2)

This is a strictly intellectual ideal. Identity is formed within forms, the form and frame of culture and tradition. Without frame and form, identity disintegrates. The trick is to open up the form without exploding it. We do this by addition, which means that you have to start with one culture.

Cultures Get Stuck and Become Unglued

In the West we live in a world in which we experience ourselves as having too many choices, even if most are between Coke and Pepsi. When tradition is in fragments (not the same as choices, though they are often confused), sometimes it seems that all we can do is cling to the ruins, or dance on them. We forget what it is like for most of the world most of the time, that for others life is not a surfeit of possibilities but a prison.

Cultures get stuck, becoming incapable of correcting themselves. This is more likely to occur in homogeneous cultures than heterogeneous ones, but it can happen to any culture (Niebuhr 1960). To liberate itself, avant-garde elements within the culture turn outward, and sometimes backward as well, re-interpreting their history, calling on suppressed strands. This strategy can only work, however, when the stuck culture has adequate receptors, analogous to those chemical receptors in the brain that receive certain chemical stimuli.

"Adequate" is not a question of numbers but of conceptual fit: the existence of precursor concepts, able to make sense of related foreign experiences. The lack of adequate cultural receptors for evil is, I have argued, the reason the Christian concept has not caught on in Korea, even among most Christians. Biological analogies only go so far, however. Receptors in the brain are not transformed forever by the chemicals they take up. Cultural receptors are. It is part of the metabolic (to mix biological metaphors for a moment) process mentioned earlier, in which foreign ideas become part of the culture—only, however, when they are received in the first place.

Consider the sad state of Korean poetry according to one observer. Born and raised in the West, he is a well-known translator into English of many volumes of Korean poetry and several novels. Korean poetry, he says, seems to have no future.

> Korean poetry has worn itself to the bone. Korean poetry began as an en-
> counter with the West, first of all Baudelaire, and Korean poets need to
> travel and read and get renewed. The spontaneous gush is no longer enough,
> and there is no model for anything else. How many different ways can you
> describe a bamboo leaf? Korean academics and poets want to translate Ko-
> rean poetry into English. That's how you get a grant. It's not what's needed.
> What's needed is the translation of Western poetry and fiction into Korean.

This translator is not a man who misunderstands, or fails to appreciate, Korean poetry. He grasps the Buddhist aesthetic behind the "spontaneous gush": don't shape, don't intervene. It is akin to the Buddhist ideal of sudden, unforced enlightenment. He understands that the nature of Korean poetry is not mere nature. Nature symbolizes a circular metaphysics:

everything changes, and everything returns. This description fits Ku Sang's "St. Christopher's River" poems.

> The river flows on,
> neither heart nor body,
> it flows, an essence of nothingness. (Ku Sang 1989, 111)

The reader wants harmony; the poet gives it to him. Koreans still read lots of poetry, and they read poetry to have hope: hope of a beyond, which in Korea tends to be a circular image, a flow that returns to its source to start all over again. A homeless man at Seoul Station said he went to sit beside the river Han that flows through Seoul. "It moved. And here I sit." Flow is hope, and he is hopeless.

The translator is still critical, arguing that the Korean poetic aesthetic is becoming emptier and emptier as it fails to draw on and reflect changes in the culture and society, lacking sources of renewal. It is not that Korean poetry is becoming irrelevant, if relevant means that Koreans still read poetry. But Korean poetry risks becoming sterile, isolated from the real lives of those who read it, and so takes on the qualities of a comforting cliché, like those "Chicken Soup for the Soul" books that sell so well in the United States.

> I am ontologist.
> Sometimes I walk the Himalayas.
> I see clouds.

A drunk in Insadong, an area of artists and antique stores in downtown Seoul, recited this original poem for me as he shook my hand, offering me a drink from a bottle of soju he and half a dozen friends had been sharing. Some Koreans are still drawn to Westerners. Are all Koreans poets? Was this a spontaneous gush, an overworked form available to any drunk? Does it prove what the translator had been saying? Or does it instead represent the kind of world we should all wish to live in, where even, or especially, drunks spout poetry?

It is hard to know. What is clear is that traditions fail in different ways. When tradition fails in Korea, it fails through stasis, the tradition becoming more rigid and empty as it cannot accommodate the changes. Globalization is no exception to this generalization, but rather it is the most telling instance. Not just Koreans' stubborn, nationalistic resistance to the reforms demanded by the IMF, Western economic powers, and Japan, but by becoming globalization in order to defeat it is another version of the same strategy, that of a culture so rigid and scared it cannot imagine truly changing, but only being broken. Koreans treat evil in the same way, bringing it so close it cannot be other.

One sees the Korean practice of all or nothing (or rather, all and nothing) in surprising places. One place is Korean pottery and sculpture. It is either indistinguishable from Western pottery and sculpture (there are more sculptures of trees, however), or it looks just like the pottery and sculpture of one thousand years ago, an unregenerate tradition. One might argue that this simply represents the principle of "and," the paratactic aggregate: the goal isn't to synthesize integral forms, but to place them side by side, one enriching the other by its mere existence. I do not see the mutual enrichment in the case of Korean sculpture, though one might cite the works of Lee Seung-teak as counterevidence. In general, however, the most creative blending is taking place, it seems, not in the arts (at least not these arts), but in life, where the brilliant Oriental doctor, the fortune-telling therapist and the yoga instructor are experimenting with their lives.

Some Say the World Will End in Fire; Some Say in Ice

As Robert Frost reminds us, either is quite sufficient, the stultification of ice or the chaos of an overheated society. In Korea the cultural container is too tight, threatening to crush its contents, isolating the culture from the world until the world finally bursts through, shattering the inflexible container. In the United States the container is too loose, not providing enough guidance or coherence, the pieces falling apart into zero gravity. It is the distinction between hwabyŏng disease and borderline personality disorder. Globalization as enlightenment would mean that societies threatened by ice might borrow some fire by looking out. Those threatened by fire are more likely to benefit from looking in, to lost traditions.

Societies threatened by stultification will have an easier time of it. It is generally easier to open up an existing container than to create a new one.

Certainly this seems to be the case with Korea. No matter how challenging the difficulties, Korea faces an easier task than that faced by the United States. Koreans must open what exists rather than put the pieces back in a box that has been torn to pieces. The difficulty, and danger, is that Korean culture will not be opened, but flattened, by globalization.

A discussion of Korean poetry is a good place to return for a moment to the original Korean poem, the Tao. The Tao is everything and nothing. It is the empty womb, sterile dead and terrifying. It is the womb that is one with its child, so filled with life it is inseparable from it. In the Tao are joined life and death, all and nothingness, form and void, woven together so tightly that they cannot be known separately. This is the point, of course, and this is why Koreans cannot know evil. Evil depends on separation; in some respects it is separation.

Koreans approach globalization as though it were the Tao. I think they approach every threatening thing this way—that is, everything that threatens to annihilate because it does not recognize one as a fellow human, a fellow Korean. There is nothing more frightening than not being noticed, said William James. Globalization does not notice.

The Tao does not notice. It does not care about straw dogs (*Tao Te Ching*, number 5). To such a threatening experience Koreans assimilate themselves, becoming the threatening other, and so humanizing it, including themselves, otherness becomes self-object. The strategy has served Korea well, but against globalization it may have met its limits. The globe contains many possibilities. Unlike the Tao, these possibilities are not formed and framed by its container. If Koreans are unable to form and frame globalization with their own traditions, they will be lost. I believe they know this, and it is why they are so scared. If there were a Korean word for evil, it would be globalization.

Conclusion: You Take the Good Parts . . .

"You take the good parts and the rest you throw away," says an eighteen-year-old student at Bankok's Thammasat University (*Far Eastern Economic Review* 1996, 51). He is talking about borrowing from Western culture, and he is wrong. It is not how experimentation works, at least not the experimentation that leads to enlightenment. It is not enough to stand at the crossroads, picking bits of this and that as the lives of nations pass by.

For enlightened experimentation to work, there has to be a frame and form: not just principles of selection and exclusion, but a pattern. Not in order to fit everything into the pattern; that is not the point. We need the pattern in order to have principles of selection. How can one choose the good parts if one does not know what to value anymore? It is why globalization is so threatening: not just because it changes lives, but because it transforms values. Nietzsche called it the transvaluation of values, good become evil and evil good. At least Nietzsche knew what the principle of selection was: abundant life.

Koreans are lost because they have lost the principle of selection. If a foreigner may be permitted, I would suggest chŏng, not the chŏng of "just we two," but the mutual affection and overlapping egos that Hahm Pyong-choon writes of, the basis not just of friendship but authority in "old Korea." To be sure, much exploitation has taken place under the guise of chŏng. About that Janelli (1993) is just right. But that is really the point. Unless the claims of chŏng are given their due, Koreans are likely, if backed into corner, to prefer new forms of warm authoritarianism to the icy polar darkness of rationalization.

Some Koreans devalue chŏng for this reason. "I voted for Kim Young Sam due to chŏng" said one. "It was the wrong reason. I wasn't being rational." By "chŏng" he means regional ties (chiyŏn), still surprisingly strong. For this new Korean, chŏng is the logic of old Korea, inseparable from relationships of almost feudal dependence. In place of chŏng, however, he does not talk about rational self-interest but ujŏng (the term contains the word "chŏng"), by which he means friendship, a relationship among equals.[3] For this new Korean, it is not a subtle distinction but an obvious one. It is the difference between the hierarchical legacy of Confucianism, and a "Koreanism," as he calls it, that might take its place. It is an important difference, but not all the difference in the world.

I am not as convinced as some Koreans that there is a strong egalitarian countercurrent to the patriarchy and hierarchy that is generally associated with Korean Confucianism. Brandt (1971) and Janelli and Janelli (1982) locate this egalitarianism in the community spirit of the Korean village.

This new Korean cites the Tonghak rebellion before going on to argue that Taoism is itself a teaching of egalitarianism, finding it in the first several stories of the *Chuang-tzu*. My view is that Taoism is egalitarian only in the sense that it would obliterate all distinctions, including those between being and nonbeing. This is not a political teaching.

Although there is a strong strain of individualism among Koreans, this is hardly the same thing as egalitarianism, as Tocqueville reminds us in the West. Nor is the sharing that the men of Pagoda Park and Seoul Station talk about the same thing as egalitarianism. Tangunism is perfectly compatible with traditional hierarchy. Chŏng is not as easily assimilated to familiar political distinctions as this.

Aristotle's (*N. Ethics*, bks 8–9) concept of political friendship is inapplicable in the United States today not because the term is old fashioned but because we live in a mass society in which the term no longer has a referent, the citizen of republican virtue. Chŏng still has a referent, the presence of the old Korea in the new—or rather, the presence of old Koreans in new Koreans. Unless Koreans think, talk, and plan carefully, this referent will go the way of the Western citizen.

In many Asian countries, the most formidable bulwark against overweening Westernization is the nation. How effective this approach will be is unclear, but in the case of Korea it is moot. In Korea the nation has largely abandoned this task, deciding that the best defense is a good offense, becoming globalization in order to defeat it. Recent nationalistic reaction, some instigated by the government (particularly government bureaucrats, eager to retain their powers), is only a blip on the screen in this regard.

The field is wide open for Korean intellectuals to take the lead. Unfortunately, their situation often resembles what Tu Wei-ming says about

> the plight of those modern Chinese intellectuals who are emotionally attached to their *history* but intellectually committed to imported *values*. . . . In their identification with the past an intellectual justification is absent, and their identification with the present is devoid of an affective strength. (Tu Wei-ming 1978, 221)

Fortunately, there are numerous exceptions in Korea. I spoke with them.

Silence is a great thing. I experienced much closeness and communion in silence with Korean friends. But silence can be deceptive, the silence of mutuality transformed into the silence of denial and fantasy in the blink of an eye. Koreans must, I think, begin to talk with each other about their values before there are no choices left. This, too, is enlightenment, enlightenment not as light but conversation. Even when it is about regrets.

Research Appendix

J ust over 250 Koreans were interviewed from all walks of life, all age groups, and all the major religions.

Some interviews lasted as little as twenty minutes. These were usually the interviews with the man or woman on the street. Several dozen took more than three hours. In about two dozen cases, I interviewed the subject a second and third time. Most were interviewed individually, but about fifty were interviewed in groups, at "evil dinners," and in classrooms. Many members of these groups were also interviewed individually.

Preliminary Interviews of Korean Americans

Thirteen Korean Americans were interviewed in the United States, in order to develop the questions. Korean Americans are overwhelmingly Christian (80 percent or more according to most estimates), and this was born out in my small sample. All were between the ages of twenty and thirty-five.

Their responses were not markedly Christian. On the contrary, the pattern came closest to the older women who worked in the restaurants of Shinchon. Evil is the choe-pŏl cycle: if you do something bad, it will come back to harm you, or someone you love. Why these younger Korean Americans, most of whom came to the United States as children, held to views most closely associated with older Korean women who claimed no religion (most of the older women were brought up in families where at least one parent was Buddhist) is puzzling.

Selection and Distribution of Informants

In Chapter 1 I describe the strategies employed to interview Koreans from all walks of life, all social classes, and different regions of the country. No single problem of research occupied me more than that of finding a diverse group of Koreans to talk with. Although I did not speak with a random sample of Koreans, I spoke with a disparate one.

Because of the large number of subjects interviewed at Hankuk University of Foreign Studies, the average age of informants was younger than the population. Because I spoke with many experts and professionals, the sample was better educated than the population.

Nevertheless, many older and poorer Koreans were interviewed. The trick, as it turned out, was finding venues in which my assistant and I might approach Koreans in public, such as restaurants, coffeehouses, and public parks. This is not a usual practice, especially among older Koreans. In this regard, being a Westerner was an advantage. I was expected to be crass and insensitive. Still, approaching Koreans on my own was far less successful than with my interpreter, who presented my card and explained my mission.

Religion

Statistics on the number of adherents to Korean religions are unreliable. The *Korean Christian Yearbook* for 1990 gives a figure for all religions of 49 million believers out of a population of 41 million (Underwood 1994). Since about 50 percent of Koreans claim to belong to no religion, these figures are more than a little inflated. There is, however, another way to look at them. Many Koreans belong to more than one religion. Membership in more than one religion is not so much inflation as multiplicity.

The 1985 census (the last year the Korean government included a question on religion) gives the following percentages:

16.1% Protestant
4.6% Catholic   (total = 20.7% Christian)
20% Buddhist
1.2% Confucian
0.8% other
57.4% no religion

A recent Gallop Poll set the number of Christians (including Catholics) at 21 percent and Buddhists at 22 percent. The Agency of Statistics recently gave the following breakdown (Kim Byung-kook 1998, 20):

23.2% Buddhist
19.7% Protestant
6.6% Catholic
0.5% Confucian
0.2% Won Buddhism
0.1% Chondokyo
0.5% others
49.3% no religion

These percentages are roughly mirrored among my research subjects, though it should not be concluded that the bare majority of informants who were nonbelievers were uninfluenced by their religious background. Frequently they were.

It is easy to overestimate the power and influence of Christianity in Korea, partly because it is so evangelical. "It is said that twenty-seven of the forty largest churches in the world are in Korea and there are certainly many churches with congregations of over 10,000" (Underwood n.d., 11). The Full Gospel Church in Seoul claims 800,000 members! Until about 1960, most Christians were from the laboring and lower classes. Today

Christianity is the religion of many movers and shakers in Korean society. Their prominence, however, does not necessarily make the Christian worldview more influential. That many influential Koreans are Christian does not automatically mean that Christianity is an influential worldview in Korea, especially insofar as evil is concerned.

Andrew Kim writes that "today about one third of South Korea's 45 million people are Christian" (1995, 34). This estimate, though, seems to take churches' reports of their membership figures at face value. I interviewed many subjects who were recent converts to Christianity and at least as many who had been Christians but no longer were. Catechumens, as they are called (new members of the church who are examined and enrolled after six months), are particularly likely to leave the church but remain on the rolls (Underwood 1994, 74).

Upon observing the widespread presence of shamanistic elements both in Buddhist Temples (most have smaller temples dedicated to local deities, as well as the mountain god) and in Christian worship (the emphasis on *pok*, or blessings, for example), one is tempted to say that Korean religion is syncretic. Grayson, however, argues that Korean religion is not so much syncretic as eclectic and plural, although these qualities are not due to a love of tolerance (Grayson 1989, 271–272). At one time or another, each of the major religions (excluding shamanism) has tried to suppress the others. Like religious toleration in the West, Korean religious pluralism is the result of long and sad experience.

Even today, this pluralism can be exaggerated. Koreans deal with conflict by suppressing it. For many Buddhists, my affiliation with a Christian university made me suspect. Only after attending the Buddhist temple for months did they begin to express their anger to me at what they regarded as Christian anti-Buddhist desecrations. A number of Korean short stories have as their theme families torn apart by religious differences.

As far as the nonbelief in evil is concerned, Koreans are indeed syncretic, although the less ambitious term "uniform" is more apt. Except for a small number of Christians (about one-quarter of all Christians interviewed), there was almost no correlation between an informant's religion, or lack of religious affiliation, and his or her views on evil. This result occurred not because Koreans were all over the map on the subject, but because they were not.

Questions

I almost always asked the questions on globalization first, unless the informant had heard I was studying evil and could not wait. This was usually not the case.

1. What does globalization (segyehwa) mean to you?
2. How is globalization affecting you? Korea?
3. How do you wish globalization would change your life?
4. What do you most hope for Korea's future? What do you most fear?
5. How are you different from your parents?

Questions Regarding Evil

6. Tell me about a personal experience that has to do with choe or ak?
7. How do you understand the terms choe and ak? (Even in interviews conducted in English, I used the Korean terms first. If the informant switched to the English term, I did too. If not, I waited a little while before using it.)
8. If you do choe (crime), do you always get pŏl (retribution)? Why?
9. What is the worst thing (kkŭmchik-han il) there is?
10. What does "heavenly" (ch'ŏn, hanŭl) retribution mean? Do you believe in it? Do most Koreans?
11. How do you understand the Western concept of evil?
12 Why do people do bad things? (Here I allowed, but did not encourage, the informant to distinguish between bad intent and bad behavior, saak-han haengwi.)
13. Do you have a religion? Did you once? Do your parents? Does any religion influence you?

Questions Regarding the Self

14. How would you answer the question "Who are you?"
15. To whom do you belong?

16. What does the phrase "we Koreans" (always given in Korean as uri han'guk saram) mean?

17. What is the worst thing that could happen to you?

18. Do you think Koreans have a "group self?" What does this mean? What is the opposite of a "group self?"

19. Why do Koreans use the term "we" (uri) so much?

Although the questions were designed to address the three areas of evil, self, and globalization, the informants did not, fortunately, keep to this distinction. Nor did I after a while, finding in many of the questions about evil answers to questions about the self, and vice versa.

This list of questions could be misleading if it were read as suggesting that I asked Koreans to answer a questionnaire. I asked the same questions in order to have comparability of results, but the interview was conducted as a conversation. Many additional questions were asked, and questions were sometimes omitted. The goal of having conversations with Koreans about evil, the self, and globalization was more important than covering every question.

Sometimes I learned most when I asked nothing but only listened to what Koreans said among themselves at "evil dinners" and in other small groups. Koreans did not, for the most part, try to mislead me, but they put things in terms that a Westerner might understand, such as "tell me the relationship, and I'll tell you what's evil." That in itself can be misleading.

In effect, three different versions of "what is the worst thing" question were asked.

What is the worst thing there is? (question 9)

What is the worst thing that could happen to you? (question 17)

What do you most fear for Korea's future? (question 4)

I had expected the answers to questions 9 and 17 to be similar, the first question a way of leading into the second. This is not the way it worked out. Answers to "worst thing there is" were conventional, such as murder and rape. Answers to "the worst thing that could happen to you," although not varying a great deal in their theme (mostly alienation and loneliness, as discussed in Chapter 3), were more personal, as might be expected. Yet another question, "What do you most fear for Korea's future?" although not intended as a version of "the worst thing that could happen to you" question, was answered that way by most informants. This result suggests the degree to which Koreans identify with the fate of their country, using the same term, *hanminjok*, to refer to the "Korean nation" and the "Korean people."

In addition, a large number of informants (over 25 percent) were asked the following questions:

20. Would it be evil if North Korea possessed nuclear weapons?
21. Were the soldiers who killed civilians in Kwangju evil?
22. Have you heard of hwabyŏng disease? What causes it? Do you know anyone who has it? Is it a Korean disease? (This question was asked of all older women, who make up over 90 percent of those seeking treatment for the disorder, as discussed in Chapter 4. It was also asked of many other informants, including men.)

Korean professionals and experts, including Buddhist monks, Confucian scholars, Christian ministers, and Catholic priests, as well as professors, psychologists, and psychiatrists, were often asked to make a distinction between how they would answer as individual Koreans and how they thought the average Korean would answer. Generally there was not a great deal of difference on the questions about evil, more on the questions about globalization and self.

On my return visit, after the economic crisis was well under way, I asked three additional questions:

23. How has it been for you since the economic crisis?
24. How do you see your future in Korea?
25. Who is to blame for the economic crisis?

I did not ask questions like "Is the IMF evil?" There is little to be gained, I have learned, from tendentious questioning. The only apparent influence of the economic crisis on Koreans' views of evil was the suggestion by several that social chaos following an economic collapse (not this crisis, but worse) would be ak. All in all, I am glad I did the bulk of my research when the depth of the economic crisis was not yet apparent—that is, when economic issues were not quite so urgent.

Language Issues

My Korean is not fluent. As a result, I missed much. I would have missed more had I not worked with a translator. There are nuances of language, including body language, that only a native speaker can convey. What people believe is not always as important as how they believe it, and ascertaining the significance of such distinctions required a subtlety about the language and the culture that I did not muster on my own.

I worked with the same translator throughout both phases of my research project. We spent hundreds of hours working together, at least as many before and after interviews as during, trying to organize and make sense of the responses. A graduate of Yonsei University's Graduate School of International Studies, Lee Yoonkyung is in many ways a coauthor of this work. She was not only my translator but my ideal native informant, as the anthropologists put it.

Many Koreans, particularly students and professionals, speak excellent English, and in these cases I conducted the interviews in English. In most cases my translator attended these interviews as well, partly in order to help with difficult words, partly in order to keep current with my work, and partly so she could tell me if I was hearing different things in English than in Korean. In most cases I was not. She also attended the dinners.

Central to my strategy was approaching so-called average Koreans in restaurants and on the street. Younger Koreans are used to this sort of thing, but older ones are not. Our usual approach was for my translator to carry a pile of my business cards printed in Korean. She would approach strangers, present my card, and explain my project while I stood back a couple of steps and looked benign. More often than not it worked. Often, especially in Pagoda Park and Seoul Station, a small crowd formed around us. Some individual interviews became, in effect, group interviews.

The romanization in this book follows the McCune-Reischauer System of Romanization. Korean names are rendered as each name is most frequently romanized in texts. The result is a considerable variation in style.

Occasionally I have indulged in minor redundancies in terminology, such as "Mount Namsan," or "hwabyŏng disease." It is a common practice. North Americans, for example, refer to the "Sierra Nevada Mountains."

Conversational Ideal and Confrontational Practice

The interview strategy was guided by the conversational ideal. Find a nice place to talk, if possible: restaurant, coffeehouse, or park when the weather turned warm. Some informants were interviewed in soju bars, which are more like coffeehouses than true bars (soju is a strong, clear potato wine, often mixed with fruit drinks). Many professionals were interviewed in their offices, but with many others we went to a restaurant. A few informants came to my house on a university campus.

A pleasant, relaxing place to talk was the ideal, but it was not always possible to arrange. A few interviews were conducted on street corners, others in taxis, still others while sitting on the floor in Seoul Station. The most pleasant setting was a Buddhist monastery high on Chirisan Mountain. The coziest was under umbrellas in the warm rain at Pagoda Park. The strangest was a restaurant that specialized in hosting shamanistic séances.

A comfortable and pleasant environment made it easier to challenge the informant without his or her taking offense. Rather than simply accepting a statement, I would generally ask why, frequently "arguing" with the informant, not to win the point, but to get at the reasoning involved.

To say "arguing," though, puts it too harshly, particularly in a culture that lacks a dialectical tradition. Many Koreans are not used to being argued with. "Why?" "I don't understand." "Explain that again." "I don't follow your reasoning." "That doesn't make sense to me." "I don't get it." "Doesn't that contradict what you just said about . . . ?" These are the questions I used to challenge informants, all the while trying to respect the informant's right to define his or her experience.

Although Koreans are unused to a culture of argument, they are not averse to emotional and intellectual encounters with relative strangers. There was an advantage to studying the "Latinos of Asia," as Koreans sometimes characterize themselves.

Time, food, and drink, and a conversational setting eased things considerably with many informants. Nevertheless, the greatest variable was not the setting but the informant him or herself. I had fascinating interviews in the backseats of taxis idling on noisy and polluted street corners, and boring interviews during fine meals. In a sense, though, no interview was boring. Even a boring interview was data, and on reflection some boring interviews turned out to offer fascinating clues. Each interview was a piece of the puzzle. It was also a new clue, the puzzle never ending.

Essays

In addition to the interviews, about 150 students at Hankuk University of Foreign Studies wrote essays on the topics of evil, self, and globalization. All essays were written in English. Koreans are often more revealing in writing than conversation (at least with Westerners), and I was surprised at the intimacy of the responses. I spoke with these students in small groups about their essays, and I individually interviewed a couple dozen whose answers were striking in some way.

Notes

Chapter 1. "Tell Me the Relationship . . ."

1. Benedict (1946, 190) quotes Sir George Sansom. "Throughout their history the Japanese seem to have retained in some measure this incapacity to discern, or this reluctance to grapple with, the problem of evil." One should be careful about extrapolating from one Far Eastern country to another, and especially from Japan to Korea, but in this case it seems warranted. What is unwarranted is the assumption that it is an "incapacity." When we organize the world in such a way that evil cannot exist, it is not an incapacity but a creative act.

2. For many it is a given that different value systems, languages, and the like are incommensurable. There is no way one could even begin to compare Eastern and Western views of evil. In fact, incommensurability is no logical given but an empirical claim, as Harold Brown (1983, 3) points out. The proper question, says Feyerabend (1975, 244–285), is not whether two different theories, languages, or cultures can be compared. If we are clever enough we can compare anything with anything. The question is how much is lost in the translation. The answer, suggests Feyerabend, is not logical but historical and empirical, to be decided and debated on a case-by-case basis. Thomas Kuhn (1977, 300–301) holds to a similar view.

3. Many Koreans claim that there are no homeless individuals in Korea. To prove it, they use the romanized English term to describe the phenomenon. Instead, the "homeless" are men too alienated and ashamed by their unemployment to go home. This was not my experience at Seoul Station, where many told of circumstances that rendered them quite literally homeless—without abode, and without parents, wife, or

children able to take them in. What is true is that the Korean homeless do not look very different from working-class Koreans with homes.

4. Following Wittgenstein (1961, 6.53–7), I do not distinguish between term and concept, as though the concept were a more abstract but powerful term. I use "term" and "concept" synonymously.

5. Culture, says Raymond Williams (1976, 76), "is one of the two or three most complicated words in the English language." There is little to be gained here from defining the term more elaborately. What is important is that culture is made from below by those who participate in it, and it is remade every day in every interaction. Consequently, culture is not an explanation of anything, as in "Confucian culture explains the persistence of rigid hierarchy in the chaebŏl." Culture is not the *explicans* but the *explicandum*. It is what is to be explained, not an explanation.

6. Some have explained the difference between East and West in terms of the need of nomadic tribes that gave birth to Christianity for rules, laws, and a third-party god to keep order, including sexual order, in the tents at night. In such an unsettled environment, anarchy was an ever present threat. In the agrarian, settled East, a more loosely woven tradition was order enough, the social situation not so unsettled as to need all these rules and gods.

It is a fascinating idea, and worth thinking about. Certainly there must be some reason that East and West evolved so differently, and finding these reasons in the actual material circumstances of people's lives is always a good bet. Nevertheless, it is hard to see how the answer could ever be more than historical speculation, even as it raises pertinent questions for the present. In Korea the power of the social web to deny evil depends not on its looseness, but its tension. Rather than trying to explain the origins of the Korean nonbelief in evil, I shall map its absence. This may not be the whole story, but it is a start.

7. The attitude of Koreans toward Confucianism is complex and contradictory. Many blame it for Korea's weakness and national humiliations. President Park Chung Hee, the late dictator, accused Confucianism of being incompatible with economic development, technological progress, and the accumulation of wealth. In "Reflections on Our Nation's Past," Park argued that Confucianism encouraged a mentality of vassalage, lack of independence, indolence, lack of enterprise, malicious selfishness, and lack of a sense of honor in the Korean people.

His successor, President Chun Doo Hwan, while agreeing with many of these criticisms, found in Confucianism (or at least the idea of Confucianism as ideology) a bulwark against the blind struggle for wealth and unbridled egoism (Robinson 1991, 219–220). Can one even imagine American presidents involved in a similar debate over the influence of Locke or Jefferson perhaps? In any case, most Korean men seem to vacillate between these two positions. Many Korean women are more ambivalent still.

Chapter 2. The Self Is a Conflict, Not a Continuum

1. The following statement, made in 1990, is unusually critical. "Fortunately enough, through education and contacts with Western culture, Confucian values . . . are

gradually decreasing in our society. What we urgently need to achieve at this time of transition between collectivism and individualism is the recovery of our lost individuality. The foremost part of human dignity is the growth and fulfillment of each person's individuality" (Yoon Tae-Rim 1994, 25–26).

2. I heard other versions, including that *in* shows the profile of one person, with *gan*, the term for between. I think the pictogram looks like two people, but mine is not a linguistic claim about Chinese but an interpretation of stories Koreans told about their culture.

3. As with just about every generalization about Korea, this statement requires qualification. During many years of the Chosŏn dynasty (1392–1910), Korean popular culture expressed itself in novels, the most famous of which is *The Tale of Ch'unhyang*, still Korea's favorite story according to Cumings (1997, 75). The appearance of the novel in recent years is actually a reappearance.

4. The diagram is from "Cross-Cultural Perspectives on Self-Ingroup Relations," cited by a half dozen Korean psychologists working on the topic (Triandis et al. 1988). The version in the text is from "The Emergence of Individualism in Korean Organizations," by Cho (1994).

5. The internal quote is from the psychoanalyst R. E. Money-Kyrle.

Chapter 3. "Why Do Koreans Always Say 'We' and Do 'I'?"

1. Under the category "outside of all relationships, isolated and alone," I include not only this answer, but answers referring to loss of all close relationships due to death of loved ones, but only if "to be left alone" is the implication. I also include: deceit and betrayal by friends; poverty (but only when poverty is defined as abandonment by friends and family, as it frequently is by Koreans); being excluded from the group; one's own death, but only if it is defined in terms separation from all human contact, as it generally was. About 70 percent of students gave "outside of all relationships, isolated and alone" as "the worst thing that could happen to you." About 60 percent of other respondents did. Note particularly how experiences that need not be automatically interpreted in terms of isolation and alienation, such as death or poverty, often were.

One might argue that "worst" does not mean worst in Korea; it means something like "among lots of bad things this is one." Koreans are not as precise in this regard as English speakers. For example, the "highest mountain in Korea" may just mean "very high." This would fit with the antidualism of many informants, their intentionally vague use of superlatives like "best" and "worst" subtly undercutting what they would regard as false dichotomies.

Nevertheless, I took pains to emphasize that worst meant worst. The term used was *kkŭmchik-han il*, which might be rendered as absolutely terrible thing, not *nappŭn*, which means bad. In any case, the linguistic issue is not decisive. It was informants who chose one thing as worst, even if they heard it as "merely" very bad.

See the Research Appendix for a further discussion of some of the methodological issues raised by this question.

2. Ikegami (1995) neglects only the iteration of this distinction that is some post-modernisms. If this pristine, real self does not exist, then nothing of the self is allowed to exist at all. If it is not pure and perfect, then the self is nothing at all, fragments and ruins (Tallis 1995).

3. I spoke with a dozen Korean psychiatrists (M.D.s and O.M.D.s) and psychologists about hwabyŏng disease. In addition, I asked forty-five informants about the topic, mostly those who made some reference to anger, more often older informants than younger ones. As a rule, younger informants thought they would not succumb. "We express our anger," said one, "we don't bottle it up. We aren't going to get it. It's our mothers' disease." One psychiatrist responded simply "Let them wait twenty years. Then they'll know."

Chapter 4. Evil Is Unrelatedness

1. A Korean academic familiar with the debate over Huntington's work thought that Huntington himself might be evil, though presumably he was just using my presumed belief in evil for effect. "How could a man create such conflicts? What's the point of setting countries against each other? You want to know what's evil? That's evil." Evil, from this perspective, is the creation of differences by stating them. No—my Korean friend might reply—not by stating them but by exaggerating them, that is how evil is made.

2. Actually, it should be called the "practical fruit of karma." Karma is the process, pŏl the fruit. But this misuse of the term "karma" is now irrevocable, at least in the West.

3. The Sapir-Whorf hypothesis, as it has come to be known, states that distinct linguistic communities possess distinct and incommensurable cognitive realms (Sapir 1929). The hypothesis is probably true, though there is no reason to assume it must be. It is an empirical, not a logical, claim, even though it is frequently treated as linguistic determinism. Certainly the hypothesis is frequently true, and I might seem to have assumed it as far as evil East and West is concerned. In fact, I have done no such thing. I have "discovered" it, if one can discover something that is already widely known. The incommensurability is empirical, not logical. As such it is a question of degree.

4. There are few cultural hosts for Indian concepts either. Indian Buddhism possesses a concept of hell that rivals Dante's *Inferno*. Located beneath the earth, eight hells match the torture to the crime. The primary source is *The Sutra of the Remembrance of the True Law*, officially a Hinayana text, but with strong Mahayana influence. This text was the inspiration for Genshin's description of hell in *Essentials of Salvation*, a Japanese text that served as a basis for Pure Land Buddhism, also present in Korea (Matsunaga and Matsunaga 1972). Although Pure Land Buddhism is present in Korea, it is a relatively minor sect, and little trace of this way of thinking is found there. The vast majority of Korean Buddhists are Son (in Japanese, Zen) Buddhists, for whom the concept of hell is absent.

5. "Ten million separated families" is a cliché, used to emphasize the sufferings of a divided nation. Taken literally, it implies that almost every South Korean has a relative

in the North. It is probably more important as an estimate of South Korean feeling than actual surveys, which run lower. After the Korean war, South Korean authorities estimated that three million North Koreans moved South from 1945 through 1953, almost one-third of the population of the North at that time. The figure seems too large. A recent survey puts the number of first generation of separated families at 400,000. Whatever the actual number, every year it is getting smaller, the generations more distant.

6. I am using incest as metaphor, but one does not want to abandon the terrible reality to metaphor. Korean law states that only the victim has the legal right to sue the abuser. The psychological, familial, and social difficulties involved in suing one's father in a traditional society are, to say the least, immense. The result is that there are no reliable figures on the prevalence of incest. A member of Korea Women's Hotline states that the problem is widespread, particularly with stepfathers and live-in lovers.

7. The term is archaic, how kings were once referred to. The kidnappers picked out the name from a Hong Kong gangster film, "The Noblest and the Highest," which was popular at the time.

8. Whether the Confucian quality of some responses is seen as similar to Socrates' position depends on how one interprets Confucius. Although many see Confucius as a teacher of rational humanism, and in this regard much like Socrates, Herbert Fingarette (1972) constructs a quite different, and to my mind more compelling, Confucius. Confucius could not promote self-cultivation because he could not imagine a self to cultivate. The human being is a sacred vessel who obtains humanity from this performance of ritual.

Chapter 5. Should Koreans Believe in Evil?

1. The original meaning of "ak" as ugly is based on the doctor's own research into the Chinese origins of the term. The term "ak" is itself a Chinese character, composed of two smaller characters, one meaning "under," the other meaning "mind." "Ak" is literally "under-mind." The doctor's linguistic history is not widely accepted, but origin is not the issue here. As argued in Chapter 2, the linguistic study of origins and meaning is often little more than metaphor. Metaphor is, however, just what I am looking for.

2. Natural evil is today a moribund category in the West. This was not always so. Ra^c the Old Testament term we translate as evil, could as readily refer to illness or natural disaster as malevolence.

3. Korean Buddhism came from India through China, giving Taoism yet another chance to influence Korean beliefs. "More than one, less than two" is as much a Buddhist teaching as a Taoist one. This aspect of Korean religious culture is indeed syncretic.

4. I put forth the Taoist interpretation of the Korean disbelief in evil in articles in two journals published in Korea (Alford 1997a; 1997b). A number of Koreans responded.

5. Cumings (1997) makes a similar observation about Korean families.
> When I lived with a Korean family having two small children, I was not so surprised at the obvious love the parents manifested for them, but was flabbergasted by their indulgence. Both kids were happy, free birds who roamed

the house at will . . . hearing no raised voices and suffering virtually nonexistent punishment. At length they would collapse in their parents arms at night. To an American . . . this looked like a recipe for making adults with no superegos, loose cannons who would soon bedevil civil society. But there was nothing of the sort; soon the schools provided all the discipline necessary to young people who were as healthy mentally as any parent could hope. Much earlier, Hamel made similar observations: "Parents are very indulgent in their Children," he wrote, "and in return are much respected by them. They depend upon one anothers good Behaviour," providing an ultimate corrective to childhood abandon (p. 58).

Hamel was a seventeenth-century Dutchman shipwrecked in Korea. Some things change slowly. But they change.

6. Rhi is quoting from M.-L. von Franz, a Jungian, in *Shadow and Evil in Fairytales*.

7. Many attempts have been made to explain away the harshness of this stanza. Cao Daozhong's claim that the truly humane do not consider themselves that way would seem to miss the larger point (Cleary 1991, 135). The Tao is not humane because it does not care about humans. It does not not care either. It just is. Humans must care for each other if any caring is to be done.

8. There are other, more complicated answers, such as God's Plan must remain a mystery, or that God himself is evolving in his goodness and mercy, or that God is not actually all-powerful, at least in particular cases. A world divided into a struggle between good and evil is the simplest and most compelling explanation, but far from the only one. *Encountering Evil: Live Options in Theodicy* (Davis 1981) is a fine discussion of these more complicated answers.

Chapter 6. Globalization Is Evil

1. Korean chaeböl own thousands of clothing and light manufacturing plants in Latin America and China, and they are heavily invested in Eastern Europe. If Korea is a colonial power, then we shall have to have a change of terms, globalization being what colonialism looks like when it is practiced by former colonies.

2. Samuel Huntington (1996, 57) has a material explanation. He calls it the illusion of "Davos culture," after a town in Switzerland where movers and shakers from all over the globe meet to discuss international issues. Not surprisingly, they share many of the same tastes and values, but they are hardly the world.

3. Barber notes the stimulating influence of American rock on Caribbean reggae, while regretting that reggae gets so little airtime on MTV (Barber 1995, 12). This regret, though, itself belies a McWorld standard. The right standard is whether Caribbeans influenced by American rock were able to enrich their musical production and appreciation, perhaps finding new forms to express their lives, what I call enlightenment. To know this, one would have to talk to Caribbeans, not because theirs would be the last word but because it is certainly the first step toward understanding, where we should start. If we do not listen, we will not only miss something interesting, but we are more likely to impose McWorld standards on our criticism of McWorld values. The

McWorld mind likes quick insights and superficial similarities because they are all that is necessary to sell—but not to understand.

4. A distinction should be drawn between theories of globalization, and the use of abstract terms of description as though description were theory. My complaint is with the latter approach. Roland Robertson (1990) and Albert Bergesen (1990), among others, represent the former approach, that of global theory. Convinced that we require a new theoretical paradigm to understand globalization, they start not from the interaction of nation states, but from the very nature of global interaction itself. About this approach, Mike Featherstone (1990, 5) says, "The world becomes a singular place with its own processes." Change "singular" to "single" and you have the distinction between a theory of globalization and its simulacrum, which too frequently turns the world into a *single* place. There is nothing wrong with grand theories of "globality." What is so troublesome about the approach of so many who write about globalization, such as Moses (1995) and Castoriadis (1991), is they way they use abstract, theory-laden terms in order to *describe* the world, using diversity and otherness as nouns rather than adjectives, as theoretical entities rather than stimuli for observation and description.

5. "Globalization" is also a political code word for holding down wage demands and appeals for increased political participation, so that Korea can remain economically competitive under the directed investment model it has followed so successfully until recently.

6. Selected by a national exam (at least until very recently, when some universities began using their own admission exams), Korean students generally do not choose where they are to study, though some may have several choices. The result is that not every student at Hankuk is dedicated to foreign study. Students there are actually more representative of Korean students as a whole than they would be otherwise.

Chapter 7. Globalization as Enlightenment

1. Fredric Jameson (1998, 75–76) also compares globalization to Hegel's philosophy, in this case the dialectic of Identity and Difference. When people are puzzled, they up the philosophical ante.

2. Hwang Chin-i wrote poetry reminiscent of Sappho's in its lovely longing. This is "Long Winter Night."

> I'll cut a piece from the side
> of this interminable winter night,
> and wind it in coils beneath
> these bedcovers, warm and
> fragrant as the spring breeze,
> coil by coil
> to unwind it the night my lover returns. (O'Rourke 1998, 42)

3. "Ujŏng" contains the word "chŏng" and may be translated as friendship. Although I was inclined to call it a weaker form of chŏng, several Koreans corrected me. "No, not weaker," said one. "Just different. Ujŏng is chŏng between friends." In other words, it is still chŏng.

References

Note: Classical sources, Greek and Chinese, are cited in the text by line, book, or chapter. Citations to the *Analects* are according to the Legge text, the translation from Brooks and Brooks.

Adorno, Theodor. 1968. "Sociology and Psychology," part 2. *New Left Review* 47: 79–97.
——. 1974. *Minima Moralia: Reflections from Damaged Life*, trans. E. F. N. Jephcott. London: NLB.
Alford, C. Fred. 1988. *Narcissism: Socrates, the Frankfurt School, and Psychoanalytic Theory.* New Haven: Yale University Press.
——. 1997a. "Koreans Do Not Believe in Evil: Should They?" *Korea Journal* 37 (Fall): 226–240.
——. 1997b. "Why Not Believe in Evil?" *Transactions of the Royal Asiatic Society, Korea Branch*, 72: 13–22.
——. 1997c. *What Evil Means to Us.* Ithaca: Cornell University Press.
American Psychiatric Association. 1994. *Diagnostic and Statistical Manual of Mental Disorders.* 4th ed. *[DSM-IV]*. Washington, D.C.: American Psychiatric Association.
Barber, Benjamin. 1995. *Jihad versus McWorld: How Globalism and Tribalism Are Reshaping the World.* New York: Ballantine Books.
Bauman, Zygmunt. 1989. *Modernity and the Holocaust.* Ithaca: Cornell University Press.
——. 1991. *Modernity and Ambivalence.* Ithaca: Cornell University Press.
Bellah, Robert, Richard Madsen, William Sullivan, Ann Swidler, and Steven Tipton. 1985. *Habits of the Heart: Individualism and Commitment in American Life.* Berkeley and Los Angeles: University of California Press.

Benedict, Ruth. 1946. *The Chrysanthemum and the Sword: Patterns of Japanese Culture.* Boston: Houghton Mifflin.

Benjamin, Gail. 1997. *Japanese Lessons: A Year in a Japanese School through the Eyes of an American Anthropologist and Her Children.* New York: New York University Press.

Benjamin, Jessica. 1977. "The End of Internalization: Adorno's Social Psychology." *Telos* 32 (Summer): 42–64.

——. 1978. "Authority and the Family Revisited: Or, A World without Fathers?" *New German Critique* 13 (Winter): 35–57.

Bergesen, Albert. 1990. "Turning World-System Theory on Its Head." In *Global Culture: Nationalism, Globalization and Modernity,* ed. Mike Featherstone, pp. 67–81. London: Sage.

Bion, Wilfred. 1970. *Attention and Interpretation.* London: Tavistock.

Blanchot, Maurice. 1986. *The Writing of the Disaster,* trans. Ann Smock. Lincoln: University of Nebraska Press.

Boyd, J. W. 1975. *Satan and Mara: Christian and Buddhist Symbols of Evil.* Leiden: E. J. Brill.

Boyne, Roy. 1990. "Culture and the World-System." In *Global Culture: Nationalism, Globalization and Modernity,* ed. Mike Featherstone, pp. 57–62. London: Sage.

Brandt, Vincent. 1971. *A Korean Village.* Cambridge: Harvard University Press.

Brodbeck, May. 1968. "Methodological Individualisms: Definition and Reduction." In *Readings in the Philosophy of the Social Sciences,* ed. Brodbeck, pp. 280–303. New York: Macmillan.

Brooks, E. Bruce, and A. Taeko Brooks, trans. 1998. *The Original Analects: Sayings of Confucius and His Successors.* New York: Columbia University Press.

Brown, Harold. 1983. "Incommensurability." *Inquiry* 26: 3–29.

Brown, Norman O. 1966. *Love's Body.* New York: Vintage.

Castoriadis, Cornelius. 1991. "Reflections on 'Rationality' and Development." In *Philosophy, Politics, Autonomy,* ed. David Curtis, pp. 175–198. New York: Oxford University Press.

Chai, Ch'u, and Winberg Chai. 1973. *Confucianism.* New York: Barron's.

Cho Nam-Guk. 1994. "The Emergence of Individualism in Korean Organizations." In *Psychology of the Korean People: Collectivism and Individualism,* ed. Gene Yoon and Sang-Chin Choi, pp. 209–232. Seoul: Dong-A Publishing Co. [published on behalf of the Korean Psychological Association].

Cho Sehŭi. 1990. "A Dwarf Launches a Little Ball," trans. Chun Kyungja. In *Modern Korean Literature: An Anthology,* ed. Peter Lee, pp. 328–367. Honolulu: University of Hawaii Press.

Ch'oe Inhun. 1990. "The Gray Club," trans. Peter Lee. In *Modern Korean Literature: An Anthology,* ed. Peter Lee, pp. 125–149. Honolulu: University of Hawaii Press.

Choi Sang-Chin and Choi Soo-Hyang. 1994. "We-ness: A Korean Discourse of Collectivism." In *Psychology of the Korean People: Collectivism and Individualism,* ed. Gene Yoon and Sang-Chin Choi, pp. 57–84. Seoul: Dong-A Publishing Co. [published on behalf of the Korean Psychological Association].

Chung Chong-Wha. 1995. Introduction to *Modern Korean Literature,* ed. Chung, pp. xxv–xli. London: Kegan Paul International.

Cleary, Thomas, trans. 1991. *The Essential Tao and Chuang-tzu*. San Francisco: Harper-Collins.

Clifford, Mark. 1994. *Troubled Tiger: Businessmen, Bureaucrats, and Generals in South Korea*. Armonk, N.Y.: M. E. Sharpe.

Crane, Paul. 1978. *Korean Patterns*. 4th ed. rev. Seoul: Royal Asiatic Society.

Cumings, Bruce. 1997. *Korea's Place in the Sun: A Modern History*. New York: W. W. Norton.

Dallmayr, Fred. 1996. *Beyond Orientalism: Essays on Cross-Cultural Encounter*. Albany: State University of New York Press.

Davis, Stephen, ed. 1981. *Encountering Evil: Live Options in Theodicy*. Atlanta: John Knox Press.

Devereux, George. 1980. *Basic Problems of Ethnopsychiatry*, trans. Basia Miller Gulati and Devereux. Chicago: University of Chicago Press.

Eckert, Carter, Lee Ki-baik, Lew Young Ick, Michael Robinson, and Edward Wagner. 1990. *Korea Old and New: A History*. Seoul: Ilchokak Publishers [for Korea Institute, Harvard University].

Far Eastern Economic Review. 1996. "Just Like Their Parents," December 5, pp. 50–52.

Featherstone, Mike. 1990. "Global Culture: An Introduction." In *Global Culture: Nationalism, Globalization and Modernity*, ed. Featherstone, pp. 1–14. London: Sage.

Feyerabend, Paul. 1975. *Against Method*. London: New Left Books.

Fingarette, Herbert. 1972. *Confucius: The Secular as Sacred*. New York: Harper and Row.

Foucault, Michel. 1980. *Power/Knowledge: Selected Interviews and Other Writings*, ed. Colin Gordon. New York: Pantheon Books.

———. 1984. "What Is Enlightenment?" In *The Foucault Reader*, ed. Paul Rabinow, trans. Catherine Porter, pp. 32–50. New York: Pantheon.

Freud, Sigmund. 1961. *Civilization and Its Discontents*, trans. James Strachey. New York: W. W. Norton.

———. 1962. *Three Essays on the Theory of Sexuality*. 4th ed., trans. James Strachey. New York: Basic Books.

Fukuyama, Francis. 1992. *The End of History and the Last Man*. New York: Free Press.

Gandhi, M. K. 1997. *Hind Swaraj*, ed. Anthony J. Parel. Cambridge: Cambridge University Press.

Gewirth, Alan. 1978. *Reason and Morality*. Chicago: University of Chicago Press.

Gilligan, Carol. 1982. *In a Different Voice: Psychological Theory and Women's Development*. Cambridge: Harvard University Press.

Gouldner, Alvin. 1965. *Enter Plato*. New York: Basic Books.

Grayson, James. 1989. *Korea: A Religious History*. Oxford: Clarendon Press.

Greene, William Chase. 1964. *Moira: Fate, Good, and Evil in Greek Thought*. New York: Harper and Row.

Habermas, Juergen. 1973. "Zu Nietzsches Erkenntnistheorie (ein Nachwort)." In *Kultur und Kritik: Verstreute Aufsaetz*, pp. 239–263. Frankfurt a.M.: Suhrkamp.

Hahm Pyong-choon. 1986. *Korean Jurisprudence, Politics and Culture*. Seoul: Yonsei University Press.

Han, Suzanne Crowder. 1991. *Korean Folk and Fairy Tales*. Seoul: Hollym.

Horkheimer, Max. 1972. "Authority and the Family." In *Critical Theory*, trans. Matthew O'Connell et al., pp. 47–128. New York: Seabury Press.

Horkheimer, Max, and Theodor Adorno. 1972. *Dialectic of Enlightenment*, trans. John Cumming. New York: Herder and Herder.

Hsün Tzu. 1963. *Basic Writings*, trans. Burton Watson. New York: Columbia University Press.

Huntington, Samuel. 1996. *The Clash of Civilizations and the Remaking of World Order.* New York: Simon and Schuster.

Hwang Sunwŏn. 1990. "Cranes," trans. Peter Lee. In *Modern Korean Literature: An Anthology,* ed. Lee, pp. 90–95. Honolulu: University of Hawaii Press.

Ikegami, Eiko. 1995. *The Taming of the Samurai: Honorific Individualism and the Making of Modern Japan.* Cambridge: Harvard University Press.

International Herald Tribune. March 3, 1997, pp. 22–23.

Jameson, Fredric. 1998. "Notes on Globalization as a Philosophical Issue." In *The Cultures of Globalization,* ed. Fredric Jameson and Masao Miyoshi, pp. 54–77. Durham: Duke University Press

Janelli, Roger. 1993. *Making Capitalism: The Social and Cultural Construction of a South Korean Conglomerate.* Stanford, California: Stanford University Press.

Janelli, Roger, and Dawnhee Yim Janelli. 1982. *Ancestor Worship and Korean Society.* Stanford: Stanford University Press.

Jansen, Marius. 1980. *Japan and Its World: Two Centuries of Change.* Princeton: Princeton University Press.

Kagan, Robert. 1998. "What Korea Teaches." *New Republic,* March 9: 38–47.

Kang Sinjae. 1990. "Another Eve," trans. Kim Seyŏng. In *Modern Korean Literature: An Anthology,* ed. Peter Lee, pp. 184–202. Honolulu: University of Hawaii Press.

Kant, Immanuel. 1949. "What Is Enlightenment?" In *The Philosophy of Kant,* ed. Carl Friedrich, pp. 132–139. New York: Modern Library.

——. 1959. *Foundations of the Metaphysics of Morals,* trans. Lewis White Beck. Indianapolis: Bobbs-Merrill.

Kierkegaard, Søren. 1957. *The Concept of Dread.* Trans. Walter Lowrie. Princeton: Princeton University Press.

Kim, Andrew. 1995. "A History of Christianity in Korea." *Korea Journal* 35, no. 2: 34–53.

Kim Byung-kook. 1998. "The Crisis of a Success: Party Politics in Confucian Democracy in Korea." *Papers of the First International Conference on Liberal, Social and Confucian Democracy,* pp. 1–43. Comparative Cultural Studies Center and *chontong kwa hyondai,* Yonsei University.

Kim Jong-Woo, Lee Jo-Hee, Lee Seung-Gi, Eom Hyo-Jin, and Whang Wei-Wan. 1996. "A Clinical Study of Hwabyŏng." *The Thesis Collection of the 18th Annual Convention of Korean Oriental Medicine,* pp. 11–23 [original in Korean].

Kim Joo-young. 1997a. "In Search of a Bird," trans. Hyun-jae Yee Sallee. *Koreana,* vol. 11, no. 1 (Spring): 89–99.

——. 1997b. "Searching for Ch'ŏrwŏn," trans. Bruce Fulton and Ju-chan Fulton. *Koreana* 11, no. 1 (Spring): 100–109.

Kim, Luke. 1996. "Korean Ethos." Unpublished ms.

Kim Sung-Hae. 1985. *The Righteous and the Sage.* Seoul: Sogang University Press.

Kim Sŭngok. 1980. "A Cup of Coffee," trans. Lee Sangok. In *Meetings and Farewells: Modern Korean Stories,* ed. Chung Chong-wha, pp. 148–177. New York: St. Martin's Press.

——. 1990. "Seoul: Winter, 1964," trans. Peter Lee. In *Modern Korean Literature: An Anthology*, ed. Peter Lee, pp. 216–232. Honolulu: University of Hawaii Press.

Kim Tae-kil. 1990. *Values of Korean People Mirrored in Fiction*, vol. 2, trans. Kim Heung-Sook. Seoul: Dae Kwang Munwhasa.

Kim Tongni. 1990. "The Rock," trans. Kevin O'Rourke. In *Modern Korean Literature: An Anthology*, ed. Peter Lee, pp. 66–74. Honolulu: University of Hawaii Press.

Kim Young-Moo. 1993. Introduction to *The Sound of My Waves: Selected Poems of Ko Un*, trans. Brother Anthony of Taizé and Kim Young-Moo, pp. ix–xiii. Ithaca: Cornell University East Asia Program.

Kim Young Sam. 1995a. "Reforms to Propel the Nation into Globalization." In *Korea's Quest for Reform and Globalization: Selected Speeches of President Kim Young Sam*, pp. 126–134. Seoul: The Presidential Secretariat.

——. 1995b. "Outlining the Blueprint for Globalization." In *Korea's Quest for Reform and Globalization: Selected Speeches of President Kim Young Sam*, pp. 268–273. Seoul: The Presidential Secretariat.

Knutson, Thomas. 1996. "Korean Communication Practices: The Moon Knows." *Korea Fulbright Forum* 12 (May): 1–20.

Ko Un. 1993. *The Sound of My Waves: Selected Poems of Ko Un*, trans. Brother Anthony of Taizé and Kim Young-Moo. Ithaca: Cornell University East Asia Program.

Kohlberg, Lawrence, C. Levine, and A. Hewer. 1983. *Moral Stages: A Current Formulation and a Response to Critics*. New York: Karger.

Kohut, Heinz. 1984. *How Does Analysis Cure?* ed. Arnold Goldberg. Chicago: University of Chicago Press.

Ku Sang. 1989. *Poems*, trans. Anthony Teague. London: Forest Books.

Kuhn, Thomas. 1977. "Theory Change as Structure Change." In *Historical and Philosophical Dimensions of Logic, Methodology, and Philosophy of Science*, ed. R. Butts and J. Hintikka. Dordrecht: D. Reidel.

Lasch, Christopher. 1979. *The Culture of Narcissism*. New York: Warner Books.

Lee Seung-Gi, Kim Jong-Woo, and Whang Wei-Wan. 1996. "A Case Study of Hwabyŏng." *Journal of Oriental Neuropsychiatry* 7, no. 1: 173–180 [original in Korean].

Lee Soo-Won. 1994. "The *Chong* Space: A Zone of Non-Exchange in Korean Human Relationships." In *Psychology of the Korean People: Collectivism and Individualism*, ed. Gene Yoon and Sang-Chin Choi, pp. 85–99. Seoul: Dong-A Publishing Co. [published on behalf of the Korean Psychological Association].

Lee Tae-dong. 1996. "Absurdity and Human Consciousness." *Korean Literature Today* 3 (Winter): 90–114.

Lee Tae-dong and Brother Anthony. 1996. Preface to *Korean Literature Today*, 3 (Winter): 3–4.

Lewin, Roger, and Clarence Schulz. 1992. *Losing and Fusing: Borderline Transitional Object and Self Relations*. Northvale, N.J.: Jason Aronson.

Lewis, Catherine. 1995. *Educating Hearts and Minds*. Cambridge: Cambridge University Press.

Lifton, Robert Jay. 1983. *The Broken Connection: On Death and the Continuity of Life*. New York: Basic Books.

Lukes, Steven. 1973. *Individualism*. Oxford: Basil Blackwell.

Macpherson, C. B. 1971. "The Social Bearing of Locke's Political Theory." In *Life, Liberty, and Property: Essays on Locke's Political Ideas*, ed. Gordon Schochet, pp. 60–85. Belmont, California: Wadsworth Publishing.

Mahler, Margaret. 1968. *On Human Symbiosis and the Vicissitudes of Individuation*. New York: International Universities Press.

Mahlsook, Han. 1983. *Hymn of the Spirit*, trans. Suzanne Crowder Han. Seoul: Art Space Publications

Marcuse, Herbert. 1970. "The Obsolescence of the Freudian Concept of Man." In *Five Lectures: Psychoanalysis, Politics, and Utopia*, trans. Jeremy Shapiro and Shierry Weber, pp. 44–61. Boston: Beacon Press.

Matsunaga, Daigan, and Alicia Matsunaga. 1972. *The Buddhist Concept of Hell*. New York: Philosophical Library.

Mlinar, Zdravko. 1992. Introduction to *Globalization and Territorial Identities*, ed. Mlinar. Aldershot, England: Avebury.

Moon Chung-in. 1995. "Globalization: Challenges and Strategies." *Korea Focus* 3, no. 3: 62–77.

Moore, Burness, and Bernard Fine, eds. 1990. *Psychoanalytic Terms and Concepts*. New Haven: Yale University Press [for the American Psychoanalytic Association].

Moses, Michael Valdez. 1995. *The Novel and the Globalization of Culture*. New York: Oxford University Press.

Niebuhr, Richard H. 1960. *Radical Monotheism and Western Civilization*. Lincoln: University of Nebraska Press.

O Yong-Su. 1995. "Echoes," trans. W. E. Skillend. In *Modern Korean Literature*, ed. Chung Chong-wha, pp. 263–297. London: Kegan Paul International.

O'Rourke, Kevin. 1981. Introduction to *Ten Korean Short Stories*, trans. O'Rourke. Seoul: Yonsei University Press.

——. 1998. "Hwang Chin-i: Folk Heroine and Poet." *Koreana* 12, no. 1: 40–43.

Pagels, Elaine. 1995. *The Origin of Satan*. New York: Random House

Park Myung-Seok. 1994. *Communication Styles in Two Different Cultures: Korean and American*, 2nd ed. Seoul: Han Shin Publishing Co.

Parkin, David. 1985. "Introduction." In *The Anthropology of Evil*, ed. Parkin, pp. 1–25. Cambridge, Mass.: Blackwell.

Rawls, John. 1971. *A Theory of Justice*. Cambridge: Harvard University Press, Belknap Press.

Rhi Bou-yong. 1980. "Dealing with Evil in Korean Fairytales: A Psychological Implication." *Korea Journal* 20: 18–29.

Ricoeur, Paul. 1969. *The Symbolism of Evil*, trans. Emerson Buchanan. Boston: Beacon Press.

Rilke, Rainer Maria. 1981. *Duino Elegies*, trans. Gary Miranda. Portland, Oreg.: Breitenbush Books.

Ritzer, George. 1996. *The McDonaldization of Society*, revised edition. Thousand Oaks, California: Pine Forge Press.

Robertson, Roland. 1990. "Mapping the Global Condition: Globalization as the Central Concept." In *Global Culture: Nationalism, Globalization and Modernity*, ed. Mike Featherstone, pp. 15–30. London: Sage.

———. 1992. *Globalization: Social Theory and Global Culture*. London: Sage.

Robinson, Michael. 1991. "Perceptions of Confucianism in Twentieth-Century Korea." In *The East Asia Region: Confucian Heritage and Its Modern Adaptation*, ed. Gilbert Rozman, pp. 204–225. Princeton: Princeton University Press.

Roland, Alan. 1988. *In Search of Self in India and Japan*. Princeton: Princeton University Press.

Rozman, Gilbert. 1991. Introduction to *The East Asia Region: Confucian Heritage and Its Modern Adaptation*, ed. Rozman, pp. 1–42. Princeton: Princeton University Press.

Said, Edward. 1994. *Orientalism*, with new Afterword. New York: Vintage Books.

Sapir, Edward. 1929. "The Status of Linguistics as Science." *Language* 5: 207–214.

Schmidt, James. 1996. "Introduction: What Is Enlightenment? A Question, Its Context, and Some Consequences." In *What Is Enlightenment? Eighteenth-Century Answers and Twentieth-Century Questions*, ed. Schmidt, pp. 1–44. Berkeley and Los Angeles: University of California Press.

Scholte, Jan Aart. 1996. "Towards a Critical Theory of Globalization." In *Globalization: Theory and Practice*, ed. Eleonore Kofman and Gillian Youngs, pp. 43–57. London: Pinter.

Southwold, Martin. 1985. "Buddhism and Evil." In *The Anthropology of Evil*, ed. David Parkin, pp. 128–141. Cambridge, Mass: Blackwell.

Steinberg, David. 1997. "Stone Mirror." *The Korea Times*, February 18.

Tallis, Raymond. 1995. *Not Saussure: A Critique of Post-Saussurean Literary Theory*. 2nd ed. London: Macmillan.

Thurow, Lester. 1998. "Asia: The Collapse and the Cure." *New York Review of Books*, February 5: 22–26.

Tocqueville, Alexis de. 1956. *Democracy in America*, ed. Richard Heffner. New York: Mentor.

———. 1980. *On Democracy, Revolution and Society: Selected Writings*, ed. John Stone and Stephen Mennell. Chicago: University of Chicago Press.

Tomasz, Julie, ed. 1993. *Fodor's Korea*. New York: Fodor's Travel Publications.

Triandis, H. C., R. Bontempo, M. J. Villareal, M. Asai, and N. Lucca. 1988. "Individualism and Collectivism: Cross-Cultural Perspectives on Self-Ingroup Relationships." *Journal of Personality and Social Psychology* 54: 323–338.

Tu Wei-ming. 1978. *Humanity and Self-Cultivation: Essays in Confucian Thought*. Berkeley: Asian Humanities Press.

Underwood, Horace G. 1994. "Christianity in Korea." *Missiology: An International Review* 22 (January): 65–76.

———. n.d. "A History of the Korean Church." Unpublished.

Wallerstein, Immanuel. 1990a. "Culture as the Ideological Battleground of the Modern World-System." In *Global Culture: Nationalism, Globalization and Modernity*, ed. Mike Featherstone, pp. 31–55. London: Sage.

———. 1990b. "Culture Is the World-System: A Reply to Boyne." In *Global Culture: Nationalism, Globalization and Modernity*, ed. Mike Featherstone, pp. 63–65. London: Sage.

Watson, Burton, trans. 1963. *Hsün Tzu: Basic Writings*. New York: Columbia University Press.

Weber, Max. 1951. *The Religion of China*, trans. and ed. Hans Gerth. Glencoe, Illinois: Free Press.

Williams, Raymond. 1976. *Keywords: A Vocabulary of Culture and Society*. New York: Oxford University Press.

Winch, Peter. 1964. "Understanding a Primitive Society." *American Philosophical Quarterly* 1, no. 4: 307–324.

Winnicott, D. W. 1986. *Holding and Interpretation*. New York: Grove.

Wittgenstein, Ludwig. 1961. *Tractatus Logico-Philosophicus*, trans. D. F. Pears and B. F. McGuinness. New York: Humanities Press.

———. 1967. *Philosophical Investigations*. 3rd ed., trans. G. E. M. Anscombe. New York: Macmillan.

Wong, Eva, ed. 1997. *Teachings of the Tao*. Boston: Shambhala.

Yi Ch'ŏngjun. 1990. "The Target," trans. Kim Chongch'ŏl. In *Modern Korean Literature: An Anthology*, ed. Peter Lee, pp. 233–251. Honolulu: University of Hawaii Press.

Yi Hyosŏk. 1990. "The Buckwheat Season," trans. Peter Lee. In *Modern Korean Literature: An Anthology*, ed. Lee, pp. 40–48. Honolulu: University of Hawaii Press.

Yi Mun-yol. 1995. *The Poet*, trans. Chung Chong-wha and Brother Anthony of Taizé. London: Harvill Press.

Yi Sang. 1990. "Wings," trans. Peter Lee. In *Modern Korean Literature: An Anthology*, ed. Lee, pp. 49–65. Honolulu: University of Hawaii Press.

Yoon, Gene, and Sang-Chin Choi, eds. 1994. *Psychology of the Korean People: Collectivism and Individualism*. Seoul: Dong-A Publishing Co. [published on behalf of the Korean Psychological Association].

Yoon Tae-Rim. 1994. "The Koreans, Their Culture and Personality." In *Psychology of the Korean People: Collectivism and Individualism*, ed. Gene Yoon and Sang-chin Choi, pp. 15–26. Seoul: Dong-A Publishing Co. [published on behalf of the Korean Psychological Association].

Youngs, Gillian. 1996. "Dangers of Discourse: The Case of Globalization." In *Globalization: Theory and Practice*, ed. Eleonore Kofman and Youngs, pp. 58–71. London: Pinter.

Yun Hŭnggil. 1990. "The Beating," trans. Ch'oe Haech'un. In *Modern Korean Literature: An Anthology*, ed. Peter Lee, pp. 310–327. Honolulu: University of Hawaii Press.

Index